About the author

Both Ruth Skrine's parents were doctors. Ruth's first career ambition was to be a nurse, but her mother would not hear of it and insisted she train as a doctor. So Ruth spent a long and fulfilling career in medicine, working in general practice, often moving house with her prison governor husband and her daughter, and eventually becoming a specialist in family planning and psychosexual medicine. She was chair of the Institute of Psychosexual Medicine for three years, and led training groups for doctors under its aegis, as well as editing a series of books on the subject and writing one herself, *Blocks and Freedoms in Sexual Medicine.* Since her retirement she has gained an MA in creative writing and has written poetry, short stories, and a novel in addition to this memoir.

GROWING INTO
MEDICINE

The Life and Loves of a Psychosexual Doctor

Ruth Skrine

Book Guild Publishing

Sussex, England

LUCAN LIBRARY
TEL: 6216422

First published in Great Britain in 2014 by
The Book Guild Ltd
The Werks
45 Church Road
Hove, BN3 2BE

Typesetting in Garamond by
YHT Ltd, London

Printed and bound in Great Britain by
CPI Group (UK) Ltd, Croydon, CR0 4YY

A catalogue record for this book is available from
The British Library.

ISBN 978 1 909716 77 3

For my daughter

HELEN

The love of my life – second only to

my husband

RALPH

Contents

Author's Note

Working in medicine, especially in the sensitive areas of family planning and psychosexual medicine, I had to keep a distance between my private and my professional life. Now that I have been retired for several years such separation is no longer necessary. Reliving my life story in memory has provided an opportunity to put these two sides of myself together and produce a personal record of living and doctoring in the last two thirds of the twentieth century.

I am grateful to my daughter Helen for agreeing to the publication of this book. Like her father she believes I should do what I want with my own life, despite the fact that her memories of childhood and her view of our marriage are bound to differ in many respects from my own.

Ever since attending the MA course in creative writing at Bath Spa University in 1999–2000, Sally Bramley, Lucy Maxwell Scott, Ellen Sentinella and I have met to discuss our work. They have visited my house regularly in order to workshop our writing (and share a meal). My thanks go to them for all their support and helpful criticism.

Lindsay Clarke of Frome Somerset and Sybil Ruth of the Literary Consultancy provided valuable professional advice.

My most sincere thanks go to my niece Tiki (Alison) Levine of Charlottesville, Virginia, USA for her dedicated reading of early drafts. Her encouragement ('wow', 'really?' 'no!' in the margins), and her honest and helpful critical remarks kept me going through the struggle to turn my memories into a readable story.

1

The Early Cast List

Daisy White came into my life in 1932, when I was three years old. My parents employed her as a second maid. I have been told how shy I was when she arrived. I could also have been told that I peeped round the solid banister at the bottom of the stairs, refusing to say a word to her for three days. But no one could have told me the feel of the well-defined edge to the wooden newel post, still imprinted on my palm. A further echo on my hand is the stone edge of the loggia pillar. I was sitting on the step, pressing my fingers into the reassuring coldness of the corner. My mother stood on the lawn by the tea table, angry and fraught as she prepared for some visitors. When I read that autistic children prefer to carry hard objects with edges, instead of the more usual cuddly toy, I feel a stab of recognition. The most 'normal' person can show traces of psychosis.

At this time my brother Arthur was rising seven and my sister had not yet been born. I wonder what Daisy thought of our household, professional and middle class but not wealthy. My general practitioner father had a few landed patients including one titled family, but at some establishments he was expected to use the servants' entrance. He worked long hours. Morning surgery ran from 9–10 a.m. but frequently went on till 11, and then again from 6–7 or 8 p.m. with emergency visits afterwards. The queue of patients often overflowed the waiting room and spread into the drive where they perched without complaint on the coping slabs that lay at the top of beautifully built dry stone walls with holes for blue patches of aubretia.

1

Daisy never moaned when he was late for supper (most days) or was too tired to eat the plate of food that had been saved for him. 'I'll do you some scrambled eggs,' she would say as she heaved herself out of the chair in the small maids' sitting room adjacent to the kitchen.

My father's practice was scattered, his patients living in market towns, villages and isolated houses and cottages. They admired him for his obstetric skills, as did the local consultants. Most of the babies were born at home or in a small maternity unit in the village of Corsham, three miles from our home in Chippenham, Wiltshire. He attended the delivery of every baby born to patients in his practice. Lying in bed I would hear his car go out and watch the headlights sweep across the ceiling. The house never felt quite safe until the engine had changed its tone at the entrance to the drive and the beam had made the return passage. During the depths of the night, when most babies seemed to be born, I would snuggle deeper into the blankets and the security of home.

Daisy valued her sleep but must have been woken frequently by his car. Her room was next to the one I shared with my sister Elizabeth, known as Biz. Both rooms overlooked the drive but again I never heard Daisy complain about him. Her first priority was that The Doctor should do his work in as much comfort as possible. However, if we disturbed her with talk or laughter too early or late she banged repeatedly on the wall. When the tomcats started their caterwaul in the spring she would throw her shoes from the window, always singly but in such numbers that several pairs would be waiting to be collected from the drive in the morning.

Daisy had left school at fifteen and had gone into service in Bath for a year or two before coming to us. Her mother lived in an isolated cottage outside Wootton Bassett, where the water was collected from the well in a bucket lowered on a long, forked pole. Occasionally, when Daisy had her day off, we visited. I can remember no surprise or shock about the rural poverty. She also accepted the established social order. Certainly I never felt that she resented our position, though recently my sister-in-law Ruth (she became Ruth Hickson soon after I got married and relinquished the name) told me that Daisy had confided to her that as children we had been less trouble than the family in Bath. The children in that household wore frillier clothes so the ironing took longer. She shared my mother's contempt for women who dressed their girls up like dolls.

Despite being raised in a safe and loving home I can trace the dilemmas of my life, the struggle for independence of thought and an adequate philosophy of life, back to my parents. The latter was not made easier by my mother's strident atheism. Both of them, in their different ways, were such strong characters that I can only start to approach my memories of them through Daisy who, although important in her own right, does not evoke such complicated emotional responses – and through animals and places.

Animals were always an important part of our lives, with one or more dogs, cats and various small animals in cages or on the lawn in runs made by my father. Daisy tolerated them all with equanimity, perhaps because her brother Bert, a farm labourer who lived with their mother for his whole life, always had at least one dog to retrieve the rabbits he shot for the pot.

Our first dog was a Welsh terrier called Jimmy, who was bad tempered and bit Biz on the head. I can see her standing on a mat inside the back entrance to the house, the blood spreading over her fair hair while we both yelled.

The mat was set in a special concrete depression, in front of a door leading into the garden from the 'boothole'. The term is not given in my Chambers dictionary and I don't know if I should write it as one word or two. We did not question the concept and I assumed it was common parlance. I now realise it suggests some sort of cupboard. In reality it was a decent sized room with a separate toilet. The shoes were kept in a rack and the wellington boots usually lined up tidily. There was also a cupboard that reached to the ceiling where flower vases, dogs' leads and gloves were stored. By the side, a table was used for shoe cleaning. In the corner a basin had, in addition to the ordinary taps, one with a thin spout that jutted out high above. When they designed the house my parents had chosen it specially so that they could fill flower vases and buckets more easily. For me it provided a cure for hiccups. I would hold my breath until nearly bursting, then twist my head and gulp water from the raised tap before breathing in, an adaptation of the advice to drink from the far side of a cup. Both tricks stretch the diaphragm before swallowing. I remember the panic when I had my first attack away from home. I could not believe the jerks that wrenched my body would ever stop without the help of that tap.

When he came in from gardening, my father scrubbed his hands at the basin, the palms and backs, each finger separately, then the nails from every possible angle. The procedure lasted at least five minutes. When I became a medical student and entered the operating theatre, I did not have to be shown how to scrub up – I had watched the process there in the boothole. Now that resistant organisms are so common I could make a fortune if I had a video of the routine my father had perfected long before antibiotics were discovered.

The dog Jimmy was reputed to be a good guardian. My brother Arthur was less than three years old when he wandered out of the garden and down towards the A4, a very busy road. When a neighbour tried to carry him home, Jimmy growled so hard that the only thing she could do was shoo child and dog together back up the hill and into the drive. After Jimmy, I was given a dachshund, named Gerda to chime with her German heritage. She was a placid creature, allowing me to decorate her back with Hewletts antiseptic cream when I was confined to bed with measles. The pleasure of squeezing long white lines, then a wavy pattern across them until the whole tube was used up, is with me still. When Daisy discovered what I had done she removed the worst with paper towels before carrying Gerda into the green bathroom.

The house had three bathrooms. The green one, between the nursery and the spare room, was used by the children as well as for the weekly wash, when the clothes were boiled in a large, gas-heated cauldron and removed with wooden tongs. The place filled with steam and the pervasive odour of carbolic soap. The blue bathroom near my parents' bedroom was specifically for their use. We were encouraged to go in while they bathed. My mother would hang her used sanitary towel on one side of a chair back and the clean one on the other. I am more embarrassed by the memory than I was at the time when, as she intended, I accepted menstruation with no sense of shock. However, this did not help me to cope when my own periods started while I was still in the 'nursery wing' at Hinton, the house in Somerset that I also loved. My boarding school had been evacuated there and I was the first of my class to be afflicted by 'the curse'. It took me three days of stained pants before I found the courage to consult the matron. My mother had sent me to boarding school with cotton pads that could be washed, not realising that modern girls used disposable towels.

The height of excitement in the blue bathroom was when our father submerged the whole of his head. Two or three times a week he soaped the crown and then disappeared under the water, blowing bubbles from his mouth as he did so. When he ran out of breath he shot up like a breaching whale, to much laughter and clapping of small hands.

The third bathroom was at the end of the corridor beyond the room for the two maids. It was poky, being under the eaves and for their use only. A similar space opposite was used to store suitcases until it was converted into a darkroom for Arthur when he started to develop his own photos. As I grew up, I felt awkward about the social stratification epitomised by these hygienic provisions.

After the episode with the cream, Daisy encouraged me to help with Gerda's bath. I knelt by the side, working the shampoo into a delicious, slippery mass of foam while the dog stood still, pleased with all the attention. My enjoyment of such sensory experiences was in sharp contrast to my mother who needed her fingers to be clean and dry. She never let us eat sandwiches on the beach, as any grain of sand between her teeth made her shudder. She preferred the rocks with their pools, taking no pleasure in the messiness of sand, while I revelled in every squish and squelch.

Bertha, a Dalmatian puppy, arrived during the war and was Biz's dog. She was very beautiful. As she grew to maturity her developing black spots became more numerous than considered ideal by breeders. They formed an enchanting tick shape on her forehead. Unfortunately she barked whenever the doorbell rang, creating great havoc. My mother's shouting only encouraged the noise, in the same way that it exacerbated our sisterly screaming.

Daisy was firm with small children but she was also gentle and full of common sense. No one could have told me about the pleasure when she did my hair. It was long and blonde and always in knots. Her patience was inexhaustible. She would sit in her chair while I stood between her legs. The slow stroke of the brush, the teasing comb that helped her fingers untangle the muddles, produced a particular delicious swooning in my head. It was the most sensuous feeling I experienced for many years, only reproduced later at boarding school when we would tickle each other, slowly and with the lightest touch.

I must have been about three or four when I would cross my legs and squat down in the middle of the road when we passed a particular tramp on our daily walk. Despite my psychosexual training and experience I am still upset to admit that the warm feelings were associated with daydreams of him beating my dolls. Here was another shadow, like that of the autistic person clutching at hard edges, which I would prefer to deny.

A third fleeting taste of derangement occurred during the few weeks after my husband died. Although I could work through a whole morning I could not stay in town to shop for more than a few minutes before fleeing for home. I would have expected these passing hints of autism, sadomasochism and agoraphobia to allow me to empathise more deeply with sufferers. But I find they merely highlight the chasm between my experience and that of others, only serving to deepen the sense of how impossible it is, without an imagination more powerful than mine, to see the world truly from behind someone else's eyes.

Daisy knew that my dolls were very important. I pushed them

about the garden in a dolls' pram with a brown hood, raised and lowered by a lever at the side. It was stiff, the joint waiting with malign intent to trap my finger. When forced down it fixed the hood so taut that the folds were smoothed away, leaving the surface tight enough to act as a drum. Or I may be muddling it with the big black pram in which I was left in the garden to sleep, a routine demanded by the protocol of the times, until I was at least two years old. During the psychoanalysis with which I indulged my seventies I remembered the dark space under the hood and the fear of being alone.

In my old age, when I crave large gulps of silence and aloneness, I am surprised by that fear. Daisy knew how much I needed company. When I was confined to the spare room with recurrent tonsillitis she would find reasons for a chat, arriving to clunk the vacuum cleaner against the feet of the bed, sending a friendly judder through the mattress. Or she would bring me a glass of fresh squeezed orange juice ordered by my mother before she left for work. The 'bits' were never strained out: that would have been a waste of good nourishment. I hated their feel against my teeth but forced it down for the sake of Daisy's visits. On a table by the bed an elephant bell, brought home by my father from India after the First World War, was left for me to ring in an emergency. I never had the courage. Asking for help did not – does not – come easily.

That gong was rung by Daisy to summon us for meals. At the weekend it would bring my father and brother from the workshop, my mother from the flower border, my younger sister Biz from… I don't know where. Often she would be out across the fields, talking to the farmers she met or to the tramps, solitary men who wandered about with broken shoes and torn carrier bags. Even the resonant elephant bell would not reach that far. But it could reach to our swing, fixed to 'the' oak tree.

No other tree can rival that expanse of indented leaves, that crenellated trunk with its huge branches. My father had screwed two thick eyes into the largest arm that stretched out across an expanse of rough grass. A modern child, familiar with the metal stands of park swings, could not imagine the height of that branch with the swing so far below. Later, it was flanked by a very thick climbing rope, a trapeze and a rope ladder provided for the more athletic Biz.

I would tie one of my 'people', a doll or a teddy bear, to the seat of the swing and push until I could reach no higher. If the person fell off, he or she was chastised – hard, usually physically with my hand or a convenient stick, but verbally as well. 'You must go into the corner until you are sorry. *Can I come out yet?* No, you are not sorry enough. *But I'm hungry I'll miss lunch.* Naughty girls don't deserve lunch. You must stay until you are truly, truly sorry.'

But the swing was also a place of escape, where I could pretend I was running away from home, where I could release those forbidden words, *It wasn't me... I didn't do it... I hate you.* And a place to drift, to see snow-covered mountains, rivers, strange landscapes beckoning to be explored...

Daisy sometimes had to come to the end of the path leading to the tree, ringing the gong with increasing force, before the sound broke into my reverie. Then dust rose from the bare earth as my feet dragged to bring the rhythmic motion to a stop. When I eased my fingers straight, white indentations remained, relics of sustained pressure.

Another important member of the household was the gardener. To him was given the unpleasant task of drowning extra kittens within a few hours of their birth. Our female cats had large litters. My parents considered they could find good homes for two by putting notices in the waiting room, but no more. Originally my father would use chloroform to kill them but when it became difficult to obtain the anaesthetic he delegated the job with relief. I learned that one should respect animals and treat them with great kindness, but kill them quickly if they were suffering, or if one could not provide them with a happy and caring home.

Each morning, while my father was ensconced in the consulting room working his way through morning surgery, the gardener would clean his car. A concrete base in front of one side of the double garage had been built with a slope from each corner towards the drain in the middle. The detailed design was an example of the meticulous care my parents took when they built the family home in two acres of raw field. The house was also intended to be a base for their medical practice. They called it Green Gables for the grey-green colour of the tiles. I don't know if they were aware of the famous book at that time but at least they did not call either of their daughters Anne.

One of the other regular jobs performed by the gardener was to clean my father's shoes. The high polish was an important part of his persona and dear to me. In my analysis I became enormously attached to the scruffy footwear of my analyst. During the five years we met, I only remember one day when they were polished: I felt deeply betrayed. All father figures should stay in character.

The first gardener I remember was called Slaney. I don't think even we children called him Mr although his successor Mr Harlow, one of Daisy's many relatives, was always addressed properly. At various times, members of three generations of her family worked in the house or garden.

It was Slaney who responded to my screams when my brother Arthur put a worm down my neck, perhaps driven to desperation as I trailed him about, asking questions and wanting to help with whatever he was doing. I must have been about five and had a horror of things that wriggled. I had been given a triangle of ground beside the greenhouse for my garden. Much as I longed to prove myself by growing radishes and cornflowers, the first worm that appeared would send me running to the swing, not to try again for several months.

Slaney looked for the worm under my blue aertex shirt but could not find it. He carried me in to Daisy who sat me on the kitchen table and discovered it nestling under the band of my skirt. Despite her cuddles and reassurances my screams, which had started in panic, continued for many minutes. I had to make sure that Arthur realised the enormity of what he had done.

Screaming was an activity Biz and I raised to the level of an art, although this was usually in the presence of my mother rather than

Daisy. Anything my mother said raised the pitch and volume. Only my father, wandering into our bedroom to mend the light or embark on a story from his day, could stem the flow. He was not interested in the causes of our ructions, in the rights and wrongs of the case. He would capture us with the news that the floods were out at Christian Malford, three new puppies had been born to Mr Green's mongrel or his 'swag' for the day was half a dozen eggs and a simnel cake. 'What is simnel?' I asked, knowing I did not like it but wanting to show I had recovered enough to take part in a conversation. Arthur bears witness to the fact that Biz continued her storms longer than I did. She was not only younger but has always had a more passionate nature.

Perhaps we screamed with my mother because we saw her mainly in the evenings when we were tired. Or perhaps Daisy's more placid nature forestalled such tantrums. Certainly her ability to be calm in all situations was useful in a doctor's household. If the secretary were out she would answer the phone. One gentleman rang asking to speak to the doctor. She told the caller he was out on his rounds.

'Is Mrs Hickson in?'

'I'm afraid she is working at a clinic.'

'Well, perhaps you can tell me, can my wife get up?'

On another occasion a grateful patient wanted to know if the doctor would like a book for Christmas. 'Oh, he has plenty of books,' was her reply. An understandable response in view of the fact that she had to dust them all.

All memory is story. We are selective in what and how we remember, changing the truth, whatever that may have been, as we relive our experiences. Some of these 'Daisy stories' are the product of family folklore. She could be irritating but we loved her and she was a part of us all.

It seems strange, in view of my ferocious play with my dolls, that during my entire childhood no adult ever raised a hand to me. What punishment I remember was being sent to my bedroom or the threat of a treat removed. Once, Arthur and I turned on the bath taps and got distracted by a pillow fight. The bath overflowed. We emerged covered in feathers to find the water leaking out under the door and making its way down the stairs. The ceiling of the sitting room below had to be replastered. We were told we would not go to the pantomime that year, but when the time came the threat was not upheld.

So forgiving was the atmosphere that I never consciously felt the discipline to be severe. However Jenny, my second cousin and my best friend for ever and ever, who will play an important part throughout this memoir, was deeply shocked when my mother woke us from sleep one evening to tidy the boothole. The idea of shattering that silence which seeps through a house after the children are asleep, was something her mother would never have considered. We were nine or ten at the time but Jenny, who was always fond of my mother, has remained surprised by that act to this day.

Four years my senior, my brother Arthur seldom misbehaved unless I led him astray. He must have found it a trial to have such a devoted sister. He spent much of his time in silence, designing and making things. I was not good with my hands, or interested in how things worked. Indeed, I was not interested in things or facts at all – only in the feelings of those around me. One of the excitements of writing in my later years has been to discover that I need a modicum of facts, that it can be fun to track them down. In those early days all I wanted was to make people happy and to make them like me, especially Arthur and my father.

To this end I would spend hours standing in cold garages staring into the bowels of car engines. I would nod as my father explained the pistons, spark plugs and distributor. In keeping with his passionate belief that girls were of equal value to boys, he wanted me to understand the workings of all things mechanical. To please him I pretended to listen, fidgeting my cold toes inside lace-up shoes.

As the months and weeks of 1939 passed by, I had little awareness of the gravity of the world situation. Jenny was sent to stay with us for six months. She lived in London with her physician father and artistic mother (my father's first cousin) who noticed she was frightened by the talk of bombs and invasions. Everyone agreed that she needed some time in the country.

Within days we had an imaginary riding school and were cantering our ponies to the swing and stabling them in the garage as soon as my parents' car had gone out. Later she went to Canada with her mother and three siblings. Our friendship had that deep solidity that can survive long periods of separation, the worst of which is her present Alzheimer's disease.

But rumours of war began to penetrate even my sheltered life. Each day my father would arrive at lunch with the news that someone else had given up hope now... Mr Smith at the garage, Mrs Palmer who had a son in the civil service so she should know, Professor Treeby who was retired but spoke and read German fluently. I hardly bothered to listen and somehow my parents managed to hide their anxiety. My mother's discussion about a possible new car held more interest for us children.

Everyone remembers what he or she was doing on 3 September 1939. As 11 o'clock neared, Daisy was in the kitchen listening to the news on a speaker connected to the radio in the sitting room by an extension wire. Arthur had a small portable wireless and the governess was keeping Biz out of the way. I was sitting in a high-backed chair in the sitting room with my parents. It stood on one side of a handcrafted fireplace, the bricks chosen for their particular terracotta patina, in front of the piano and an enormous standard lamp with a shade painted by a talented aunt. It depicted a deer, starting with its birth and following its life cycle as you walked round the light.

My perch was not particularly comfortable. Although padded, it was not exactly an easy chair. I sat very upright. My father was in his big chair, the one with wooden arms, carved round the edges into a pattern where half moons appeared to have been gouged out, leaving raised, smoothed rectangles separated by narrower indentations. My mother was in her usual place on what she called the chesterfield, a sofa in today's language, next to the fire.

While the Prime Minister was speaking I did not realise it was a declaration of war. I merely thought, 'Oh, Mr Chamberlain has given up hope now.'

When he reached the end my father got to his feet and switched off the set. The silence hung curdled in the room before my mother cried out, 'I'll have that car. I'll need it.'

2

My Mother

One day as I was lying on the couch in my analyst's room I found myself reliving the sense of being shattered into tiny pieces when my mother shouted – that feeling that could be soothed by feeling a sharp edge against my palm.

'Perhaps,' said my analyst, 'it is like a singer who strikes a note so exactly in tune with the inner vibrations of a glass that it shatters.'

I lay still, a feeling of warmth seeping through my body. Could I have had that kind of resonance with her? There were no words then or now to describe the feeling of relief that some part of me might have been in tune with her rather than being for ever discordant and therefore not good enough. It was a turning point in my life.

While introducing the reader to some of the significant others of my early childhood I have deliberately kept my mother in the shadows. She was not the lurking kind. Both in herself, and in my memory, she will overwhelm the others if she is not given some separate space.

Joan Whitelock was born in 1899 to a Birmingham solicitor. Her mother, my grandmother, had intense, twinkling blue eyes and was loved by men of all ages – and by me. She was known as Mum's Mum to her grandchildren. My mother would have considered any form of address such as *mummy, granny, nanny* both sissy and lower class. For someone who had great sympathy for the communist party during much of her life, my mother had a surprisingly well-developed feel for the nuances of the English class system.

Her hair always fell to her waist. As a child she was expected by her Edwardian mother to wear it loose, which she hated as it got caught in the twigs and branches of her favourite climbing trees. After her death I found some letters from her father addressed to 'Dear Johnny'. I never knew she had been called Johnny. Perhaps her parents gave out mixed messages about the sort of person she should be. Being a family with strong feelings about the continuation of the name, I suspect they were disappointed when she was not the boy for whom they had to wait another eighteen years. That boy, my much beloved Uncle Miles, did not die until the end of 2011. He grew to appreciate his sister Joan. Not long ago he told me she was a passionate woman. Until that moment I had not attached that adjective to her, using instead words like strong-willed, fervent and fierce.

But yes, she was passionate, she loved and hated passionately and held to her beliefs with unwavering passion, the most strident being her atheism. Always despising hypocrisy, she told me that her hatred crystallised during the First World War. It had been reported that at the beginning the padres were not sent into the trenches but kept behind the lines. She thought this was a cowardly cop-out. Two young men of whom she was fond were killed in the early months and she believed the church, while preaching self-sacrifice, was a sham.

Her hatred reached paranoid heights. White was anathema to her as being the virginal choice of brides who were, in the main, not virgins. She would plant no white flowers in her garden. One of the most important moments of my life was the only time I defied her: over my own wedding. She had bought me a pale blue dress with a little jacket and presumed I would be married in a registry office. Unfortunately I had fallen in love with the only son of a very conventional family.

'You can't possibly want to parade through some church in white,' my mother said. 'But you must do as you want.'

'Of course you must want a lovely white wedding with everyone wishing you well,' my future mother-in-law cooed. 'But it is your day; you must do what you want.'

I did not care what sort of wedding I had. All I wanted, as usual, was to make everyone happy. That was impossible. Daisy, who by then had lived with us for almost twenty years, was expecting a lovely party at Green Gables and felt personally deprived. In contrast, I had known all my life that my mother would not be at my wedding. I accepted the fact – but her inability to understand my position when the time came was hurtful. In the event I decided that she would forgive me in time, but I did not want to start my marriage by alienating the family of my future husband.

Jenny's mother offered to host it for me and I walked down the isle of a church in London wearing a long white dress. My father paid for everything and gave me away, dressed in the obligatory morning suit. From the start of the discussions he had managed to support me without wasting energy arguing with my mother. We children believed for many years that she bullied him, but my wedding was just one of the occasions when he cared enough to stand firm and take no notice of her passions. Biz and Jenny were bridesmaids in what now appears to be hideous scarlet satin. During the ceremony my mother took Daisy's spaniel dog in her car to look for the source of the Thames.

My belief that she would forgive me was mistaken. In the year before she died she was still writing in her diary that she could not understand why I had chosen to be married in that way and that she would never forgive the woman who helped me to such a disgusting show and so much wasted money.

I can now take some pride in the steadfast way she held to her convictions, although my friends are baffled and shocked by the story. If she were alive, my mother would be horrified to see the lavish weddings of the twenty-first century, especially when so many marriages fail despite the money spent. For my part, I envy the choices that are more widely available. No one was upset when my American niece Tiki was married on an isolated island, the only witnesses being the officiating officer and a couple of strangers who happened to be passing.

My mother's reaction to my wedding was the latest incident in the long-standing battle about her own. Joan did not want to get married in church but family pressure was so great that she gave in, saying she would do so if she could do everything else her own way. She chose to be married at 8 o'clock in the morning wearing what she always called a tweed coat and skirt. When I found a picture after her death I discovered it was in fact a grey striped affair, rather smart. Miles remembers riding his bicycle, together with his parents on theirs, across the cricket pitch to the church in the village of Whitchurch, near Reading, where they lived. He was six years old at the time and played trains in the aisle during the brief service. Afterwards he was allowed to ride home to the family breakfast in the dickey, the space that opened at the back of my father's precious two-seater car.

Joan had gone out of her way to accommodate her parents but in so doing she felt she had compromised her beliefs. She was furious when she discovered that her mother had sent pieces of wedding cake in the traditional small silver boxes to their friends and acquaintances. A marriage was a private affair between the two of them and should include no one else. To support this she had only invited her immediate family, whereas my father had a larger contingent. My grandparents found the exclusion of their friends hard to forgive. I fear that for them too my wedding opened old wounds, though my grandmother valiantly stood in for her daughter in the photos.

Despite her disagreement over anything that involved the church, Joan adored her parents, especially her father, known to everyone as D. This was a shortening of the nick-name Diddles, which I believe was given him by my mother's sister. She was a few years younger than Joan and at one time she rode a child's scooter round their garden and became known as Scoot or Cooty for the rest of her life. Artistic and a bit fey, she was never able to hold down a job for long. She loved singing and play-acting and I was acutely embarrassed when she wanted me to join her in performing in front of the family and neighbours. I think D found her a trial and perhaps in consequence paid more attention to my mother. He often went abroad in the winter for the sake of his weak chest and on one occasion Joan joined him in Tenerife. Her memories of this holiday with him gave her intense pleasure, perhaps because at some level she was jealous of her scintillating mother and of their relationship.

I found D a bit forbidding. At six foot five inches, and already developing a stoop when I was a young girl, he had a slow, legal way of talking. It took me a long time to recover from his monosyllabic fury after I made the mistake of copying my Aunt Cooty and called him 'Diddles'.

For my mother, her father was always the person she consulted about any important decision. After the postman delivered my disappointing higher certificate exam results, my future education was in doubt. Before my mother could voice an opinion, she bundled us all into my father's car and told him to drive fifty miles to consult with the one person whose opinion she could trust. My father made no complaint. I don't know if that was because he seldom argued with her or whether he also valued my grandfather's considered views.

My mother qualified as a doctor from University College Hospital. When she was a senior student my father, Eric Hickson, was the obstetric house officer. Joan was not one of the very first wave of women doctors but the only one in her year, hard to believe now when more than half of medical students in Britain are women. She felt she had to compete against the men at every stage, maintaining that women in medicine always had to be better. Yet her diaries, and some of my memories, suggest that her tough approach was won at some cost. It is clear that she had an instinctive dislike of the messiness that is an integral part of looking after bodies. When they settled in Chippenham she decided to specialise in eyes. Perhaps this choice was more than a matter of convenience, the eyes being a long way away from the dirtier parts of the body.

For many years, until the onset of the NHS in 1948, she worked two mornings a week for no pay at the Bath eye infirmary on Lansdown Hill with the surgeon Mr Colley. She was not herself a surgeon but wanted to keep in touch with proper medicine, diagnosing and treating those conditions that were amenable to medical rather than surgical interventions and doing much of his follow-up work. Her boss was an active member of the communist party and had a strong influence on her political ideas. Although she never joined any party, at that time she described herself as a socialist.

Meanwhile she made money by testing the eyes of children at school, an important job taken over by nurses many years ago. My mother also saw children privately at home. She had a flair for spotting what Dr Apley, in his book *The Child and his Symptoms*, called 'the child as the presenting symptom of the mother', where the child shows the symptoms of the mother's neurotic worries. A common complaint was headaches and by listening and advising she saved many children from the indignity of wearing unnecessary glasses.

As I think back to this painstaking aspect of her work I am reminded of a man I met many years later in a psychosexual clinic. He was in his late thirties, with the problem of impotence. I could find no physical cause for his difficulty and he needed little encouragement to talk about himself. He sat behind thick glasses and told me how his father had been in the army and as a boy he had attended many different schools. At each one he was bullied anew. As he told me about his anguish at being labelled 'four eyes' wherever he went, tears ran from behind the frames and down his face to drop onto his clenched fingers.

My mother also held baby clinics and was a strong believer in breast-feeding. She thought that test weighing before and after feeds was useful although it is now thought to add to the mother's anxiety. For her it was a time-saving device that allowed her to put the baby down at the earliest opportunity. I can imagine her squirming if my tiny lips and fingers played with her nipple instead of getting on with the job of sucking.

Her sense of the right way to behave was very strong. The doctor's children must behave with decorum. We were never allowed to eat ice cream in public, except on one occasion when an erudite cousin, a professor of economics who looked the part with an extensive black beard, bought us cornets and encouraged us to follow his lead and lick them with enthusiasm as we walked down the high street.

Clothes were particularly important to my mother. She took immense trouble with her own, fussy about the exact shade of blue, such a favourite colour that it appeared to my child's eye to carry some sort of moral worth. For work, she invariably wore a 'suit', a skirt with a matching jacket, a tradition I emulated for the whole of my professional life. In winter the material was tweed. If it were very cold she put a matching long coat over the top. Once Crimplene and other synthetic materials appeared they made a useful alternative for the summer. She invariably changed into a dress before supper. When she travelled to London for a medical meeting or a day shopping she wore a small hat. She and Mum's Mum spent hours working on those hats, adding and removing delicate feathers, tiny artificial flowers and wisps of veiling.

I hate hats. When my husband was invited to a garden party as a reward for his time in the prison service, I was obliged to buy one. I considered it small enough and thought the fluff of feathers standing up at the back rather fetching. When I showed it to my mother she made a face. 'Well, I suppose it will do but of course you will remove that nonsense at the back.' I was in my fifties at the time but agreed to do so, not admitting that I thought the decoration the only thing that provided any spark of life to my outfit.

The first long dress I ever bought for myself was pale green satin with an off-the-shoulder frill. I have never loved a garment so much, until I went home to show it off. 'You look just like every other typist,' my mother said, her class awareness kicking in full blast. I wanted to look like every other typist, only I hoped a bit prettier. She wanted me to look different, elegant and above all tasteful.

The greatest humiliation came when I cycled home from university in Bristol with Jenny and my sister, who was on a tandem with one of her friends. She had borrowed it from the postman in Street where she was at school. I chose to wear three-quarter-length jeans, imagining them to be the most sensible choice, as they would not catch in the chain. When we arrived at Green Gables my mother threw open the front door, and her arms, to welcome us with her usual enthusiasm.

'Come in, come in. You must all be tired and thirsty...' she stopped in mid-sentence and her eyes widened as she looked at my legs. 'What HAVE you got on?'

'I chose them specially so they wouldn't get caught in the chain.'

'How could you?'

The others watched as my face began to burn. 'I was trying to be sensible...' I had expected praise. Her attack on me in public fractured my world yet again. I struggled on, bending to touch a bare ankle. 'Look, I don't need cycle clips.'

'Go upstairs and change into something decent immediately. Leave them in my room. I will burn them tomorrow.'

I propped my bicycle against the wall and pushed past her towards the stairs watched by three pairs of incredulous eyes. I heard her voice change again behind me.

'Come in,' she repeated. 'Lime juice is waiting for you in the sitting room and then I'm sure you will all want to swim.'

The next morning the bonfire was lit. By the time we came down to breakfast black smoke was billowing across the garden reminding my friends of my disgrace.

Only much later did I understand that such garb was associated in her mind with girls who stood on street corners trying to attract the boys. These were not necessarily prostitutes but 'those sort of girls', ones with loose morals who did not know how to behave. After I had been married for several years I was surprised by her reaction when I told her I thought I had fallen in love with someone other than my husband. Her response was to say that it was possible to love more than one man at the same time. She added that one could not help one's feelings but must take responsibility for ensuing actions.

From someone with strong moral values, at a time when sexual fidelity was held in high regard, I felt her response as warm and generous. I should have remembered that she was a product of the twenties. She told me once that she and my father had decided they should each try sex with another partner in case it was better. My brother and I believed she probably did have some such experience, but we imagined our father spending a night alone in some dingy hotel. Like all children we did not find it easy to imagine the sexual lives of our parents and cannot envisage him embarking on such a premeditated escapade.

My mother wanted her children to be people who took sensible decisions. The last time I remember her giving me unsolicited advice she was living in a granny flat at the back of my house. I was on my way out and she said it was going to rain and I should take a mackintosh. This time I flared up, saying that, in my mid-fifties, I thought I was old enough to know when I needed a waterproof. I did not take one and it did rain and I got wet – but by then we could laugh about it together.

Today's reader may find it difficult to imagine the importance of appearance. She longed for us to be dressed properly but also to have the suave, easy manners of the upper classes, those she had met in her adolescence at tennis parties and at Henley. For this she should have chosen a different partner. My father, coming from solid Quaker stock, was kind and endlessly gentle but not bothered by such superficial polish. But despite her attempts to turn us into the sophisticates we could never be, she was often embarrassingly graceless herself. She was a large woman, abrupt and more direct than social nicety demanded. In retrospect I wonder if an awareness of this made her particularly anxious for us to shine.

My mother's social life centred round the world of medicine and doctors. On principle she never went 'out to tea', an activity common among bored middle class women in the 1930s who had servants and seldom worked. But she was always hospitable to doctors. Chippenham had a small cottage hospital, run by GPs with visits from consultants in Bath. Some operations were performed there and, if my father diagnosed a patient with appendicitis or other fairly straightforward emergency, he would call a surgeon out and give the anaesthetic himself. My mother provided cocoa, coffee or fruit juice, which waited in the sitting room in jugs or thermoses, a pile of sandwiches by the side, ready for them however late they finished.

Visiting consultants ran outpatient sessions at the hospital, a service that spared patients the tedious bus journey into Bath, twelve miles away. Domiciliary visits also provided an opportunity for medical contact. My father invariably accompanied the consultant to the patient's house and my mother encouraged them to come home for a meal or drink afterwards. She liked to be included in discussions about the case, which provided a way for both of them to keep up to date with changes in medicine. Alas, the general practitioner of today makes very few home visits, and I understand that if a consultant does visit the house the GP seldom accompanies him. Such personal contact and mentoring by the bedside appears to have been lost for ever.

One chore that doctors working in the NHS do not have to face is 'doing the bills'. This was a family affair that took place twice a year. My mother brought out the low table with drop sides that was usually used for the tea tray. Now it was laden with one heavy drawer after another, carried in from the consulting room. These contained the patients' notes. As each brown folder was scrutinised for the number of visits and bottles of medicine my mother suggested what the family should be charged. Those patients with money were charged what it was thought they would pay, while those without were asked for a small token fee. The job took several long evenings and at least one weekend. I enjoyed feeling useful as I stuck on the stamps, moistening the backs on a damp sponge that sat in an old tobacco tin.

Every day my father discussed his work with my mother, often over the lunch table in a vocabulary that we children did not understand. Because the practice was run from her own home, and in the early days she often helped out with surgeries and visits, she played a decisive role in the way it was organised. One day, when she was living with me during the last years of her life, she confessed to a

24

serious mistake. As a result of some misunderstanding, a specimen of urine was thrown out before it had been tested for sugar. The patient, a young boy, died of undiagnosed diabetes, an avoidable death for which they never forgave themselves.

On hearing this story, and especially following my psychoanalysis, I can appreciate how much they supported each other. My previous understanding of their relationship as one of unequal power was flawed. Her quick temper and passionate beliefs added life and sparkle to his placid and dependable nature, on which she depended for her stability.

James Hillman, in his book *The Soul's Code*, suggests that parents, especially the mother, have become too important, too powerful a myth in our psychological understanding. I never saw my mother as being responsible for the person I became, but my ambivalent feelings towards her, or the figure of her I had built into myself, were uncomfortable and limiting. Although my friends say they can see little change in me since my analysis, I know the effect on my subsequent life has been profound. When they ask why I spent so much time and money the answer is a lame one. 'Because I now have the confidence to write books,' I reply. 'And I can appreciate, understand and feel nothing but love for my difficult mother.'

3

The Wrack of War

The month after war was declared I celebrated my tenth birthday. I had no understanding of its horrors. 'Wrack' is too strong a word for its effect on my life, for I continued to be protected and privileged. I was fed, clothed and loved and lost no one dear to me. The adolescent turmoil that was looming might well have been just as powerful during peacetime. However it is possible that the anxiety of those around me, never openly expressed, heightened my tendency to dramatise my feelings.

Until the war started I was educated at home. The role of the governess was well defined. She looked after our clothes, taught us in the mornings and took us for walks in the afternoons. Lunch was eaten round the dining room table with my parents but she always gave us supper in the nursery and then ate her own on a tray in her room. The food was provided for her by the two maids.

My favourite governess was Miss Fox, who taught me to swim in our pool in the garden, an unusual feature in those days and an important part of my childhood. It had been dug a year or two earlier by my parents with the help of the gardener and one other labourer. I liked to believe that my efforts with a sandpit spade helped the success of the project.

The pool was filled at the beginning of summer by two hoses from the house. The process took three days and I watched with growing excitement as the level rose. The system had no pump or filter and went green within a few weeks, despite liberal doses of chlorine disinfectant. Leaves and dead worms accumulated at the bottom making me unwilling to put my feet down. Once or twice during the season it was emptied and cleaned out. The water drained away into the rough land downhill from the house. On one occasion workmen who were digging up the road at the bottom were mystified by the water that was filling each hole as fast as it was dug. When my father learned of their puzzlement he hurried to replace the bungs in the waste pipe. Later in the war it was valued by the defence services as a source of static water they could use against the fires expected to rage through the town if we were bombed or invaded.

My parents invited many children to swim, although my mother tried to reserve the late afternoons, when she came in hot from work, for her own use. She would proceed with slow breaststrokes, her head and shoulders held high out of the water as she made her stately progress once round the edge. At those times we kept out of the water, fearful of splashing the unprotected plait wound round her head.

When Miss Fox thought I could manage without my rubber ring, a precursor of today's arm bands, she set me to swim from the deep end, six feet six inches deep, across to the steps at the shallow end, a distance of about twenty feet. After three strokes I sank. For some reason she was standing on the edge fully clothed but did not hesitate to kick off her shoes and plunge in to rescue me. I can see her now, climbing out to toss the dripping hair out of her eyes, laughing as she picked an apple from one of our many trees and took an enthusiastic bite.

Before long I too was swimming a sedate breaststroke though I never managed a satisfactory crawl. I learned to dive and always made myself enter the water head first. Jumping caused too much of a splash and annoyed the adults, while walking down the steps was an ignominious activity reserved for old ladies like my mother (then in her thirties). Until well into middle age I could not admit, even to myself, that I hated diving.

As soon as war was declared the last governess, Miss Taylor, a rather prim person who tried to teach me to sew, left to do more important war work. To my child's mind the term always referred to making munitions in a factory, but I cannot imagine her in such a rough and arduous setting. Many clerical jobs needed to be filled by women as the men left to join the forces.

My parents were too old to be called up but younger doctors disappeared in quick succession. Patient loyalty was essential for the livelihood of the doctor and many, forced to leave for active service, feared they would have no practice left when they came home. My mother offered to take over the work of a single-handed doctor in a village three miles outside Chippenham, promising to hold it together so she could hand the business back intact when he returned. She ran surgeries, made home visits and was on call night and day. Not knowing the neighbourhood, and not being mechanically minded, her new car was invaluable, especially as all the signposts had been removed in preparation for the expected invasion.

Many years later she told me how appalled she had been to find the consulting room had no couch and the only place she could wash her hands was in the yard under a cold tap. Some filthy instruments were hidden in a dust-laden cupboard and she had found a washable, reusable condom hanging behind the door. The comparison with the surgery premises my parents had built in their own house was stark. My father had a curtained couch with washable towels, changed for each patient (there were no rolls of paper in those days). A dispensary was equipped not only with large glass stoppered bottles with their array of coloured medicines, but also with another couch, sterilising equipment, special antiseptic soap over the sink and constant hot water. I have learned from a recent paper that such inequality of services continued into the 1960s.

In addition to all the extra medical work, my parents took part in a fire-watching rota at an observation post nearby. Their experience of working in hospital, where nights on call were followed by a full day's work, provided good training for their exhausting lives at that time. Without Daisy their situation would have been impossible. She was by this time their longest-serving maid and she was promoted to the essential job of cook/housekeeper. Apart from my mother's one brief visit each morning to the kitchen, when they stared into the fridge together deciding what we should all eat that day, Daisy ran the household.

Following the departure of our governess, my parents decided to send me to boarding school and Biz to a local day school. I went to Oldfeld, a school owned and run by my father's mother. She was a forward-looking educationalist who had started the school when my grandfather failed in business, and had made it a great success. The buildings had been purpose built with the girls sleeping on one side, the boys on the other and communal rooms in the middle.

At ten years old I had never attended any sort of school, my only experience of mixing with children outside the family being those few who 'came for tea', and the occasional girl who joined us for lessons from time to time. Being related to the staff at Oldfeld, I was a natural target. After a few weeks it was decided that I was the one to be 'beaten up'.

The attention was unremitting. No single child dared to stand against the crowd and take my side. In the classroom the ends of my plaits were dipped in full inkwells; in the playground they were tied round my neck in a noose; in the dining room boys snatched food from my plate or spilt gravy and peas down my front, then jeered at me for being a messy eater. In the corridors I was jostled and pushed against the walls.

The worst place of torture was the dormitory where each girl had a chamber pot under the bed. Again, my plaits were the first things to be forcefully dipped in as soon as any steaming urine was available. My cuddly toy, a dog that acted as a pyjama case, was immersed each night until he smelt so bad that I had to take him into the grounds and throw him behind a hedge. When I was sent a special pack of cards they were dropped ceremoniously, one by one into the liquid and I was made to fish them out so that they could be dropped in again. Once I collected a smooth stone from the field so that I had something to hold during the night – something that could not be permanently soiled – that I could wash and dry each morning.

Arthur had been at the school before and is unaware of any such organised bullying at that time. I wonder now why I couldn't tell my parents. It might have been the certainty that I would not be believed, especially as they thought so highly of the school and my grandmother who had created it. My fantasy is that I would have been told I was a wimp and needed to toughen up. Perhaps the manners of the day did not encourage children to share their feelings, even where the parents were progressive. When I mentioned it to my mother fifty years later she was horrified. I never told her any details and only let myself remember them with my analyst. He suggested that the violence and terror being enacted across the channel was invading the microcosmic society of the school.

The school was in Swanage, on the south coast, and in those early months of 1940 an invasion was expected any day. The staff would watch for ships and planes from the roof. It is not surprising that they had no time to notice that tension and fears were being projected onto me in acts of cruelty.

At the beginning of the following term I managed to run a temperature for several weeks. At first this was genuine but I became adept at keeping it up artificially. First I rubbed the thermometer furiously with my tongue but that didn't work. Then I put it under the hot tap in the bathroom but the glass broke and I had to scrabble on the floor to collect the evasive blobs of mercury. The best way was to take a mouthful of hot water when I heard my father's step on the stairs and swallow it as he opened the door. Although he worried about the swinging readings for which he could find no cause, he never discovered what I was doing. After several weeks my parents decided to ignore the thermometer and return me to school.

'Do I have to go?' I asked as my father manoeuvred my trunk down the stairs.

'It can't be as bad as all that, can it?'

There was no way I could explain.

As I slunk into an empty desk at the back of the classroom I held myself rigid.

One of the boys looked up and saw me. 'You're back.' He paused and looked from the top of my head to my newly polished house shoes. Slowly, his eyes came back to my face.

I gritted my teeth and waited for the torment to begin all over again.

'We've decided not to beat you up this term.'

I put my elbows on the desk and let my head sink into my hands.

The girl next to me turned. 'It's because of the war you know. The state of the country.'

With that laconic announcement, delivered as if she was suggesting the rain might hold off that day, she returned to her exercise book and my world somersaulted back to normality.

The school closed before the end of the summer term. Several members of staff were to take the remaining children to Canada and both Biz and I were due to be evacuated with them. Two school trunks lay half packed on the floor of our bedroom. We could jump from the trunks, backwards and forwards, roll off, hide behind them. I would line my dolls up on top. Day after day we waited for the news of our departure date.

Each week Daisy made a Victoria sponge cake. She would allow me to clean out the bowl with my finger. A character in one of my unpublished novels, based in part on my memories of her, leaves a blob of the mixture on the wireless switch as she turns off the report of the sinking of the *City of Benares*. The ship had left Southampton with a cargo of children taking the route to Canada intended for us. The date was 17 September 1940 and we were due to sail any day.

That evening, as we were lying in bed, Biz and I heard our father's soothing voice and sobs that must have been coming from our mother, a sound we had never heard before. We crept out of bed, down to the sitting room and into her arms on the sofa.

'Don't worry darlings, I won't let you go.' She never called us darling. 'Whatever happens we'll stay together,' she said. 'We shall keep the family together, and die – if necessary – together.'

Once my parents had decided to keep us in this country, my mother arranged for me to go to her old school, St Felix, which had been evacuated from Southwold in Suffolk to a large mansion house in Somerset. Hinton House, Hinton St George was the seat of the Poulett family. The Earl at that time was distraught that his home had been commandeered for a horde of schoolgirls. Stories of his fury were retold from one girl to another with glee. A load of coal had been dumped in his beautiful courtyard and he was said to be demanding that each cobble be taken up, scrubbed and replaced in the same place. Needless to say, this did not happen and the rumour probably had no basis in fact.

I loved that house. For many years afterwards I could have led you through the attics or into the byways of the long avenues with my eyes closed. I did not need to go 'out of bounds' to find my own private places where I could stretch my eyes or contemplate the details of a leaf. My favourite spot was at the top of a bank behind thick rhododendron bushes with a view out over fields of flax and sugar beet. I remember thinking that if I ever lost the lift of spirit and sense of wonder produced by a distant horizon, or yellow lichen on a log, I would kill myself.

I never shone academically, my marks hovering just above or below the centre of the class. I learned little and consider myself ill educated. I have blamed poor teaching, believing that all the good teachers had left to do more important work for the war. In retrospect, my ignorance probably had as much to do with my temperament as with the quality of the lessons. There was little space for facts in the territory of my inner world, occupied as it was by emotion.

Most of the time I was in the throes of being 'gone on' some older girl. I would trail round after her, waiting in corners and behind doors to bump into her 'accidentally'. My greatest love of that time eventually got annoyed and told me, quite gently, to stop following her around. My world collapsed and I wrote home saying I was so unhappy I would run away.

Petrol was scarce, so my mother, despite intense fatigue, struggled onto a train. She had to stand in the corridor, squashed between servicemen and their kit bags, from Chippenham to Crewkerne. Then she took a taxi, a luxury to be indulged only in the most extreme emergency, arriving at the Poulett Arms in Lopen Head in time for me to join her for supper. This pub was used by parents on their rare visits and boasted a bowling alley which we enjoyed on happier occasions.

We talked of small things while I worked through a plate of meat and vegetables followed by treacle pudding, expecting her to ask questions at any moment. Instead she told me about the animals at home, the flowers she would plant for next year, the potatoes they planned to grow on the land designated for a tennis court after the war. Gradually, a sense of foolishness replaced my misery. After the meal we sat alone in a small sitting room in front of a wood fire. Only then did she ask, 'Do you want to talk about it?'

I could not find any sufficient reason for putting her to so much trouble. I had not broken up with my best friend, or been hit by a member of staff or even found worms wriggling in the toilet after I had used it. My only problem was that some girl had told me to stop following her around.

'No. I don't think so. I'm all right how.'

My mother was silent. Then nodded her head and changed the subject. She never mentioned it again.

I appreciated her forbearance. I was deeply ashamed that my stupid heart had caused her so much trouble: at the same time, her concern sustained me – and does so still.

Petrol rationing was introduced in 1942. At first there was a small basic allowance for social purposes but later this was removed and only essential workers were able to use their cars. Doctors were of course essential, but the police were strict if they thought the doctor was cheating. The only way my parents could get away from the house was by visiting their caravan, which they had parked in a field belonging to a successful farmer and patient. My father could drive the three miles and leave the car in his yard on the pretext of making a medical visit to the family. The van was parked down by the river Avon, an idyllic spot where they could seize a few hours' peace away from the constant ringing of the telephone and its demands.

Arthur had a small tent of his own while Biz and I lay down on mattresses in the canvas lean-to attached to the side of the van where our parents slept. One night during the Easter holidays we were all in bed when we heard thunder, though it was a clear night with stars and searchlights scanning the sky. We ran out in our pyjamas and bare feet to stand and watch the flashes of light, which preceded the worst of the explosions. My parents and Arthur realised that bombs were dropping, probably on Bath. I thought the lights were pretty but something in the tense way the adults turned from side to side made me cling to my father. At one particularly loud crash my mother also threw her arms around him, perhaps wondering if our own house had been hit. In the morning we learned that one stick of bombs had dropped on Chippenham, killing two of my father's patients.

As soon as it was light we packed everything away and went home. Back in my own bed I slept through a second night of noise. By the Monday morning it became clear to my parents that the rumours were true and Bath had been the target.

In her diary, which has now been published under the title *Carry on Coping*, my mother gives a vivid description of driving round Bath with thermoses of coffee and two spirit stoves in the back — looking for distressed doctors. She was trying to get to the Eye Infirmary on Lansdown Hill where she still worked. There was glass and debris all over the road. She passed many fire engines with hoses. Her journey goes on, constantly diverted and *still in streams of traffic unable to stop — no one asking for a lift and everyone following their own business grimly.* Many fires raged, including one church.

After two hours she reached her goal. The infirmary had no windows and there was blood on the steps, for it had been turned into a first aid station. She went in and found the matron rendering first aid and the waiting hall full of beds. *Dirt, dust, broken glass and mess indescribable. Cooking on open fires.* After a while, when my mother could not find anything medical to do, she went home.

As I read her account of that day I remember her standing in the hall on her return. She was grey and monosyllabic with dust and

35

fatigue. Daisy came out of the kitchen to tell her that the Colley family, two parents and three children, were leaving Bath and their damaged house and due to arrive at any moment. My mother was of course welcoming but she writes that Arthur and I were cross at having to give up our single rooms, though we tried to be good about it. For me, the day feels like a vacuum, filled with waiting and not understanding.

An unexploded bomb in the Circus in Bath, where most of the medical specialists lived, was not removed for two weeks. When at last the people were allowed back to inspect the damage to their property, my parents went over to help their friends try to make their homes habitable.

As I edited her diary for publication I read again of the passion with which my parents followed every twist of the war, and the ups and downs of every battle, of their fatigue and anxiety. I wish I could tell them that I do, at last, value the extraordinary shelter they provided for their children through those agonising years. A few years ago I had typed out the first two chapters of this diary and sent them to an exhibition of wartime memorabilia on show in Bath. One day I went in and recognised the sheets in the hands of a young man engrossed in her words.

'Excuse me,' I said, pointing to the pages in his hand. 'Do you know if there is another copy?' I could not remember how many I had provided.

He immediately held them out. 'Do have this – it is the most wonderful story. This woman doctor is driving round Bath on the day after the Blitz. Her descriptions are amazing.'

I waved them away, swelling with pride as I blurted out, 'That was my mother.'

4

'You Can't Want to Be a Nurse'

As I write I am looking at a small flip diary, the back and front covered in leather, the whole held together by a piece of perished elastic. At the top, two screws allow for new pages for each year. This object lived in my father's pocket all the years I knew him. Each morning he would take it out to see what repeat visits and appointments were booked. Then he added new calls, ticking them all off as he worked his way through the list.

He started to take me with him on his rounds when I was about seven years old. I stayed in the car, making up stories in which I was always the central, heroic character, a practice I only stopped entirely in my forties. As I sat in the car waiting for him to finish his call, I was sometimes frightened by local children, especially when we were in the poorer areas of town and I imagined they were looking at me in a hostile way. Once, when he took me on a visit to Lady Waldegrave, his only titled patient whom he attended for the first five of her confinements, I was so frightened by some geese in the drive that he took me in and left me in their enormous drawing room. After a while I became convinced that he had forgotten me. Tears were streaming down my face when he returned. To cheer me up, Lord Waldegrave rushed from the room and came back dressed in his robes. Throwing the train over his shoulder he boomed, 'What ho, Iolanthe?' He and my father began to sing the number about when Britain ruled the waves and the house of Peers 'made no pretence to intellectual eminence or scholarship sublime'. My father looked so happy that I was soon happy too.

Once I reached my teens he sometimes took me into the house to see a patient. By this time both my parents were hinting that I should train as a doctor. I had no wish to do so for I knew I would have to work hard and take more responsibility than I felt capable of shouldering. What I really wanted was to be a nurse but I did not dare to say so for a long time. I longed to make people comfortable in bed, bring them hot drinks and sympathy, not run the risk of misdiagnosing a life-threatening emergency. However, my father's patients were tolerant when they heard I might be going to follow in his footsteps.

My memories of a particularly busy Saturday remain with the clarity of a fine engraving. An agitated woman phoned for a visit to her husband who was in pain. She led us up to a cluttered but clean bedroom. I watched as my father sat on the edge of the double bed, his hand on the man's wrist as he asked for details. Then he took out the metal thermometer case with its screw top from a wallet, which also held his pen and pencil torch. He rinsed off the surgical spirit in the bathroom. After kneeling by the bed to look at, feel and listen to the man's abdomen, he told me to go back to the car.

Twenty minutes passed before he rejoined me. 'Thank goodness they had a phone. It has taken ages to make the arrangements.'

'What's the matter with him?'

'Acute appendicitis. I couldn't find a surgeon free to come and do it here so he has to go into Bath. Further for his wife to visit but I can't help that.' He turned on the engine and we drove off. 'This was a fairly classic case but I did a rectal examination anyway. I thought he might be embarrassed if you stayed.'

I knew what he was talking about and was only too glad I had escaped.

'The appendix is a great mimic,' he went on. 'In a case like this the diagnosis is not too difficult. If it is tucked away behind the caecum it can be the very devil.'

We got home to find a call to the hospital. Here he let me scrub up and put on a gown and mask so that I could hand him instruments as he cut the patient's hair and cleaned a nasty scalp wound, taking infinite care before putting in the stitches. As he finished, a message arrived to say he was wanted in a house in Sheldon Road. When we got there we found a boy, delirious with a high temperature and a very red, swollen ankle. My father looked serious, sent for an ambulance and rushed back to his workshop to make a splint to support the ankle during the journey.

The first of the sulphonamides, prontosil, had been discovered in 1935 and by the beginning of the war my father was using what he called M&B for infections. Penicillin was not manufactured till 1942 and I don't know whether it would have been available by injection for the serious infection in the bone, osteomyelitis, that we had just seen.

When I was even younger I went with him into the maternity home in Corsham to look at the babies. But he delivered most of his patients in their own homes. I was about thirteen when he allowed me to watch my first baby being born. The delivery took place in a farm labourer's cottage across three fields, where I got out to open and shut the gates, glad to be of some real use.

The birth was a joyful experience. For the first time I heard my father's mantra, 'Is it a little John or Mary? Ah, it is a Mary,' as he looked at the genitalia. In the days before ultrasound scans and genetic testing the sex of every baby was unknown until it was born. To a relative he would say, 'Put the kettle on will you? Mother could do with a cup of tea and so could I.' If it was a first baby the use of the word 'Mother' at that particular moment felt poignant and apt.

The maternity home in Corsham closed eventually and a converted house in Chippenham, called Greenways, was opened in time for my own daughter to be delivered, in 1959, by my father.

The practice of providing medical care to one's family was not considered unethical or even risky. Certainly, I would have trusted no one more than my father. He worked closely with the matron, a very experienced midwife who, knowing I was a doctor, asked me when I was in labour what pain relief I would like. I was in no state to take decisions, so after a pause she said, 'A dose of your father's tipple, I think.' I did not know or care what it contained. Anything recommended by my father would have worked for me.

I suspect the magic potion he recommended was similar to chlorodyne, a famous medicine patented in the nineteenth century by Dr John Collis Browne. It contained an alcoholic solution of opium (laudanum), tincture of cannabis and chloroform. My father certainly prescribed it freely, often mixed with other agents from the dispensary jars. I have been told that in the 1960s it was available as a recreational drug, often with a special room set aside for its use. At some stage the cannabis was removed and the dose of opiate reduced so that my father complained the remedy became a shadow of its former self. However, when my sister started travelling, and then emigrated to the US in the early sixties it was still reasonably potent, especially for the treatment of diarrhoea. She took a bottle of the tincture with her. She tells me the dose was ten drops. When a favourite cat had a severe tummy upset they added two drops to a dish of cream. My father had provided her precious supply, probably illegally, and she used it so sparingly that when I checked the facts with her recently she said there was still some left in her cupboard – fifty years later.

As I was growing through my early teenage years the opportunity to share medical experiences with my father made me feel special, a need perhaps in all children with siblings. One of the happiest times of my life was one Christmas Day. By family tradition, presents were put on the windowsill in the dining room and opened after break-fast. The parcels were few by today's standards, one each from our parents, perhaps two or three in brown paper from aunts or grandparents, and a small one from Daisy. On that morning my father asked us to wait before we dived in to rip off the wrappings. From his outside pocket he produced an envelope.

'This is for you,' he said, handing it to my mother. She opened it and found a book token.

His hand disappeared again and came out with another envelope for my brother containing a five-pound note. With the third offering in his hand he turned to my younger sister. 'Here you are Biz, not quite so much for you as you are younger.'

As I watched her pull out a one-pound note my eyes filled with tears. I came next in the pecking order, how could he forget me? I heard his voice.

'I have no envelope for you, Ruth, I have spent all my money. But perhaps this would do instead.'

I lifted my eyes to see him reach into a pocket inside his suit jacket made by order to carry his stethoscope. The parcel he produced contained a wooden flute.

'You never told me that was what you were doing in London,' said my mother, in a hurt voice.

I had been trying to get a note on his flute during the summer holidays and he had encouraged me. Without discussing the matter with anyone he had chosen one for me to have as my own. It was that reticence, as if his feelings for me were too private and important to be shared even with his wife, which still brings a lump to my throat.

His flute has a story of its own. He bought it when he was a medical student and took it with him to India after he had qualified and joined the RAMC. On the way the boat was torpedoed. Over the Tannoy the order came to abandon ship. He disobeyed and went below to collect his flute. By the time he came back on deck another ship had drawn alongside and they were pulling the men from the water. Because he was the ship's doctor he was wanted aboard in good condition so they put him in a net and threw him, clutching the instrument, from one vessel to the other.

I inherited both that flute and another from him, so that when I wanted to start playing again in my sixties I had three to choose from. To my delight the experts said his original instrument was the one worth repairing and I played it for several years, until I changed to a silver one which was less sensitive to moisture.

At school, singing took precedence. The music teacher was inspirational, insisting with great ferocity that we watch her baton, a habit so ingrained that I bless her every time I play with a conductor. She made me leader of the choir, a job I relished. If she had taught me the flute as well I might have persevered. As it was, once I left school I only picked it up in a desultory way, stopping altogether when my husband winced and my dog howled, waiting to return to it when they had both died.

Making music with others is now one of the great joys of my life. I have few regrets about the way my life has evolved for I have had more than my share of luck. But I am sad not to have reached a higher standard of flute playing when I was young. Those who reached grade seven or eight in their youth seem able to return to an instrument later in life and regain their original standard. As I never rose above grade five or six I cannot hope to improve above that level, which is not good enough to play the first flute part in an orchestra.

During those years, when I was very close to my father, my relationship with my mother remained complicated. I believed that Biz was her favourite. Not only was she the youngest but she was more intelligent and her stories made my mother laugh with delight. I still winced at a sharp word. My mother knew of my sensitivity and tried to curb her tongue. 'Ruth does feel her feelings so,' I heard her say once when I should not have been listening.

My poor spelling has haunted me all my life. Children at boarding schools were expected to write home, usually once a week on Sunday. In her reply my mother wrote out my misspelt words at the top of her letter with the faults underlined. I am not dyslexic and during my psychoanalysis I realised the extent of my fury. The suggestion that my failure to learn was an unconscious expression of spite made a lot of sense. My mother had been trying to help, only wanting her daughter to be able to take her place in the educated world, but I waited for her to be genuinely interested in my news, not critical of the way I reported it. My brother reacted to the same treatment by vowing never to write more than a few words in any letter and I felt particularly honoured recently when his Christmas letter ran to two pages.

In the holidays I mooched around Arthur in the nursery, which he had now been given as his own room, and in the workshop where he continued to make things. We rode out together on our bicycles, often to Hullavington airfield where we lay in the hedge and watched the planes leave and return. It had been opened in 1937 and became the Empire Training School in 1942. At that time seventeen different types of plane are listed as being seen there. No wonder Arthur was so keen to develop his skills in identification!

There was so little traffic on the roads that we were quite safe on our bicycles. Indeed the lanes were so quiet that my mother used to exercise the two dogs by running them behind the car for a mile or two. Gerda the dachshund got tired first and was lifted back into the car, while Bertha with her long Dalmatian legs could keep going much longer.

Daisy continued to cook for us all and run the household. In time, Arthur and I became irritated by her efforts to control us. One day we ran away. Leaving a note, we took our bicycles and went to the caravan. Arthur tells me that on our journey we bought three potatoes but I remember raiding the store cupboard in the van for tins of sardines and baked beans: not a very imaginative or courageous revolt. As the evening drew on and the light faded, I began to regret our bad temper and was relieved when my father arrived. He explained how dependent the family was on Daisy, how impossible it would be for our mother to manage without her and asked us to be more tolerant. Shamefaced we followed him home. When I read my mother's account of the episode in her diary, of her belief that there was right on both sides, I realise how intensely she wanted to provide us with a happy home. She even considered getting rid of the invaluable Daisy as soon as her own medical work was no longer essential.

In a happier joint venture, Arthur and I visited our grandparents by ourselves. They owned a double skiff. Family holidays during wartime were usually spent in the caravan, parked in their garden, which was large enough to hold a croquet lawn, tennis court and cricket pitch. Our joint expeditions on the river were happy interludes. My mother had been given a punt for her twenty-first birthday so we had a choice of craft. She associated the stretch of water upstream from Pangbourne with her own happy adolescence and was relaxed while we were there. D, dressed in white flannel trousers, emblazoned jacket and neckerchief, with either a Cambridge Trinity College cap or a straw hat called a boater on his head, had taught us how to behave in a boat. One must not drag one's fingers in the water; always pull in to the side before changing places; never have more than one person standing up at the same time.

Few cabin cruisers spoiled the peace, only the wash from the Salters steamers, plying up and down to Oxford, disturbed the smooth ride. I could scull by the time I was thirteen, feathering my oars with some skill and looking with disdain at people in tub-like rowing boats who chopped at the water in ungainly bites. During our visit we were allowed to take the skiff out by ourselves. Eating our picnic lunch on the move we got to the furthest limit ever reached by a family party, even with two strong men at the oars, going through Goring and Cleeve locks to the islands above. Over supper that night, Mum's Mum quizzed us on our day. 'We got to the islands,' Arthur said, with a straight face. The atmosphere chilled as it was assumed he was referring to the Harts Wood islands, barely half an hour upstream. All through the meal I was bursting to let the truth out, for even my loving grandmother was looking disappointed. Only when we reached the end of the meal did my brother say laconically, 'Oh, not those islands, the ones above Cleeve.' Our backs were slapped, Mum's Mum searched out palms for blisters and D poured a small glass of sherry, not only for Arthur but also for me. I had at last, with Arthur's help, done something to gain his respect.

When Arthur left school he joined the Fleet Air Arm, a branch of the Royal Navy responsible for its planes. He had hoped to be a pilot but was prevented by his red/green colour blindness. When he and a friend visited me and Biz at school in Somerset, in their naval ratings' uniform, they caused a stir for we seldom saw men of any kind. We were allowed to walk with them round the grounds, followed by the admiring glances of all the girls we passed.

We were an extremely protected group, never let out of the grounds unless we walked in a crocodile with two senior prefects. The main impact of the war was food rationing. We all had our own tiny pats of butter and jars of jam that we collected from a tray each day. Although the diet was nutritionally adequate we did feel hungry. As I stood in the queue watching the helpings of tart being served out, I tried to judge if I would get one with the extra pastry edge, or even better, a precious corner. Missing out felt like a major deprivation.

I do not remember ever reading a newspaper or discussing the war or politics, our only contact with reality being the red eyes of an occasional girl coming to terms with the loss of a father or brother. Our concerns were which house would win the hockey shield and who would play the part of Viola in the performance of *Twelfth Night* planned to take place in the sunken garden.

As my School Certificate exam approached, discussions at home about my future became more intense. One day my mother and I were sitting on the seat at the end of the swimming pool, my father standing by her side contemplating the murky water. I took a deep breath. Aiming my remark at his shoulder, not looking at my mother, I said, 'What I really want... is to be a nurse.'

She exploded. 'You can't want to be a nurse. If you are going to work with people you must do it properly – as a doctor.' She leapt to her feet and looked down at me. 'No daughter of mine is going to be a handmaiden to someone else. That is not why we have gone to so much trouble to give you a good education.'

My father said nothing but I knew that if I gave in and followed my mother's choice he would be happy. His ideas about equality for women included them training for a profession; nursing did not have the same cachet. My determination to make my own choice seeped away.

In my heart I have often thanked my mother for her intransigence. I have never regretted the decision, even if it was made for the wrong reasons. I was not called into medicine by some long-standing wish to heal the world. I was lucky that the need to please my father and avoid antagonising my mother led me into a profession that offers many choices. A surgeon does not have to be brilliant with people, for his or her patients are asleep much of the time. Pathology is even further removed from interaction with living people. On the other hand, general practice depends as much on the art of communication as on pure science. I enjoyed that field, and my good fortune led me to the niche of family planning and psychosexual medicine that fitted me particularly well. In addition I must admit that a well-paid job is useful, especially if one wants to work part time while raising a family.

The announcement of peace in Europe was expected on 7 May 1945. My mother's account of that time forms the climax of her diary. She describes feeling drained of emotion, very different from her experience in 1918. Then she joined her father and roistered round the city, revelling with the crowds as the maroons went off and they all celebrated their belief that there would never be another war. But in 1945 she just felt numb, with no sense that civilisation was fundamentally decent. She was acutely aware of the state of Europe with its starvation and physical ruin, and the fact that we still had to fight the Japanese and Arthur would be involved in that battle.

At school someone had smuggled in a wireless and at 8 o'clock, when we were preparing for bed, we heard Churchill say that the next day would be a national holiday to celebrate VE day. Cheering broke out in the stateroom dormitories, five huge connected rooms with 15–20 beds in each. As the noise subsided Miss Williamson, the headmistress, stood in the sunken garden outside, and raised her voice in condemnation. She was disgusted by our unruly behaviour and we would not be allowed to take part in the national holiday but would have to work a normal day as a punishment. Even at that moment of national rejoicing we were kept isolated from the wider world. I can only think that she felt threatened by the noise, panicked into a fear that the mass of nubile femininity would become unmanageable. It is only now that I can see how challenging her job must have been, with a diminished staff, families uprooted and a camp of American servicemen nearby. The restrictions I found so irksome were prompted by understandable concerns for our safety.

5

Teenage Years

True to form, my results in the School Certificate (subsequently O levels and then GCSE) were mediocre. I only sat seven exams, a feeble effort compared to many children nowadays with ten or eleven subjects. I obtained six credits and a distinction in geography. My husband teased me about this as I was still muddling the East and West Indies when we got married. To my deep regret I had given up history when we reached Ur of the Caldees for my mother did not think it an important subject. My profound ignorance about the past added to my sense that I was stupid. Reading historical novels I just followed the romance, as I had no milestones around which to build the extra knowledge to be gleaned from such stories.

St Felix School moved back to Southwold in the autumn of 1945. The purpose-built red-brick buildings and well-marked playing fields lacked the private corners in the house and garden at Hinton St George, where I could find small but precious slivers of solitude. But I came to appreciate the romantic, windswept coast and undulating dunes of Suffolk, especially after I saw an unidentified bird flapping over the dykes, disappearing in the dips to emerge a few seconds later. Not long afterwards I spent a weekend at Flatford Mill, immortalised in Constable's painting, but by then converted into a nature study centre. From my careful notes of the bird's markings the tutor could identify it as a short-eared owl. Whenever I see a reproduction of *The Hay Wain* I am reminded that I slept in the room behind that window in Willy Lott's cottage. It was in there that, when a friend's hair caught light from a candle, I was able to smother it before the flames had done more than frizzle the ends.

Little of what I was taught in school remains in my mind. Just once, I felt a stab of recognition. I was driving across the plains of Alberta. Nodding donkeys dotted the yellow, autumnal landscape, exact replicas of the picture on page twenty-three in my geography book. The isolated excrescences stood as evidence of the oil wells below.

During the Christmas holidays, in the last year before I left school, I went to my first dance, held at Corsham Court. I wore a floor-length blue dress lent by the wife of a local doctor, with my long hair pinned up with kirby grips into curls all over my head. It should have been the most romantic occasion but turned into something of a nightmare. Biz and I were good friends with Richard Awdry and his younger brother Philip. That night Richard was, in my view, the most handsome boy in the room. He was also literate and amusing – but he spent the whole evening dancing with a pretty brunette. I sat behind a pillar discussing the dissection of dogfish with another schoolboy, both of us feeling too plain and nervous to dance: and if I had taken to the floor my hair might have come down. A picture from the local paper shows the guests crowded on a staircase, and there is Richard with his brunette and I a few rows behind, looking anxious.

Before the war such parties, even in much smaller private houses, had been common. My parents had given one in Green Gables. They rolled the carpet back in the nursery, sprinkled powdered chalk on the floorboards and put 78 rpm records on the gramophone. I must have been eight or nine at the time and was allowed to join in with Arthur provided we promised to go to bed promptly at 9 o'clock. The last dance, Sir Roger Decoverley, was moved forward so we could take part before we were banished. I was both proud and furious when I overheard someone say, 'The little dears, so good of them to go to bed without making a fuss.'

* * *

Back at school after my visit to Corsham Court, my three sixth-form subjects had been dictated by my mother's decision that I should be a doctor: biology, physics and chemistry. The only one that held the slightest interest for me was biology. We had a good teacher who was married and marginally more interested in the way living things, including human beings, worked. I learned physics by rote, messed up the practical chemistry exam and did not reach the required standard for the place in the second year of the medical course that I had been offered at Bristol University. Luckily they had forgotten to state in their letter that my exemption from the first MB was dependent on my grades. My father created a fuss and they were forced to accept me into the first year. I am ashamed that I only managed to get into university because of an administrative fault.

Before I took up that place I negotiated two important milestones. In two hours during the summer I became an adult... or so it felt to me. At that time women with long hair wore it up, the plaits wound into bangs over the ears or round their heads. Only children wore them hanging down. This rigid distinction allowed no opportunity to oscillate between being a child and a grown up. When I insisted that I wanted my plaits cut off my mother eventually agreed, but only if I went to her special hairdresser in London, where he was to put a perm in the remaining hair. I sat in the chair with my mother standing by my side as we watched the long strands fall to the floor. In the mirror, she looked devastated. The man applied lotions and papers and curlers and a disgusting chemical smell filled the room. Once it was washed off and my hair had been dried I watched the head in the mirror turning from side to side, unable to accept that it belonged to me. With no experience of brushing short hair, let alone helping it into any sort of style, it was a tangled wreck by the next morning.

I remained dependent on a perm until my seventies when I found a hairdresser who could cut in such a way that she discovered a hidden wave. What bliss to be able to go out in the rain without the fear of becoming a corkscrew mess. However fashionable such a look might be today, it was an embarrassment in waiting for me, necessitating ugly waterproof hoods in the pockets of every coat.

My other important experience that year was a trip to France with Arthur. Apart from staying with relatives there had been no previous opportunity for me to travel anywhere without my parents. We put our bicycles on the train to Avignon and rode down the Rhone valley. After a few days we reached the Mediterranean at Sete but could find nowhere to stay for the night. Out of the town we found a flat spot at the edge of a vineyard. We were not equipped for camping but slept on our Macintosh coats. I was terrified by noises in the next field... clearly murderers, thieves or at the very least bad-tempered French onion men in flat caps, who floated in my memory from the days before the war. I clung to the long-suffering Arthur until, as daylight finally arrived, we discovered a herd of cows munching along the hedge.

We continued up into the Pyrenees by putting our bikes on the top of buses. I was no good at pedalling my bike uphill. Earlier I had gone to the Wye valley with three school friends, ending the trip on the back of a lorry because I could not keep up. I have never known if this was because I had a particularly heavy bike or whether my heart/lung capacity is not large enough for my body; or perhaps I am just a wimp.

Again, in the mountains we had trouble finding a room. By then there were piles of snow by the roadside and I was terrified of another night in the open. At the fifth hotel I burst into tears. Immediately the end of a corridor was curtained off, mattresses and bedding found and we sat down in front of large bowls of soup. To my shame I discovered then that tears could get me out of all sorts of scrapes, including those embarrassing times much later when I was caught exceeding the speed limit in my car.

The journey down to Carcassonne was wonderful. We free-wheeled round hairpin bends, the wind in our faces as the verges sped by. Once we reached the attractive town, with its castle on the top of a hill, we again boarded the train. On the way home we bought two small cakes at a French station to take back for Biz. I discovered years later, when I tried to make them, that they were a kind of Vacherin, a mixture of meringue, hazelnuts, sweet chestnut puree and cream. This was 1947 and no one in England had tasted anything of the sort for years. The family could not believe that such luxuries were available in France, so soon after the country had been devastated and when we were still suffering severe food rationing. We all watched as my sister started to eat. Overcome by the need to be appreciative, she rushed away to finish them in private.

We had been encouraged by both our parents to make the trip. They had a passion for France and had taken various cars across the channel before the war. We had heard many tales and been shown the faded photo albums recording their meanderings, their adventures in tiny rural hotels and crossing high passes where the radiators of my father's old-fashioned cars boiled. A small statuette of Phineas, a reproduction of the wooden mascot of their Alma Mater, University College Hospital, was mounted on the radiator cap of each car in turn. When the radiator was about to boil, the cap would work loose and the mascot turned to face them.

In retrospect I think it was generous of them to use their small allowance of foreign currency to send us abroad, rather than to seize the first opportunity to escape once more on a life-giving journey. For me, travelling around rural France with no definite plans, arriving at some unknown destination, up a farm track, in a mountain village or by a river, became my vision of the ideal holiday.

In my first year at Bristol the syllabus was less demanding than the one I had already worked through at school, giving me plenty of time to adjust to a different world. My first friend was a miner's daughter from Abertillery who was experienced in the art of make-up and dealing with boys. She took me to buy lipstick and stood by while I smeared it round my mouth. We went together to dances at the Victoria rooms, now the department of music but then the student union. We girls did not dance with each other but sat around the walls until the boys had boosted their courage with enough beer to ask us to dance. Recently I met a man who had been in my year.

He told me that with a friend he devised a system whereby they could capture the prettiest girls. They would stand by the door watching as we came in, simpering and preening. Having made their choice they would rush to the bar, down a pint or two for courage and then descend on their chosen prey.

The best dance was the Paul Jones where the girls circled one way, the boys in an outside ring going in the opposite direction. When the music stopped you were expected to dance with the person opposite. If he was nice, one hoped he would ask for the next dance. If he was odious I would shoot away, often taking refuge in the ladies' room to titivate my hair yet again. I still felt intimidated by the array of powder and paint used by my neighbours with such skill.

For my first two years I lived in Clifton Hill House, one of the halls of residence. The house is at the top of a steep hill. By the time we had walked up and down twice during the day we were ravenous. Bread was rationed until 25 July 1948 so my memory of eating a small brown loaf at one sitting, from the crust at one end to the very last crumb of crust at the other, must come from that year.

Men were not allowed in the women's halls, certainly not during the evenings. Couples outside the front door, often three or four, would stand clinched for ages while those of us embarrassingly single would sprint past into the safety of the house, hoping not to meet a mouse or a rat. In retrospect the rodent that I encountered on the stairs has grown in size and ferocity. Its eyes glinted at me for what seemed to be several minutes but could have been all of ten seconds before it retreated. The only other rat I saw was trapped in one of the early washing-up machines. The shrieks of a maid drew me to the kitchens where I found it circling, frantic to get out. I calmed the frightened woman and turned on the machine, drowning it as quickly as possible. The memory of the kittens drowned at home helped my determination to do what I thought was the kindest thing.

Several young men showed some interest in me but I had no idea how to behave. My friend offered much good advice. Although I was flattered and excited by the hand holding and surreptitious kisses I soon tired of them all. I continued to yearn after Richard until he let drop the remark that he would never marry a professional woman. When he and his second wife asked me to lunch recently I found a man who was still totally charming, but who firmly denied that he had ever said such a thing.

During the Easter vacation I hitch-hiked to Scotland and back with another girl. Many people had journeyed 'on their thumbs' during the war, especially service men and women going to and from home leave. It was considered bad form to drive past without stopping. We had little difficulty getting lifts, for the habit of picking up those without other means of transport was still ingrained in those lucky enough to have petrol.

I revelled in the mix of people we met. On one occasion we climbed down from the back of a lorry, windswept and covered in dust. We just had time to buy two buns and start to eat them when a luxurious car, it might have been a Bentley, swept past. It came to a stop with a squeal of brakes and backed towards us. The two businessmen inside had growing families of their own and were amused by the cheek of our trip. The studs of our boots left indents in the deep pile of the fitted carpet.

They drove us 148 miles, with a comfortable stop for a three-course meal. I was embarrassed by their generosity, which was altruistic with no sexual innuendo. I believed that the only way we could repay all such kindness was to encourage the drivers to talk, if they wanted to, and listen to their life stories. Showing interest was no hardship. The different lives I had glimpsed when visiting patients with my father had left me thirsty for contact with different sorts of people.

At last our route diverged from that of the Bentley and we clambered out. As soon as it had disappeared round a bend in the road we took out the remains of our buns, searching our pockets for the shredded morsels. We were both eighteen but must have been growing still for despite the large meal we were hungry again.

After the restrictions of boarding school the freedom at university was heady. Despite the possibility of a widening social life I hated to have any commitments at the weekends and used any excuse to keep both days empty. I would walk alone to the centre of Bristol, where the buses started for the surrounding countryside. I took no notice of the destination written on the front but leapt onto the first one with its engine running. I always bought a ticket to the end of the line. When I got off I wandered wherever my feet took me with no interest in maps or making a plan. I wanted to be open to 'adventures'. Any chance encounter with a horse, a postman or an old woman in a cottage helped to ease the constricting ache that had built up during the years of confinement. It was not too difficult to find a bus or train, or even to hitch-hike back to the city. These excursions were tame flickers of a candle compared to the flashing neon signs of today's adolescent global travellers.

One day I got off at Brislington and followed a footpath to the river Avon where I found a rusty bell. I struck it with a piece of iron hanging by the side. In due course a man in a rowing boat arrived to ferry me across, demanding a few pence in payment.

Ever since my excursions on the river with my parents and grandparents I have loved rivers. Perhaps this was because those family holidays had been particularly happy times for my mother, and I was always sensitive to her moods. Now I had found my own river and a unique way of getting across. I was already composing a story to tell her, hoping to impress her as much by my escapades as those of my sister.

On the other side of the water a pub stood with its door open. I had never been in a pub by myself before but mustered my courage and went in to order a sandwich. It was not full of rowdy men, as I had feared. The bread was stale but I was so hungry that seemed unimportant. Afterwards I walked along the bank. Suddenly I saw something swimming in the water. Its flat head and sinuous, silvery body below the water convinced me it was an otter, though I had never seen one. All thought of my mother vanished, as I became absorbed in stalking it along the side of the river across two fields. I watched it moving from one side to the other, feeling that ineffable lift of the spirit that occasionally fills my being. The emotion is private, perhaps nearest to the essence of me, quite separate from any need to please my parents or anyone else.

Such moments are rare and cannot be produced by an effort of will. They only arrive in response to some natural beauty and only when I am alone. After my husband died they deserted me for several years. I feared the loss would last forever. Then one day I was driving along the A46 from Bath to the M4. At the top of Swainswick hill the view across a wide valley drew my eyes. There had been a heavy hoarfrost. Every twig and blade of grass was shimmering in the new-risen sun. Marion Milner, whose writing inspires me, talks about near vision and distant vision and the discipline of using both. At the top of that hill the two perspectives combined with magical effect.

These fleeting moments are the nearest my plebeian soul gets to rapture or religious experience – my analyst called them 'love'. I will not banish the word despite its amoebic ability to change shape, the lightness of a puff of wind and the density of a black hole. The ground beneath it shifts and the sky tilts but, when it pushes into these pages I will not be deterred from exploring its nuances.

6

Preparing for Medicine — and Marriage

Outside the dissecting room I braced myself, determined not to be shocked or faint or disgrace myself in front of the others. We were a disparate group, the girls straight from school, while more than half the men had served in the armed forces. Several faces were new, having been exempted from the first year, as I should have been if I had got adequate grades in my final school exam. I was in awe of the older men who had seen life and death, imagining they would have no qualms about dead bodies.

The doors opened and we walked in. Four of us were assigned to each table where a body was stretched out, the skin cold, not rock hard but resistant to the touch, firmer than dough. The features were shrivelled into anonymity. We sat on stools, two at the right arm, two the left. One person at each table read from the anatomy book while the others plied their scalpels. Two or three demonstrators moved between the stations encouraging the direction and depth of our cuts, explaining how to tease the yellow fat away from the exsanguinated arteries and the more difficult thread-like nerves.

My own nerves were under tight control. At no time, then or during the next eighteen months, did I admit to feelings of disgust. Only on waking from nightmares in which I was eating human flesh did I glimpse my private horror.

Several years after I qualified, I joined a seminar for General Practitioners run by Dr Michael Balint. He was an Austrian psychoanalyst with a revolutionary interest in what went on between doctors and patients. The psychodynamic idea, that the feelings of a therapist or doctor might have been provoked by the client or patient, allowed us to accept that feelings were worthy of study. Those meetings helped me to realise that the day I walked into the dissecting room saw the first of many defensive layers, like the outer protective skins of an onion, clamp round my vulnerable heart. I realise this metaphor is not very accurate, for most of the layers of an onion are soft and provide nutrition for the inner sprouting potential. At the time I felt constricted and needed to be able to remove those dry, brown layers in order to be able to use my inner nourishment to develop.

Doctors need defences in order to survive the job, especially when they are confronted by the suffering they see in hospitals. I discussed this many years later with GP trainers who were introducing students to patients in their first year. They suggested that in order to practise a caring and humane approach, students needed to observe compassion early in training. The experience would then remain as a core of sensitivity which could be revisited later when they were emotionally mature enough to share a larger part of the suffering of others.

Dissecting the whole body took eighteen months and we spent many hours each week on the task. I remember few of the details, neither the four facts needed about each muscle – origin, insertion, nerve supply and action – nor the course of any of the nerves that I repeated in mantra form. But a general understanding of how our bodies are made is built into my understanding of the world. A medical friend pointed out that this knowledge separates us from many other people. We know what lies under the skin of each finger, the position of our internal organs and how the vertebrae work to perform their multiple functions, keeping us upright, allowing us to bend and protecting the spinal cord: whereas, in the main, non-medics do not.

I notice I have not included the brain in the list. We dissected the head and neck last. When the time came, a laboratory assistant sawed off the top of the skull for us. After careful inspection of the contents we severed the nerves that passed through holes in the base and lifted the organ out. Slicing it into sections was a delicate job. It might have been done for us. I remember watching the special long knife sink into the convolutions as if passing through soft butter. This particular image is still disturbing, perhaps because I believe that if our cadaver had possessed a soul it had resided in that flesh.

Although we learned something about the different areas of the brain, such as those for speech and vision, the study of its gross anatomy offered no key to the magical way it functions. Recent advances in imaging the living brain have revealed wonders to rival any discoveries in particle physics, quantum mechanics or the depths of space. Even those people with no anatomical training will now have more understanding of the brain than we did in the 1950s.

When my daughter studied anatomy in the late seventies she did no personal dissection. Although detailed anatomical knowledge is obviously essential for someone who is going to be a surgeon, with medicine now so specialised many doctors never touch a scalpel after they qualify. Belatedly, it has been recognised that other subjects are more important at the undergraduate level.

I cannot leave the dissecting room without recalling one of our demonstrators whose right hand was a useless claw. Her ambition had been to work as a surgeon in some far country. She had developed an infection in one of the deep compartments of the hand, each separated from the other by a strong band of fascia. An essential part of the treatment of any infection in such a confined space is the release of pus. Her doctor inserted his lance into the wrong pocket. The resulting scar tissue was so strong and dense that it contracted the muscles and destroyed the nerves. All students who passed through the department in her time were word perfect when tested on the fascial divisions of the hand.

Physiology was the other subject in our second and third years. Much of the work was practical and consisted of testing our own body fluids. We stalked down corridors carrying pots of urine and took blood from each other's veins. I cannot forget the sickly smell of new-drawn blood when it was not smothered by disinfectant as it is in hospitals. I wonder if this tang is present in war zones or whether the stench of mud, excrement and explosives overpowers the spilled blood.

The worst part of the experimental work was swallowing a Ryle's tube to withdraw some of the contents of the stomach for analysis. At first we pushed them down each other but if that failed the staff were fierce, taking no notice of our gagging but continuing to shove, intoning 'swallow, swallow'. One girl vomited repeatedly and was eventually excused. But I was glad to have survived what was a frequent procedure for patients.

The pre-clinical departments of the hospital were scattered in various buildings, allowing plenty of opportunity for coffee, chat and a cake (if one could afford it) between sessions in the labs and lecture theatres. I continued to go to dances at the Victoria rooms, to sing in the choir and take an active part in university 'rag' weeks. One year I exhausted myself shaking a tin as I jumped on and off buses dressed in pyjamas and dressing gown. In support of our efforts, the bus company charged us no fees.

Once the second MB exam was behind us we progressed to 'walking the wards' of various hospitals. A group of students was assigned to a 'firm', usually consisting of two consultants and their junior staff. We moved through attachments in medicine and surgery at the Bristol Royal Infirmary (BRI), interspersed with other subjects. ENT was covered at the general hospital, where the air was heavy with the stench of brewing from the local industry. We were introduced to the paediatric enthusiasms and piercing questions of Professor Neal in the children's hospital, at the top of St Michael's Hill opposite the site where the new maternity hospital would be built. For our obstetrics we had to sleep in at Southmead in order to fulfil our quota of twenty deliveries. At the same time we were studying pathology at Canynge Hall under the watchful eye of Professor Hewer, his exotic bow ties jumping on his Adam's apple as he explained what we were seeing down the microscope – or not seeing.

When each student was assigned a new patient he or she had to take a history, perform a physical examination and then present the findings to the whole firm at the bedside. Some consultants were more sensitive to the listening patient than others. I was shy, finding it difficult to relax with the patient alone and even more uncomfortable talking about his signs and symptoms to the others.

I had particular difficulty hearing the heart murmurs that were the signs of diseased valves, a serious complication of rheumatic fever. That illness could follow an attack of scarlet fever, common at the time and a more serious disease before the introduction of penicillin, although some consider the streptococcus has also become less virulent. Our professor of medicine, Bruce Perry, had a particular interest in the cardiac complications. My good friend Christine Willis suffered from a bad attack at the end of our first year. She had to rest for many months and her medical training was delayed by a year.

The student common rooms at the BRI were segregated by sex. The men played bridge and if I had been given the opportunity to join them I would have played all day. My passion for cards was born playing rummy with my grandmother. She loved to gamble and her grandfather clock, inherited by my brother, was won in a card game aboard ship on one of her winter cruises. I never played for money but my daughter tells me that when her turn came to be initiated into rummy her great grandmother took her pennies with no compunction.

In my fourth year I moved out of Clifton Hill House to share a flat with my cousin Jenny. She had come to Bristol to study social work and we continued the friendship that had been so important to us before it was interrupted by the war. Clifton suspension bridge, one of my favourite places, was within walking distance. If I needed to escape, usually from my own feelings of embarrassment or inadequacy, I would storm up the path to a corner where I could gaze at the single span supported by thick cables. The water, or more often the extensive mud banks, glistened below in the light of sun or moon. On the surface of a sloping rock a bright track gleamed, with a patch of rough grass at the bottom to act as a safety stop for the generations who had used it as a slide. Leigh valley woods covered the opposite side, and the buildings of Bristol lay beyond the bridge to the left, the cranes rising like exclamation marks in several areas. The sky above could provide spectacular sunsets.

Although the war had been over for several years a great deal of rebuilding was still taking place in the city. With the wind in the right direction one could hear the thump of pile drivers. I would imagine the houses with their varied occupants: children coming home with school satchels, housewives at the doors in their pinnies, men hurrying home for tea.

Jenny and I continued to share our inner worlds in the way we had done when we had galloped our horses round the garden at Green Gables and stabled them in the garage. One evening we took a cloud-formed journey into a land of beaches and seas, rocks and mountains that led to our imagined future. Her dream was of a house in the country, children, horses and chickens, with croquet on the lawn. That dream materialised in much of its detail. My own was less clear-cut, the edges obscured by the need to fit a professional life into the jigsaw.

Perhaps my daydream was also vague because reality, in the form of my future husband, was now edging into my life. I first met Ralph at one of those dances held in the house of some friends, although I had a single previous image of him. He had attended a small school that my mother had organised at Green Gables before Arthur went to boarding school. She employed a trained teacher and asked a few children of local friends to join him in classes. I was only three at the time. Daisy told me that when they marched round the garden doing squats and stretches I would follow, remaining down to play with stones after they had risen and moved on. I can see Ralph, perhaps standing taller from my perspective on the ground, at the top of a grassy slope, a pale, freckled boy, withdrawn but in some way a presence, at least in my mind.

When I told my mother whom I had met at the dance she said, 'Whatever you do, don't marry a diabetic.' It was not perversity that made me do just that. Ralph intrigued me. He had gone into the

Rajputana Rifles, via the Somerset Light Infantry, straight from school. At the age of seventeen he sailed for India as a private. Unwilling to scrabble for a better place he slept on the dining room table. He was a quiet man who wrote poetry and had an ironic sense of humour.

He had hoped to cure his fear of heights by learning to parachute. It did not work and throughout our marriage I had to change light bulbs and fix curtain rails as he was never comfortable standing on a chair.

In 1946 he had developed diabetes, undiagnosed until he returned from India to his home in Bath weighing five stone. By the time we met at the dance he was studying philosophy and psychology at Oxford, leading a fairly isolated life, organising the local judo and boxing clubs, and listening to jazz, but doing little else while he recovered from his experiences. He did not discuss these with me, as if in some way he needed to keep me innocent, or perhaps to keep his innocence in me. After he died I discovered he had confided stories of his war to one of my friends. She told me of the time he threatened to kill an English doctor who refused to go into a cage to treat the confined prisoners. Ralph's gun did not waver – so the doctor went in.

All his life he was on the side of the underdog, one of the qualities that attracted me to him. In a railway carriage once, three men were lamenting the number of foreigners, especially coloured people, who had immigrated into the country. He said nothing until he was asked for his opinion. Then he raised his head. 'It is hard for me,' he said, 'I am a quarter Japanese.' Then he retired back to his newspaper. His landed family had been in Somerset since the beginning of the sixteenth century and may have arrived with the Vikings. But his typical, thin-lipped Skrine face could, with some imagination, have concealed a smattering of oriental blood.

After I passed my pathology exam, at the end of the fourth year, I planned a short holiday on the Isle of Sark. At that time Jenny could not come with me and as no other friend was free I decided to go alone. I joked that people would think I was going in order to decide

63

whom to marry or to recover from a broken heart. As the day drew near the humour wore thin. One evening when it was pouring with rain I burst into the flat.

'This is the most important moment of my life,' I said as I stood with my hands pushed against the closed door, water streaming down my face.

Jenny smiled at my self-dramatisation. 'Really? How do you know?'

'Ralph has just asked if he can come with me to Sark.'

'Is that such a big deal?'

'I'll have to ask my mother.' I went home the next day and put the question to her. The reply was typical.

'An excellent idea, see if you can stand each other, but I won't tell anyone outside the family.'

Such a trip alone with a man was still not considered respectable unless one was engaged.

With no cars on Sark, the smallest of the Channel Islands, we were taken to the hotel by horse and cart. When we arrived, the clerk asked if we were together. I answered defiantly that of course we were not. But no one was deceived when we spent the next days together exploring the coastal paths and beaches, almost deserted at that time of year. Inland the gorse was in full bloom, covering the hills in a sea of yellow. When we missed a path Ralph began to slip down the grassy slope towards the edge of the cliff. As if in slow motion he disappeared from sight. I peered down as an arm, followed by his head and torso, rolled into sight on the beach below. He lay still and I thought he might be dead. After a moment he stood up, shook his head and tested all his limbs. His judo training had saved him. Frozen to the cliff with fright I waited to be rescued by a passing man.

My mother had implied that we would return with the matter of our future settled one way or another. The evening of Ralph's fall, the last one before we returned, I forced the issue. I don't know whether I acted because I wanted the matter settled before we returned, or whether his fall had made me realise that I wanted him as a permanent part of my life. When he asked me what I was thinking (something couples did in those days, do they still?) I replied that I was wondering if he was going to ask me to marry him. He said yes. He could not have answered otherwise. At moments of self-doubt I have wished I had waited for him to ask me spontaneously. However, he said later that he could never have asked a girl to marry him if he had not known her as a child. 'Known' is an exaggerated description of his brief contact with me as a three-year-old. I like to think that by the time we returned to the mainland from Sark, ready to tell the world that we were engaged, he had convinced himself that he had done the asking.

I now had two more years to qualification. Jenny left Bristol with a social work degree and I moved into a series of lodgings. Ralph came down from Oxford with a third class degree. He was not surprised as he had done no work. Those three years had been spent adjusting to civilian life. The freedom of university life must have been a strain for he had lived in male societies since the age of seven and felt comfortable in a hierarchy with a well-defined role.

We had a difficult year while he looked for a job, applying to various hospitals for work as a psychologist. My parents disapproved of him living at home doing no work. In their eyes he should have laboured on the roads or in a factory if he could get nothing else. My future in-laws would have been shocked if he had done anything so menial. Eventually he applied for a job in the prison service. At the interview he was turned down yet again for the post of psychologist. Then one of the assistant commissioners said, 'Have you ever considered joining on the governing side and subverting them from within?' The suggestion appealed to him. He was appointed as an assistant governor and assigned to an open borstal, one of the special institutions for young offenders, in Yorkshire.

Now that he had a job we could proceed with the wedding and managed to negotiate all the conflicting emotional difficulties caused by my mother. I wanted us to get married and live together immediately but I still had one more year of undergraduate training.

In the Bristol medical school brochure I found a paragraph that stated a student could study for a year at some other university. I got in touch with Leeds, whose admission panel turned me down without taking the trouble to see me. But Sheffield offered me an interview. When I explained the situation they said their policy was to foster 'oddballs'.

We started our married life in one half of the upright side of an H-shaped prefabricated building, built by the RAF during the war and then taken over as a borstal. It was a remarkably comfortable building with a furnace in the middle that heated four bathrooms in the cross of the H and provided central heating to all four quarters. Washing, hung over the bath at night, was bone dry by morning, very fortuitous as any garment exposed to the air outside was covered in smuts within a few minutes.

Pollington, the nearest village, is nine feet above sea level, half way between Selby and Pontefract. Although geographically in the West Riding, the landscape is that of Lincolnshire, flat and featureless. Sea mist sweeps in from the coast. In those days before the clean air act it met the dirt-laden wind from the industrial cities to the west, depositing the resultant grime over our hut.

Each weekday I drove to Doncaster in Ralph's Austin Seven and caught the train to Sheffield. With no useful hill in the vicinity the car had to be pushed for several hundred yards when it refused to start. I blessed the groups of borstal boys who got me going on more than one occasion with much laughter and cheers as I disappeared into the gloom. Some of those journeys were the worst I have ever made. The best hope was to fit myself behind a lorry and stay within a few feet of its rear light. The car had no heater so the only way to clear the windows in winter was to scrape the ice off and I could not stop every few yards to do that. Instead I wound the windscreen open and allowed the murk to freeze on my face.

The energy needed to get into the city did not leave enough to do justice to my new university, where several members of staff took trouble to accommodate my needs. The syllabus did not match the one at Bristol in every detail. Smallpox vaccination had been covered at Sheffield before I arrived. The professor of infectious diseases arranged for me to have a private session with him. He attacked me with the scratch needle to demonstrate the technique, before insisting that I do the same to him. We both survived.

One of the great differences between the patients in Bristol and those I was now meeting was in the inmates of the medical wards. The lasting image of Professor Bruce Perry's beds is of rows of women with heart murmurs, whereas in Sheffield it was the huge men's wards that remain stamped on my memory. Almost all the patients were suffering from bronchitis and emphysema or full-blown silicosis, as a result of life-long exposure to coal dust. The hacking and coughing went on day and night. A cup-like covered spittoon, which must have held at least half a pint, sat by each bed. In the bottom a small quantity of water prevented the sputum sticking. These containers could be completely filled with deeply stained phlegm before the end of the day.

For the three weeks before the final exam I moved into digs in Sheffield and crammed. Then I returned to Bristol for the papers and clinical tests. The worst experience was the midwifery practical where the external examiner was Will Nixon, professor at UCH and a great friend of my father. He was the nephew of my father's senior partner in Chippenham and wanted to write a book. With no personal experience of general practice he had asked my father be his co-author. At the end of my case the local professor shook his head and turned away. Will insisted I be given a second case and a second chance. When I read his inscription in the copy of their book, *A Guide to Obstetrics in General Practice*, published in 1953, I had mixed feelings: *To Ruth, who after reading this book should have gained a distinction in the Obstetric Finals examination at Bristol!* I was not failing, as I had imagined, but being grilled for a possible distinction.

7

Hospital and Home

A new regulation, first introduced in 1953, the date I got my degree, required all doctors to spend a year in residential hospital jobs before being allowed to practise. I knew I must complete my training – but leaving my new husband for at least five nights a week set up many tensions. Later I was grateful that I had been caught by the new demands, for I had not been a very diligent student and would have been a hopeless doctor without the concentrated experience I gained.

The hospital nearest to our wooden hut was Pontefract General Infirmary where I was appointed as a house physician. Ralph worked in the evenings, having some time off in the afternoons to compensate. On the nights I did get home he was already back at work, not getting in till 9 or 10 o'clock, by which time I was often asleep, having been up several times during the previous nights. I had alternate weekends off but he only got one a month. On those rare occasions that we were free to go to the cinema together he wanted to watch nothing but westerns. I found them violent and hid my eyes in his jacket every time a gun was fired.

Most of his interests were alien to me. He had a passion for classical jazz, while my musical taste had not developed beyond the Gilbert and Sullivan beloved of my father. The martial arts and all things Japanese fascinated my husband, especially the Samurai code of chivalry with its emphasis on loyalty, honour and bravery. He took up archery and shot down the long corridor of our hut. He read about Zen Buddhism and headhunters in the forests of South America. He played chess.

I did not have hobbies. My energy had been focused for six years on passing exams and trying to please people. My mother gave me a subscription to a postal course in household management. Each month a copy arrived with details of cleaning, organising and cooking that should have been a great help in my domestic life. I was furious that she should imagine I had time or energy for such reading and consigned them to the rubbish bin unread.

If we had gone for any sort of pre-marital counselling surely we would have been warned against such an ill-fitting union. Some force had propelled me headlong into the alliance, at the age of twenty-two. Perhaps I was afraid of being 'left on the shelf', an unrealistic worry as I was reasonably attractive and did not lack admirers. Unmarried women were common in those days, not because they had chosen such a condition as might be the case in the modern world, but as a legacy of the First World War when the male population had been so reduced. My father's eldest sister was one of them, stuck at home to look after her elderly mother and handicapped younger brother. I might have been worried that I would become somewhat fey like my aunt Cooty if I remained single. I prefer to believe that some unconscious good sense led me to choose a man who, while not obviously the most outgoing and helpful, was a much better match for my temperament than he appeared to be on the surface.

Now in the second year of our marriage I was spending my days and many of my nights in the company of a motley collection of doctors. I am deeply grateful to Leo Mulrooney, an attractive Irishman who supported me through the first few months. We had no casualty consultant and only one junior in what would become known as Accident and Emergency. The rest of us helped out on a rota basis. The majority of patients were miners with crushed toes or pieces of grit stuck in their eyes. I learned about the rusty ring such foreign bodies could leave in the cornea if not removed adequately; but the most important lesson for me was to look for the injury that was not obvious.

One day a patient was brought in with a damaged shoulder. I

suspected a fracture, dislocation or both, and having filled out the form for an X-ray, I turned away. Leo happened to be passing. He twitched back the blanket covering the man's legs.

'What about this?' he asked, removing a temporary dressing that had been applied by the ambulance men.

I looked down at a huge laceration of the thigh. The wound was at least ten inches long and deep enough to expose the bone. Although conscious, the patient was too shocked to complain.

'It might be a good idea to X-ray this too? Then we can see about getting him patched up.'

I felt my face burning as I realised how cursory my examination had been. After this experience I insisted on examining every part of all casualties, often almost ignoring the obvious injury. As I looked for the damage I might be missing, some patients complained. 'It's not my head [leg, back, stomach] it's here doctor, my HAND,' or some other part of their anatomy in which they were feeling pain.

After a while, a second Irishman joined us. He appeared to live in order to bet on horses, but never discussed his results. If he passed his cigarettes round with a smile he had probably won. If he sidled up with a murmured 'got a spare ciggy?' I knew his luck was out. I was never a heavy smoker but I kept a crumpled packet in the pocket of my white coat for those occasions.

I had graduated from the short white coat worn by students to one that reached below the knee. It had capacious pockets for my stethoscope, patella hammer and British National Formulary (BNF) – and of course my handkerchief. (I have never managed to wean myself onto more hygienic tissues.) The coats were provided by the hospital. A clean one arrived in my room about twice a week, so strongly starched that the sleeves were often stuck together, crackling as I pushed my arms down. If it got spattered with blood, pus or excrement I had to descend to the laundry to try and find a replacement that fitted.

Of course we scrubbed up for the operating theatre but even in the middle of the 1950s we were beginning to be blasé about infections, relying heavily on the magical antibiotics. The insights gained by my ancestor Lord Lister who was the first person to argue against the idea that pus was 'laudable', and Pasteur who discovered microbes, were being ignored. Now, the increasing number of organisms resistant to even the most modern antibiotics has led to changes. When I questioned my daughter, who still works in hospital, she replied, 'No white coats. The rule is "Bare below the elbows. One plain ring, no stones. No wristwatch. Wash or disinfect hands before and after every patient contact." I think the suggestion is that you wear freshly laundered clothes every day. Many doctors in acute specialities wear scrubs now [the garb for the operating theatre]. BNF lies around on the drugs trolley. Stethoscope usually round neck – not that it gets used as much as it should with reliance on tests etc, but that is probably just me.'

Me too. I am horrified by the stories I hear from friends who been sent for tests without any clinical examination.

In Pontefract the general surgeon covered our work in casualty, but if he was in the operating theatre we had to cope until he could escape. One young man haunts me still. He had a severe head injury and was semi-conscious, suffering from cerebral irritation, making him throw himself about so violently that two porters and two nurses had to hold him down while I tried to cut the surrounding hair and clean the wound. Was that brain I could see? I could not be sure. I stitched it up as well as possible – too well. When the surgeon eventually made his way to the ward he decided to leave my sewing undisturbed. Despite antibiotics it became infected and the boy died three days later. My boss admitted to me that he should have taken the boy to theatre and done a proper job but he had been deterred by my tidy, superficial work. We were not wilfully negligent, just two human beings doing our jobs but making mistakes. As so often happens, the grieving parents were some of the most grateful I have ever met, donating a large sum of money to the hospital for the 'care' their son had received. Another defensive skin tightened round my feelings.

At the beginning of my hospital work I was the only woman

resident. Both the medical and surgical registrars had qualified in India. The former was the best doctor I have ever met. My trust in his judgement was absolute. Although he was half my father's age he was more knowledgeable. If ever I were in a large-scale disaster, that man is the person I would like by my side to make the decisions. I was particularly grateful for his help when a severely asthmatic young woman was repeatedly admitted to the ward. She was often *in extremis* and we had no steroids. I had to make do with subcutaneous adrenaline, intravenous aminophylline, given very slowly, oxygen and a tight hold on my panic. Thank you Ramu, for seeing me through those nights.

The surgical registrar was brilliant. I played chess with this man who was not even sure of all the moves but still beat me with a flourish. He was neat and quick when operating but I did not trust him to make good clinical decisions. One patient had been using an electric sewing machine and somehow got her wrist in the path of the needle which had broken and left a piece inside. My knowledge of the anatomy of the wrist was by this time rusty but I remembered our anatomy teacher and her crippled hand. I phoned to ask the registrar to come to casualty.

'That's all right,' he said airily. 'You are quite capable of getting it out.'

I knew I was not. 'Sorry,' I said, 'I'm not going fishing around in the wrist with all those vital structures so close together.'

He disappeared and the next thing I heard was that the consultant was planning to remove the broken needle in the operating theatre under a bloodless field. (A tourniquet is applied from the fingers up to remove blood from the limb and stop any more entering for the brief period of the operation.) I was shocked that the registrar had asked me to do something he would not attempt himself.

One doctor from West Africa was an enormous liability. His weekends off, when he was away from the hospital and which always lasted four days, were a comparatively peaceful time for me, even though I was doing the work of two people. At least at that time I had the authority to try and rectify his blunders. When he was present he did not examine patients or take their blood pressure but wrote down any number that he thought might be suitable. Drug prescriptions were inaccurate. He made advances to the nurses, who came to me in the belief that I could rescue them, and their patients, from the worst of his excesses. At that time there was no suggestion that I should act as a whistle-blower and report him to the authorities. Today I would be severely censured for not doing so.

Until this time, in common with many of my friends, my contacts had been exclusively white and middle class. My experience of working with doctors of different ethnic groups, brought up and trained in different cultures, taught me that such factors were far less important than individual personalities. In Britain in the twenty-first century the opportunity for that lesson will normally occur in nursery school.

Despite the lack of supervision, long hours and excessive responsibility, there were some ways in which our life was better than that of junior doctors today. We always had a nurse to help us undress the patient and move them in the bed when we carried out an examination, something I understand that even consultants cannot expect nowadays. The turnover of patients was not so fast and each ward had an experienced Sister who knew them well. We always had access to tactful but invaluable advice if we were humble enough to ask for it. This was particularly true on the children's ward. I had sat in on a few outpatient clinics and walked round the wards occasionally as a student, but I knew nothing of sick children. Paediatric care was part of the house physician's remit so I 'took over' the ward on my first day. Of course, I did no such thing. Sister told me what to do and I did it. She had held the ward together for many years and with her extensive experience she had kept the children safe from the worst mistakes of generations of newly qualified doctors.

We lived close to the wards with a housekeeper who would make us scrambled eggs and other delicacies at any time of the day. On the wards too we were fed, especially at night, with toast or more, when the staff judged we needed it. Because we carried the label Doctor, everyone in the hospital afforded us automatic deference. Like the muscles of childhood that pull bones into characteristic shapes, their expectations helped to change me from a frightened girl to a passable doctor.

At home I also had to adapt, to the strange man I had married. He had no experience of living with a professional woman and although he never made a single overt demand on me, like all men of his generation he expected the house to be cleaned and food to appear as it had always done in his childhood home. Even if he had been prepared to share the household duties in the way most men do in the twenty-first century I would not have welcomed it. I too believed that it was the duty of the woman to manage the home and indeed enjoyed doing so when I was not overtired. I could not have managed without the indefatigable Mrs Nutt. She would arrive from the village on her bicycle to 'siden up'. That activity consisted of efficient tidying and cleaning but no help with washing or cooking.

When I qualified, my parents had given me a second-hand car of my own so Ralph and I now had our own individual means of escape from the isolation of Pollington. I would buy food on my way home, cook a meal and try to leave something in the fridge for the nights I would be away. Ralph would have been quite happy to live on packet soup and toast but I always felt I was not fulfilling my job as a proper wife. He was fussy about food, the legacy of a sadistic nanny in early childhood. His instinct was to ignore the process of eating but when he developed diabetes he had to take notice, even weighing his food until he could judge the portion by eye. He disliked social meals, using supposed dietary prohibitions as an escape from eating many foods he hated. Most people did not know that diabetics could perfectly well eat liver, stewed fruit, and crab, all anathema to him. I remember cooking a lot of rabbit (myxomatosis did not spread widely in England until 1955). Steaks, fishcakes and rissoles were also acceptable, together with fried eggs and bacon – not the best diet for a diabetic already at higher risk of arterial disease. At that time the long-term risks of a poor diet were less well known. But with my need to provide something he could enjoy, I fear I would probably have ignored the recommendations.

Before my second job started I developed tonsillitis, a recurring problem since childhood. At one time I had begged my mother to let me have my tonsils removed. She was against any intervention unless absolutely necessary and the attacks gradually became less frequent. The one at the beginning of 1954 led to the only occasion when I deliberately played truant from work. I stayed at home for a week with a high temperature but then added another week of unnecessary 'convalescence'. Jenny came to stay.

Her visit was a heart-warming interlude at that time in my life. I never admitted that I was finding it hard. Indeed I took some pride in coping with what my mother thought was an impossible existence. Then and later, she was so sympathetic about my life, spent moving from what she considered one desolate prison to another, that she made a point of trying to help me make a garden at each place. Outside our hut in Pollington she planted a hedge of Berberis Stenophylla. The plants never grew in the wind and grime, but never managed to die, remaining as stunted little bushes. At times she might have wondered if they were symbolic of my life, so different from the one she had imagined for me.

After Jenny arrived the weather turned very cold and the ground froze. We went skating on a nearby lake. Having lived in Canada she circled with great proficiency while I tottered about on my mother's skates. The boots were too small but with the cold air on my cheeks I began to recover from the emotional traumas of the previous six months.

The friendship that Jenny and I enjoyed was so deep and solid that it could survive long periods of separation. But during that first visit after I was married, something had changed. Alone together in the open air we were fine. Once Ralph came in we became more stilted. The special closeness of our childhood was only recaptured after both our husbands had died.

Back at the hospital my second job was in the surgical wards. As well as interviewing new patients I had to assist in the operating theatre. I showed little talent with a scalpel and soon changed to helping the anaesthetist who had no junior staff of his own. I was also responsible for many intravenous drips. After I had inserted the needle into a vein in the crook of the elbow the arm was bandaged onto a board to keep it straight. The needles we used were metal and pierced the vein with the greatest ease. Phone calls in the middle of the night were usually to re-site a drip that was running into the tissues. I would put my white coat over my dressing gown, enter the ward bleary-eyed, and be back in bed within ten minutes. Unless there was no suitable vein left to use. Then I had to 'cut-down' at the ankle to expose the vein with an incision, a longer and more complicated procedure. The plastic cannula that allows so much more movement had not arrived before my time in hospital came to an end. I have never inserted one.

Sometimes I was summoned from my bed to retrieve the cat. Luck had given me a room with a window opening onto a large balcony, which made it possible for me to adopt her when she arrived in the hospital as a stray. She had found her way onto the ward and snuggled under a blanket until discovered by one of the nurses who threatened to throw her out. The elderly patient had been comforted by her presence and hated to think of her turned out into the night. When I offered to take her to my own room and care for her she was somewhat consoled. Every time the cat found her way back to creep into another bed, the staff sent for me. She gave birth to one family of kittens in a box by my bed, but once they were weaned she left. She was a wanderer by nature.

When summer arrived, Ralph and I spent our holiday in our canoe. Our wedding presents to each other had been the front and back halves of a double-seated kayak. The wooden struts were covered by canvas and collapsed into two bags. We had set off on our honeymoon in the Austin Seven with them strapped to the roof rack, choosing to go to the Vosges mountains, not a very suitable location for easy paddling though we did camp for two nights on an island in the Moselle river.

The norm in the 1950s was one annual two-week holiday, with

shorter breaks in lieu of Christmas and Easter. We managed to visit our parents for one or two weekends a year. The drive, only about 175 miles, took at least six hours for there were no motorways. We returned laden with bottles of soup and Christmas puddings from Ralph's mother and good advice and plants from my own.

Our next canoe trip was down the river Cherwell. The water was very low and after two days carrying our craft over reeds and across fields of new-cut hay we abandoned the effort and changed onto the Oxford canal. We became adept at portaging round locks but by that time we realised we were not comfortable in the same craft. Ralph sat at the front and I could not adapt to his quicker stroke. We invested in two singles for our excursion the following year when we embarked on a stretch of the Wye. Now we had the problem of getting in and out. In one canoe we could steady it for each other but my clumsiness made it difficult for me to step in without such help. In addition, the Wye flowed fast and we were not ready to face rapids. We were supposed to be good on rivers and were a bit embarrassed when we gave in and transferred to the more leisurely Stratford Avon.

But the rest of that trip passed in great contentment. Motorised craft were forbidden; indeed they would not have been able to travel far, as there were no locks by the weirs. We drifted in isolated silence. On the last day the air became heavy with an impending thunderstorm. As we slipped silently past a bed of reeds we saw a bittern standing, unaware of our passing. Later I hardly noticed the rain thudding on our tent and the moisture seeping in as I relived that shared moment of wonder.

I worked as the casualty officer for the first few months of my second year. That job included some minor surgery. I circumcised babies – the reek of Friars Balsam soaking the strip of lint that we tied round the mutilated organ is with me still. I also had to change supra-pubic tubes, permanent bladder drains through the abdominal wall in old men whose prostatic enlargement could not be relieved. I hated the task. The smell was overpowering and the procedure painful. One man started to whimper as he came through the door, and his shriek, as I yanked the tube out, echoed down the corridors and in my mind down the years.

Another common problem was breast abscesses. These occurred in women who were breast-feeding and are not seen so often now. Perhaps we did not recognise them in time or give adequate doses of antibiotics. It was important to break down all the fibrous compartments with a gloved finger and I used to feel brutal as I poked deep into the tissue.

During that time we had the chance to see the work of general practitioners from a particular angle. My parents' old adage that doctors were either 'poo-pooers' or 'wind-upers' was borne out. One man brought his patients in almost every day. His lack of confidence was in striking contrast to our ill-founded certainties. We laughed at him and had little understanding or sympathy for a man who had lost his nerve. Others referred serious cases with dismissive notes: 'Please see and treat'. One conscientious doctor often joined us in the common room for coffee and chat. He was lonely, but also still genuinely interested in medicine and wanted to be close to the centre of things. I often found his suggestions helpful.

My appointment as a junior medical officer in geriatrics came as a relief, although it was not without its horrors. Long wards filled with all kinds of physical and mental suffering stretched into the distance. The smell of disinfectant was overpowering but at least the place was clean. One woman had half her face eaten away by a malignancy. Some of the patients called endlessly for help, others dragged themselves to the bathrooms from which, on the male wards, men would emerge with their trousers round their ankles.

The idea that old people needed a special medical approach was only just developing. The hospital in the neighbouring town of Castleford had been the old workhouse, and was now classified as 'part-three' accommodation. The patients had been confined to bed for years without investigation, diagnosis or rehabilitation. I was lucky to have an enthusiastic consultant who was determined to sort out the medical problems of the inhabitants in order to diagnose and treat the treatable. He was one of the first specialist geriatricians who realised that rehabilitation was crucial in the fight against what were called the 'Giants of Geriatrics': Immobility, Instability, Incontinence, and Intellectual Impairment. He fought hard against entrenched positions, building a multidisciplinary team to tackle the problems.

I also worked on a ward in Wakefield, another twelve miles beyond Pontefract. By that time I had exchanged my small car for a Ford consul convertible. For me a car is a means of getting from one place to another, not an object of interest or emotion. But I loved that first vehicle that I had bought with my own money. It was pale green with a fawn hood that folded right back. I drove under the sky with the wind in my hair and the wireless blasting, so that the sights sounds and smells of hospital were blown into the ether.

I was now getting back to Pollington every evening having driven up to fifty miles during the day. It never occurred to me that our marriage was not secure although we were clearly not a close couple at the time. Our love life was pleasant although not totally satisfying until several years later when Ralph bought himself a book on sexual technique. At no time, even years later when I became more comfortable with the subject, could I have shown him, far less told him, what my body liked. My personal shyness never abated, but I hope that perhaps it helped me to empathise with some patients.

By the end of that second year in hospital, my wish to be a nurse forgotten in my passion to be a better doctor, I had been shut up for most of the days and many nights with a variety of unattached, attractive and helpful men. We worked in the highly charged atmosphere of life and death. At Christmas and for some birthdays we gave small parties in the common room where drink flowed. On two occasions I found myself tempted into a cuddle and some kissing, but it never went very far. The idea that it was wrong to seduce a married woman was still strong and the men helped me to remain faithful to Ralph in a way that might be more difficult today.

I believed I had kept these lapses well hidden. When we heard that we were to be moved to Portsmouth I was not surprised for I knew that governor grade staff were moved fairly often. It was only many years later that Ralph told me he had requested a transfer because he thought our marriage would not survive if we continued to live such disparate lives.

8

General Practice

Our quarters in Portsmouth consisted of a two-bedroom ground floor flat, outside the walls of the prison. The sitting room was long and narrow with the fire on the short wall. In an effort to get warm I sat so close that my legs developed brown marks, which took a year to fade. The kitchen looked out onto the wall of the house next door with room between for nothing but dustbins. The tiny front garden faced a busy main road. My mother planted two cherry trees; despite the pollution they flourished and were a good size when I drove past ten years later. By the start of the twenty-first century the area had been flattened and redeveloped.

I was lucky to find a post as a trainee general practitioner. The scheme had only recently been devised and was not yet compulsory. It consisted of just one year's training. Such scanty preparation must be hard for today's trainees to imagine. Now they have to work a mandatory two years in hospital, followed by three years' training for what is recognised as the speciality of general practice.

I had sampled the world of medicine outside hospital even before we moved to Portsmouth. After my first year in hospital I was free to be let loose on the public. I took a job for two weeks as a locum in Ackworth, a village three miles from Pontefract. We knew the doctors to be conscientious, although in our view from hospital somewhat over-anxious. The senior partner went on holiday, leaving his junior to keep an eye on me. Faced with the undifferentiated illnesses of general practice, most of them minor but with an occasional emergency not to be missed, I was completely lost. I hardly knew how to write a prescription, having used nothing but the bed-end charts on the wards, where my drugs were checked by a competent ward sister and again by the hospital pharmacist.

This was the moment when I started to ape my mother by wearing a coat and skirt, perhaps in the hope of annexing some of her confidence. The small BNF lived in my pocket, as it had done in my white coat in hospital. It was my Bible. I did not have the confidence to refer to it in public, as I learned to do later, but I consulted it while the patient dressed behind the curtain, on hasty trips outside the consulting room or in the car between visits. I soon realised that patients were not happy if I challenged their own doctor's advice. Wherever possible I would repeat what the regular doctor had already prescribed.

One woman stays in my memory. She was a hotel proprietor, on her feet all day. She asked for a visit because her foot was painful. Arriving at the large building I found she had slight swelling and tenderness over one of the long bones of her foot. I thought it was probably a strain but it could have been a 'march fracture', a spontaneous break due to physical stress on the foot. Coming from hospital, where we tried not to take unnecessary X-rays, and knowing the treatment would be the same, I strapped the foot and told her to rest – I don't remember discussing the difficulties of doing so when she had a hotel to run. When her own doctor came back he ordered an X-ray and it did indeed show a hairline crack. The patient was furious and considered me negligent despite the fact that the treatment was not changed.

The same problem could arise with a simple cracked rib. In hospital, provided we were sure the lung was undamaged, we were encouraged not to ask for an X-ray. In those days we applied tight strapping to the chest. (This is no longer advised because of the fear of infection in the less mobile lung.) Doing the simple task with care was one of the few occasions when one could provide immediate relief from discomfort. Another was syringing ears. A modicum of skill was needed in those days when we used a metal syringe: the appropriate pressure had to be applied in the right direction. Since then the ear irrigator has been developed. It allows electronic adjustment of pressure and the task has been delegated to nurses.

I now realise that patients need to know what has happened to their bodies, especially if a bone is broken, even if the knowledge does not affect treatment. A sprain is just a sprain, but a broken bone elicits more sympathy from family and friends and justifies a longer convalescence, even though a bad sprain can be more troublesome than a clean break.

My trainer in Portsmouth, Dr Burnham-Slipper, was a well-established and conscientious general practitioner. At that time there was little supervision of trainers. Some were exploitative, benefiting from the fee they were paid but using the trainee as an extra pair of hands to help shift the considerable burden of work. I was lucky to have found a man who gave freely of his time and took his training role seriously. For the first time since I had obtained my degree, I felt adequately supported. For at least three weeks I sat in on his surgeries and went with him on home visits. When I started to consult alone he was always in the next room, available to give advice if I was in any doubt about a diagnosis or management. When I started home visiting by myself, we met over lunch and at the end of the day to discuss cases.

The routine in Portsmouth was very similar to the one I had observed as a child. In both practices long surgeries were held twice a day, on a first-come first-served basis, the queue of patients overflowing the small waiting rooms. In Chippenham they had perched on the walls at the top of the surgery path which ran along the side of Lowden Hill. In Portsmouth twenty years later there was less room for the patients to wait and they would spill out through the small front garden onto the road.

All GPs in those days made many house calls, in response to requests for new visits, to follow up cases and to a list of regular elderly patients. However, there was no local hospital run by the GPs in Portsmouth as there was in Chippenham, where my father did a ward round each day, with an opportunity to drink coffee and talk with other doctors in Matron's sitting room.

Under the NHS, introduced in 1948, hospital medicine was advancing and becoming more organised. Because the system I was now working in was so similar to the one I had known as a child, I was not aware that general practice was falling behind, becoming the poor relation. Doctors organised their own practices, perhaps with the help of a wife or secretary. Partnerships were small, usually two or three doctors often working in different premises. Nursing and midwifery services were separate. Individual doctors and nurses might try to work closely, but the employment of ancillary staff within the practice was still a long way off. Above all, this was a patient-driven service, the doctor responding to immediate demands. Preventive medicine was limited to the vaccination and inoculation of infants, usually carried out at clinics run by the medical officer of health and his staff.

It is now twenty years since I did any work in general practice. The changes have been profound. My son-in-law Simon, who practises in Swindon, worries about the efficiency of his practice manager, reaching his targets for screening and health promotion and his work in a deanery where he oversees the trainees and trainers. With cars so widespread most patients can drive or get a lift to the surgery so he makes far fewer home visits. He often sends patients with an acute illness directly to the hospital where the range of useful interventions has expanded beyond anything my parents could have imagined.

One of the most dramatic changes is in the treatment of patients who suffer a stroke. My father had several partially paralysed patients on his routine visiting list. One lady limped about her house with a useless hand and impaired speech. I was embarrassed by her handicap but intrigued by her white cockatoo with a yellow crest that shrieked 'go away' and 'lovely boy' when we visited. She would let it fly loose and cuddle it, allowing me to stroke its back with one finger. When she first suffered her stroke she had been nursed at the hospital. But her calamity had not been considered an acute emergency for there had been no immediate treatment – patients either died or lived with varying degrees of disability. In recent years, specialist stroke services have been set up in many places. If the patient can be seen, scanned and a treatment regime started within two hours the outcome can be significantly improved.

The definition of a general practitioner that I was trained to fill was 'A doctor to the individual, his family and a practice population'. I have always thought that the roles were not totally compatible. The conflict of interests has become more severe since the rise in patient expectations, the emphasis on preventive medicine and on financial considerations, made so much more acute by the challenge of scientific advances. But the individual patient is still preoccupied by the immediate symptom or anxiety. Health education and routine screening can feel irrelevant at that moment, and the focus of the doctor's concern may be deflected. I wonder how much the pressures on the doctor to fill many different roles underlie the discontent that I hear from so many elderly friends, who feel their doctor has no time to listen or empathise. When my father visited his chronically ill patients he had little BUT time to offer. Despite the major organisational changes, appointment systems, computerised records and teamwork, the heart of primary care remains what it has always been, a meeting between a troubled patient and a doctor wanting to help.

After my year as a trainee I stayed on in the practice as an assistant. Ralph was now working with adult prisoners for the first time. Some of these were serving life sentences for murder, and his contact with them stimulated an interest that began to take the place of his concern for young people and was to last him the rest of his working life. He worked more civilised hours so we could spend most of our evenings together. There was no room for his archery in our cramped quarters but he joined a judo club. Although I was becoming more tolerant of his strange hobbies, when he filled our bedroom with weight-lifting equipment I was irritated. We still went to western films but I was getting used to the guns. Our relationship was strengthened by a couple of very enjoyable holidays driving round France and Italy. However, my personal concern was that I did not seem to be getting pregnant.

Both my parents had stressed the disaster of getting pregnant before I was qualified, but as soon as I had those precious initials after my name I had stopped using my contraceptive diaphragm. After three years I saw a consultant in Bath who gave me temperature charts to try and discover if I was ovulating, a passion-killing device of the worst sort. After a few months it showed no rise in the middle of the cycle. I was not producing egg cells. It was senseless to feel we had to perform to order. I took the various ineffectual hormones available at that time and tried to concentrate on my work.

Two patients stand out in my memory. The first was a woman in her thirties, desperately ill in the last stages of septicaemia and kidney failure. By the time she plucked up the courage to send for me she had passed no urine for two days. I called the ambulance and sat on her bed while she confessed that she had been to an abortionist, a local woman who 'helped' women in trouble. She died three days later. The unnecessary death of that patient, caused entirely by the laws and social mores of the times, has haunted me to this day. The year was 1956 and I will never forget the desperate plight of so many women before the abortion act was passed eleven years later. If one had money, or a friend with the right connections, a gynaecologist might be persuaded to perform a D&C on some pretext such as irregular periods. If one had no such advantages the back street abortionist with her knitting needle or other unsterilised implement was the only answer. Sex education was totally inadequate and the pill was still a dream in the mind of a few research scientists.

My father told me of being called to see a young girl who had delivered a baby into the toilet, having had no idea that she was pregnant. Even in the 1980s, in a suburb of Bristol, I was confronted in a family planning clinic by a twenty-year-old who came with her boyfriend. They both denied any knowledge of her 36-week pregnancy, having convinced themselves that she had been overeating.

The other patient in Portsmouth I remember with great clarity was a woman who, on several occasions, developed acute breath-lessness at night due to the failure of the right side of her heart. I treated her with slow, intravenous Aminophylline, a technique I had perfected with my asthma patients in hospital. (This treatment is not used now because of occasional ill effects.) After a time the response was a relief of symptoms that made it possible for the patient, previously standing at the window gasping for air, to return in comfort to her bed. Anxiety made the symptoms worse so I always stayed for at least half an hour. Clothed in the aura of doctor and with my nerves held firmly in check, I found it deeply satisfying to be able to provide the necessary calm.

By this time the local doctors had organised a rota system that left one of us on duty for the patients of three practices at the weekends. There could be fifteen or even twenty new calls on each of the days. We did not employ a driver as some larger groups did later. Luckily by this time I knew the geography of the town fairly well – but not well enough. One Saturday afternoon I parked outside the house of a child with earache. To my horror, when I came out there was a mass of people streaming past the car. I had not realised that the road led from the football ground. The river of humanity went on and on, and I had several calls waiting. I got in and tried to move slowly past the oncoming torrent, only to be met by catcalls of abuse and beating on the windows. I had no Doctor sign on the car and there was not a policeman in sight to help me. In the end I edged back-wards, going with the tide. I have seldom been more frightened by the strange organism that is a large body of men, all individuality lost. The composite life form is governed by different and terrifying rules. Not one man lifted a finger to help, each egging the others on in more and more insulting slurs on my sanity and my female driving.

At the end of my second year with Dr Burnham-Slipper, Ralph heard he was to be sent to the London School of Economics (LSE) for a year. Later we discovered the plan was to appoint him to an open borstal south of Birmingham, between Redditch and Broms-grove, called Hewell Grange. The future governor was to be Alan

Roberton who was studying at the Tavistock Clinic while Ralph was at the LSE. The idea was for them to learn some psychological and social theory and then devise new schemes of rehabilitation. Alan and his wife Dilla were to become our closest friends.

Ralph was not naturally gregarious; I can understand him best if I think of him as a closet hermit. A few people could turn a key and get him talking. At those times he would hold the room spellbound. But he could not engage in the normal give and take of social discourse. He would reply to questions about his life and family but would never ask a question in return. I should have tackled him about it. As always I did not, but tried to show by example how such interchanges took place, an exercise that often embarrassed him. I realise now that what appeared to be lack of interest was a sensitive attempt to protect people in the way he would have wanted to be protected. His need for personal privacy was acute. The Japanese idea that to give a present was to put the other person in your debt appealed to him. He liked the symbolic, anonymous scarf that did the rounds with no personal attachment. His restraint provided a foil to my need to ask questions, to listen, to offer sympathy, to 'wag my tail at everything' as my daughter Helen once put it. I wish I had understood the workings of this dynamic earlier in our life together. At the time I was confused, for his silences made him appear cold in public, yet I knew that he was in reality one of the warmest-hearted people I had ever met.

Leaving almost all our belongings behind in Portsmouth, we moved into a furnished flat in a doctor's house in Hendon. We had the place in return for my work in the surgery below. Soon after we moved in I was wandering round the medical bookshop H K Lewis in Gower Street and picked up a book called *The Doctor, His Patient and the Illness*. I stood still between the bookshelves as I turned the pages. Here was a writer who was asking the questions I had not even formed, about the workings of doctors and patients together. I bought the book, continued reading at home and then glanced at the latest *British Medical Journal*. There in the advertisements was a notice about a seminar to be run by the author of the book I had just put down, Dr Michael Balint, starting the next week. It felt like more than a coincidence and Ralph was excited for me. We now had a shared interest in what went on between people; his focus on those in trouble with the law, mine on those in trouble with their health.

Re-reading Balint's book all these years later I am reminded that his original aim was to study the effect of the 'drug doctor', to help us to be aware of how we use ourselves in the consultation. Much of the first part of Balint's book is devoted to ways of helping the patient to accept that there might be an emotional cause for the physical symptoms. In the face of the present belief in 'stress' as the cause for many things, the idea seems dated. Now there could be a danger that patients put symptoms of serious illness such as cancer down to stress and delay seeking a reliable opinion.

Two other ideas dominated the book. One was what he called the 'collusion of anonymity', where a worried doctor referred the anxious patient to one specialist after another, thus avoiding total responsibility. In the present system, where patients often sign on with a practice rather than an individual doctor, the opportunity for continuous personal care is so small that such a concept can have little more than historical interest. Shared care is built into the system. Perhaps the same applies to Balint's concept of what he called the doctor's 'Apostolic function'. By this he meant that in his effort to do his best for the patient, the doctor was driven to impart his own understanding of the boundaries of the illness. For instance, what symptoms warranted anxiety, what pain should be borne. Unless the doctor could become aware of his/her own belief system the approach could not be tailored to individual patients according to their needs.

Balint was experimenting with the idea of training GPs to use psychotherapy in their work, encouraging them to offer patients long interviews, up to as many as twenty meetings. The devotion of so much time to one patient provides an example of the conflicting interests of the individual and the rest of the practice population. Later, his studies of work within the short consultation were published in the important book *Six Minutes for the Patient.*

For me, the experience of studying the emotions of the doctor in response to a patient was revelatory. For the first time the doctor was allowed to have feelings; but the emphasis was not on those feelings for their own sake but for any light they could throw on the patient's condition. These ideas were developed further by Tom Main in the Institute of Psychosexual Medicine (IPM), and were to become a very important part of my work.

For the rest of that academic year I attended the seminars and did various GP locum jobs. One practice in the east of the city horrified me by the amount of undiagnosed pathology that I found. On the first morning it became clear that the doctor was a great believer in homoeopathic medicine, which he used in place of any traditional medical work. He ignored serious symptoms and never examined his patients. My horror was tempered by the pleasure of recognising the signs. During the week I discovered three advanced cancers, a case of florid heart failure, body lice and varicose ulcers, all obvious and easy to diagnose once the patient removed some clothing. Ever since I had qualified I had been afraid of missing signs; I was no good at hearing soft heart murmurs and could not always see the ear drum. Now I knew that I was not totally worthless as a doctor. I was beginning to believe that medicine had really been my chosen career.

The Asian flu epidemic of 1956/8, which started in China, is estimated to have killed two million people worldwide. This did not put it in the same category as the 1918 pandemic where the number was 50–100 million but it led to enormous visiting lists for me. I was by now working for another practice in Hendon. We might do thirty or more visits in a day, often not finishing until late in the evening. Many of the calls were easy, the most important aspect being to assess how ill the patient was. I discovered that I could never judge the seriousness on the phone, and I am amazed at how doctors and nurses now give so much advice without seeing the patient. Those people who sounded calm were often the most severely ill, while those who set my heart racing with anxiety as I reached for the door bell, especially parents, could be tending children who were happily eating and playing. Again I lacked confidence and added to my workload by often visiting the same patient two or three times a day. Admission to hospital was extremely difficult and a last resort. By the end of the day I could hardly speak for exhaustion.

Despite the fatigue I remained fit the whole time, only succumbing ignominiously to mumps the following spring, not long before our summer holiday. I phoned home and heard my mother calling, 'Ruth has mumps, isn't it lovely, she's coming home.' I did not feel particularly lovely but the warmth of her welcome was sincere, even if her words and deeds were not always tactful. I found a jug of home-squeezed lemon juice, one of her specialities, waiting by my bed. Nothing could be better designed to make my swollen parotid glands ache as they laboured to produce the rush of saliva stimulated by acidic lemons.

However the side effect of that infection *was* lovely. Ralph and I went to France, driving down through the sea of lavender growing in eastern Provence. I had no idea such an expanse existed and had never seen such profusion. The perfume reminded me of drying seed heads in the sun to make lavender bags, an occupation beloved of my mother, my grandmother and myself. Those wide stretches of colour, as blue as the Mediterranean sky, evoked the memories with added force. On our return we went back to Portsmouth to collect our belongings, which had in the meantime become covered in mould. I visited Dr Burnham-Slipper and asked him to arrange a pregnancy test, for I did not trust the one I had bought from the chemist. After a couple of days he rang to say, 'It is weakly positive, congratulations.' I knew he would not raise my hopes without due cause and had the courage to believe the unexpected had, after six years, happened at last. I had managed to conceive somewhere in one of those small French hotels, chosen from the Michelin guide with a black bird, *tranquille*, or a red bird *très tranquille,* among those heady fields.

Mumps is known to carry a risk of inflammation of the testes in adult men and occasionally of the ovaries in women. Although I had no abdominal symptoms I am convinced that my ovaries had been mildly affected, just enough to soften their covering and allow one egg cell to pop out. At about that time I heard of two medical wives who had conceived following mumps. Alas, I did not follow up my idea or collect the dates and details necessary to write a paper. But I was left with a lingering regret that a second dose of mumps was almost unheard of. Without that fillip to my ovaries I never managed to conceive again.

9

Motherhood

Once we had wiped the mould off what shoes and clothes could be saved from our flat in Portsmouth, our next move went smoothly. I felt very well and suffered no morning sickness. We had not accumulated many belongings in the small flat and had not yet acquired any animals. The semi-detached house which had been allocated to us at Hewell Grange in Worcestershire had three bedrooms and felt palatial. As soon as we had settled in I found two practices where they needed occasional help with surgeries. I was happy to be working part-time, able to adapt my hours as my girth increased.

I returned to Chippenham for the birth. It is now considered unprofessional to be a doctor to one's own family but we trusted no obstetrician more than our father. He delivered all three of his children and two grandchildren. Biz came from Virginia USA to have her first child. Before and during the war several friends and relations had stayed in Green Gables to have their babies. They were given the spare room and a midwife moved into the house, which became a temporary maternity home. Father had his instruments and dressings sterilised at the hospital in large brown drums.

For at least two weeks the household would revolve around the room where the mother rested, gave birth and then recuperated. Daisy and the second maid cooked and cleaned, the gardener picked the youngest vegetables, the secretary worked to keep the patients in the surgeries as quiet as possible and even the dogs and cats seemed to sense that something important was happening. It was without doubt not only safer than giving birth among the bombs in London but cleaner and more hygienic than the most expensive maternity home. My mother supervised the whole operation, ensuring that we children were visiting friends at the time of the birth.

Only one of the deliveries caused my father any problems. His favourite sister, my Aunt Pip, had trouble with her first child. With great skill my father delivered her with the help of forceps but sadly the baby's face was scarred. Later plastic surgery made the marks virtually invisible but my cousin must have been painfully aware of them during her childhood. My father took consolation from the fact that she had clearly suffered no brain damage, for she went on to become a successful doctor and mother.

By the time Helen was due, babies were no longer born in my parental home. My father had been appointed senior medical officer at Greenways, a new maternity home on the outskirts of Chippenham. A couple of days after she was due I heard my father telling the consultant on the phone that this was 'a precious baby' and he did not want to hang about. All babies are precious but the strain of being responsible for his first grandchild, for whom we had all waited six years, was great.

The consultant induced her and I went into labour within hours. I managed the first stage with Matron herself by my side, helped by my father's special chlorodyne tipple. He arrived at 6 a.m. to deliver her himself – and I heard again his standard, 'Ah, I see it is a little Mary.'

Ralph arrived for a brief visit. In those days husbands were not expected to be present at the birth of their children, which suited us both fine. He would have found the whole thing unbearable, and I needed to be free to cope with myself without worrying about him. Ralph liked to be in situations with which he was familiar. He was good at weddings, his experience as best man on several occasions giving him confidence, but in a medical setting he was out of his comfort zone. He managed to hold his daughter briefly, intrigued but frightened. We decided on her name but after a couple of hours he escaped back to his borstal boys. Part of me wished he had stayed longer, wished that we, the two of us who were now his family, came higher on his agenda – but without him it was easier for me to sink back into a dependent relationship with my parents. All my life I have found it difficult to be with more than one loved person at the same time, needing to adapt differently to each person.

Most of the rooms in the maternity home had several beds but one was a single, reserved for those with medical problems. When I was admitted there was no one with such a need, so I was given the privilege of privacy and beautiful views over the surrounding countryside through windows on two sides. It was a magical place to lie on that morning, 2 May 1959. Summer had arrived overnight, a cuckoo called, lambs shook their tails and a thrush flew by with her beak full of worms for her young. For the first day or two I felt a great peace, at one with fecund nature.

The skill of the nursing and the detailed care that I received during and after the birth reminded me that I had wanted to spend my life making people comfortable. I had never been in hospital and had not appreciated the relief of a new-made bed. Matron had a particular way of arranging the pillows that provided maximum support. She and the other staff were adept at applying binders round tender breasts, just firm enough to support them without reducing the supply of milk. The routine was to leave the babies with the mothers during the day but take them to the nursery at night, allowing time for bonding but giving the mother her undisturbed sleep at night: a perfect arrangement.

During her first few days Helen was a sleepy baby. Maybe the induction of labour had forced her arrival a day or two before she was ready. By the evening of the third day, when the normal post-partum blues had set in, I was getting desperate and was mortified by a strong impulse to shake the tiny bundle that refused to suck. Late in the evening I heard my father's voice and thought it was a miracle that he had arrived in response to my distress. When his voice faded I realised he had been called in to see another patient. Knowing he was in the building was a comfort and in due course he wandered into my room and sat in the visitor's chair. I burst into tears. He took little notice but talked about the small doing of his day, just as he had done when Biz and I had screamed in our joint tantrums. In due course, perhaps because I relaxed and was no longer trying to force her, Helen woke up and took a good feed.

In the obstetric book my father wrote with Will Nixon, published in 1953, the idea of early mobilisation after childbirth was just becoming fashionable. They give details of a new regime that suggests swinging the legs over the side of the bed on the first day, standing for three minutes on the second, walking round the bed on the third and journeying to the toilet on the fourth. The mother should gradually progress to discharge on day ten, though a stay of fourteen days was preferable so that lactation could be better established. In the book they discuss the practice in less-developed societies of treating labour as an incident in the day's work. They did believe we had a lot to learn from them, but their advice was still cautious. I fear the pendulum has now swung too far the other way, especially where family support is inadequate. If discharged after a stay of twelve or fourteen hours the mother may be expected to look after the house and other children, tasks I would have found quite impossible.

I stayed in the maternity hospital for a week. When I went home to Green Gables I was expected to do nothing but feed the baby and myself. I was glad of my mother's supervision. In response to some superstitious fear she had refused to buy anything for the baby until the birth was safely over. Then she had rushed out and bought dresses, nappies and a set of scales to test weigh the baby before and after every feed. At the time I thought they were helpful but now I wonder. For her, test weighing had provided a way of getting through the process as rapidly as possible. For me it was different. I wanted, as all mothers do, to provide the very best care in the world. I enjoyed breast feeding and if the requisite weight had not been gained I would sit for a long time, giving my baby no opportunity to take more at one time, less at another. I was trying to impose my will on someone who had a strong will of her own. Looking back this seems symbolic of an invasive and perhaps over-controlling style of mothering. I had no wish to emulate my mother in any way, but patterns repeat themselves however much we try consciously to break them.

Ralph came to collect us after two weeks. When we got back to Hewell Grange I walked into the sitting room and found a small black and white television set, still something of a rarity. Trying to adapt to an unfamiliar routine, and tied to the house for much of the time, I found the set a great comfort.

Despite the opportunity to be passively entertained, and to prop Helen up in front of *Bill and Ben the Flowerpot Men* from an early age, I did not take easily to motherhood. Living in a semi-detached house I was sensitive about disturbing the neighbours, so tended to feed the baby at the first cry during the night, with the result that it took her a long time to drop that feed.

Dilla, the governor's wife, was a great help. She loved babies and ground her teeth with pleasure when she saw one. If Helen would not stop crying, I carried her the two-minute walk to the governor's house, the old gatehouse which stood at the top of the drive to the large mansion that was the main borstal building. I would sit in Dilla's kitchen, where the atmosphere soothed us both. Dilla taught me various household skills I did not know I lacked, including the way to hang shirts on the line so that the wind blew down the sleeves. She walked with us through the grounds, ever patient and interested in the minutiae of my disturbed nights, washing powders and tiny changes in my developing offspring that only I could see.

The grounds were beautiful, with a lake and rhododendron bushes. One patch must have been a nursery bed for azaleas. The bushes, in different shades, were now so big and tightly packed that one could not move between them. The perfume was overpowering. We were not supposed to pick any of the flowers, but once I pushed Helen down the drive in her large pram and smuggled some scented yellow blooms under the cover. I dared not put them in the window – my husband was a member of the senior staff and I was supposed to be setting an example to the officers' wives, not stealing from prison property.

After about four weeks I was asked to do some surgeries in one of the practices where I had helped out before, some way from our home. The GP's wife offered to look after my baby while I worked. I was pleased and flattered, thinking that seeing patients would be easier than motherhood. On the second day I was waiting to collect some results at the pathology lab. There was no one behind the counter so I rang the bell. No one came. I put my finger on the bell and left it there. A startled girl appeared.

'Where have you been?' I shouted. 'This desk should be manned at all times.' Then I burst into tears and blurted out, 'I'm late for her feed.'

The poor girl had no idea what to do with this distraught doctor. It took me a while to explain that my baby was totally breast fed and the person looking after her had nothing to give her. 'She will be crying and I can't bear her to feel I've deserted her.' As I ran from the room, without the report, I realised I was not yet fit for work.

A few months later I started to do surgeries in Redditch while my neighbour Cathy looked after Helen. By this time I could manage, and it was the start of a variety of part-time jobs.

I was particularly lucky to be a professionally trained woman at that time. My parents had been passionate believers in the equality of men and women and had given me exactly the same chances as my brother. They had assumed I would train for a profession, like my mother, who had benefited from the first wave of feminism at the beginning of the twentieth century. However there was no pressure from them or from society to climb to the top of my particular ladder or to compete on equal terms with the men. I was not expected to return to full-time work, or return at all if I did not want to do so. I would have been deeply unhappy to hand over my mothering role to anyone else, despite the fact that it did not come easily. In addition, we had not built our lifestyle on the assumption of two salaries, but started modestly with what furniture our parents could spare.

I was always aware that the majority of women still had to fight for the right to equal opportunities and equal pay. But during my career I have met some women who have been left in a muddle. I remember one girl in particular whose longstanding relationship broke up because her man wanted more cherishing. She wept bitterly in my surgery, sobbing that if only she had realised, she would have enjoyed cooking for him and running the house. She had been brainwashed into thinking those jobs were beneath her. We seem to have gone through a period when social and peer pressures made women feel it was weak for them to be more 'caring' than their man. Jenny, whose views always influenced me greatly, believed firmly that small children need their own mothers. She also thought that one member of the couple needed to be prepared to bend and that this was usually the woman. I'm not sure about either of these views. Good mothering in the early months and years is vital but does not necessarily have to be supplied by the mother herself. Modern relationships are much more flexible and couples can work out differently balanced partnerships. However, the unfulfilled nurturing needs of some high-flying business or professional woman may be a high price to pay. Perhaps in the past some men with such needs also felt deprived. My husband could have been among them. I suspect that he sublimated his parental energies into the care of offenders of all ages, contributing much to society. But by expectation and by nature, I think my need to be the carer of my only child was stronger.

When Helen was three months old, Jenny got married and I was her maid of honour. I chose a most unsuitable green satin frock that showed every mark; I had to pad it with gauze to prevent my milk leaking through. I hardly dare hold my baby for she used to regurgitate milk after every feed, probably because I over-fed her. Ralph was still not confident enough to hold her for any length of time. Biz had also been invited to the celebrations and performed a most useful aunt's role of holding the baby, mostly upside down, during the ceremony and reception.

Immediately afterwards Ralph and I left for a holiday in a hire boat on the fens. We had an idyllic week, it never rained and my fully breast-fed baby had no dirty nappy during the whole time. Luckily I knew this could happen and did not worry. We passed several other boats with nappies strung out on deck. News of the age, sex and sleeping patterns of our offspring was shouted over the calm waters as we drifted past, generating a sense of solidarity. The trip strengthened our love of inland waterways, but we had to wait until Helen was able to swim before we could embark on another holiday afloat.

She was never a good sleeper and for several months between the ages of two and three years she was awake for three or four hours every night. The only way we could keep her quiet was to take her downstairs and play. Again, like the time Ralph got us moved when he thought our marriage was in danger, he showed a strength I had not expected. When I became exhausted and could not get out of bed he took over, endlessly patient and enjoying the chance to get to know his daughter for the first time. My possessiveness played into his apprehension, so that throughout our parenting life I had to be on the verge of collapse before he was able to come to my aid.

On Helen's third birthday we moved to Parkhurst on the Isle of Wight. Our house was one of the best we ever had, with airy rooms and high ceilings. It was outside the walls of the prison but set in a large garden with a tennis court, next to a similar property where the governor lived. A working party of prisoners tended our gardens and distributed plants with abandon. If my garden sprouted new clumps it meant Ralph was in favour that week and bare patches would have appeared in someone else's flowerbeds.

The men made a great fuss of Helen. On one occasion they gave her a pristine teddy bear. To her dismay it had to be returned. Staff and their families could not accept presents that could be misconstrued as bribes. One day I came home from work to discover they had made us a pond, in a most unsuitable place under a tree, and carved the letters HELEN in the concrete at the front. It had set hard by the time I arrived, making me cringe with embarrassment. Logos were not the ubiquitous presence that they are now and I had inherited the belief that carving one's name, or even initials, on a desk, tree or anywhere else was extremely vulgar.

I started to work part-time in the infant and school health service.

The medical officer of health was keen to build a good relationship with the local GPs and freed me to work for them as a locum during the school holidays. This cooperative approach was unusual at the time. Many GPs felt the public health service interfered with their patients and caused unnecessary work for them. Historically the National Health Service had been organised in three parts, Hospitals, General Practice and Public Health. Not until the 1970s did these barriers begin to break down and the attachment of nurses and health visitors to individual practices started the primary health care teams of today.

I enjoyed infant welfare clinics, though the health visitors did much of the routine work. Having a small child of my own it was easy for me to sympathise with the worries of other mothers and they appreciated the time I gave them. Many doctors are irritated by over-anxious patients but I have always been happier trying to help the worried well than the seriously ill.

School medical sessions were more of a strain. I worked to increase my paediatric knowledge, reading and attending meetings where possible. Most of the children were physically fit. My worries were directed to the school misfits. I realise now that I must have missed several cases of sexual abuse. One particular child, louse-ridden and constantly wet with urine, had clearly been sexualised, wanting to kiss me on the lips and snuggling too close at every opportunity. The signs were not well recognised at the time and the system of cooperation between social services and the medical profession almost non-existent.

Before Helen started at the local primary school, Mrs Hurford, the wife of the prison chaplain, kindly took care of her while I was at work. She was much better with small children than I was, patient and gentle with a family of her own. I am greatly in her debt and we have remained in contact with her family ever since.

I remember our stay at Parkhurst as a settled and fulfilling time. We learned to body surf in Compton bay. One memorable day in the pouring rain we went down to the beach with the Robertons. We were the only people on the wide expanse of sand and even Dilla, who normally needed strong sunlight to come alive fully, swam and laughed in the waves. We climbed back into the cars in our soaking swimsuits, there being nowhere to change in the dry. But one near disaster of my own making overshadows these happy memories.

I had gone to work leaving a bottle of cough medicine on a high shelf. Helen, now in her fourth year, decided to play nurses with the daughter of the lady who cleaned my house. She got a chair and climbed up. As the ring leader she must have drunk the larger portion, for the other girl suffered no ill effects. Helen became increasingly sleepy as the afternoon went on. I sent for our GP, Paul Hooper, who with his wife Helen became good friends of mine. He judged that my Helen was going to be all right – but the drowsiness got worse and it seemed to me that she forgot to breathe if I did not tell her to do so. I did not dare leave her for a second, even taking her with me to the toilet. Later that evening we moved her into a ward in the local hospital but she got worse during the night. At 6 a.m. both Paul and I thought she needed to be on a ventilator. No such apparatus for a small child was available on the island. He rang the shipping company to ask them to hold the first ferry across to the mainland. We raced to the terminal with sirens blazing. Paul and the Ward Sister from the hospital came with me in the ambulance while Ralph followed in his car. During the crossing Helen became so deeply unconscious that she tolerated an airway in her mouth. I suggested that we might have to use a laryngoscope to put a tube down through her vocal cords. Paul said he did not have the experience or skill to consider such a thing. Having given some anaesthetics in Pontefract I surprised myself by being prepared to try if necessary, although I had never attempted such a manoeuvre in a small child.

We waited. At that stage I told Paul that I wished I could pray. He put an arm round me and said, 'Don't worry, you have an Anglican on one side of you and a good Catholic on the other, we will do the praying for you, atheist though you are.'

Helen got no worse. By the time we arrived at the hospital I had watched every breath she had taken for the last twenty hours. The doctor on call came into the ambulance to assess her and carried her into the small intensive care unit. I could hardly believe she was now in safe hands and I could relinquish my vigil. The doctor showed us kindness beyond the call of any duty, walking us round the grounds and arranging somewhere for us to stay. I phoned my parents. When I woke from a few hours' sleep in the B&B they were in the room, having already visited Helen. They said that in their opinion she was fine and at the moment she was in no need of a ventilator. They had brought money, washing things, pyjamas, all sorts of eats and even reading matter for the two of us. We had left the island in such a hurry that we had nothing. The one thing I wanted was lipstick. I still felt undressed without it, and my mother, who did not really approve, ventured forth and bought me some.

The next morning we went into the ward to find Helen sitting up in her bed studying an alphabet book. 'Look Mummy, that is a V and that a W.' She had never identified them before. Clearly she had not suffered any lasting brain damage. I left the room and wept while Ralph sat with her identifying more letters.

10

The Tug of Domesticity

By the time we moved to Wormwood Scrubs in west London, after three years on the Isle of Wight, I had accepted that our unsettled life would make it impossible for me to get a job as a hospital specialist. I needed to remain in the sort of work that would be easily available, even if we were a long way from the big centres of population. My mother and others thought I was at a great professional disadvantage; for me it was an excuse to forgo the struggle up any academic ladder. But I had become bored by community infant welfare and school clinics. I took on some surgeries in general practice but they did not fit easily into my domestic set-up.

Ralph was still on duty every other weekend, but came home earlier than he had done when working with young offenders. I had to juggle surgeries with his hours and the regular task of driving Helen to and from school. This made me consider the possibility of training to work in family planning clinics, which were often held in the evenings. So far I had avoided the Family Planning Association (FPA), for it had been started and was run by lay women, whom I associated with the sort of do-gooders my mother despised so much. . . who wore large hats and spent their time at tea parties. My friend and colleague Heather Montford reminds me that the family planning doctors were often considered 'nice ladies in twin sets and pearls' who had taken up the work as 'something to do in the evenings'.

Such ignorant views were a parody of the truth. The FPA had been formed by dedicated pioneers who appreciated the plight of women with no access to birth control. It took time for me to realise what an enviable position I had enjoyed, growing up in a family where such matters were discussed. My father was isolated as the one GP in the area, possibly even in the country at that time, prepared to give advice and fit vaginal diaphragms, the only reasonably reliable method for the woman to use. I am sure this was prompted by his wish for women to have healthy babies, spaced appropriately, but I suspect my mother also encouraged him to provide the means for women to have some control over their own bodies. Before the 1970s doctors did not consider that it was their job to give such advice. Only with the introduction of the pill did they show a reluctant interest and it was many years before they began to offer the full range of services developed by the FPA.

When the NHS was introduced in 1948, family planning was not included. A network of FPA clinics continued to offer a service for which patients paid a modest fee. The pill was approved for use in these clinics in 1961 and the intrauterine device (IUD) made its appearance a few years later. The organisation trained their doctors and nurses well, and then employed them to run the clinics. Under the supervision of the Medical Director the basic training demanded attendance at a training clinic for at least six sessions, observing and then seeing patients under the critical eye of a training doctor. Once I had obtained the necessary certificates I started to do locum sessions and was soon appointed to a couple of permanent clinics within easy reach of the prison.

Following Helen's episode with the cough medicine I had become an even more anxious mother. This was not helped when she developed vestibular neuronitis, a viral infection of her inner ear that gave her acute vertigo. The symptoms came on one evening when I was at a clinic – where Ralph phoned me. I finished the remaining patients and dashed home convinced, for some reason, that she had a cerebral tumour. We wrapped her in a blanket and carried her to the Hammersmith Hospital, almost next door to our house. The doctor on call tried to reassure me and arranged for us to see the consultant paediatrician the next day. She did not recover as quickly as the specialist expected. He put the blame on me for being a working mother. He insisted I take at least three months off work to look after her.

It is difficult for anyone who has not suffered from true vertigo to understand what it is like. Only recently I heard of an American soldier who had fought in Vietnam and seen much active service. He said that none of those experiences had instilled the same degree of terror as an attack of vertigo. I once asked Helen if it was like the self-induced dizziness when one had spun round and round as a child, or ridden on a roundabout. She said it was nothing like it; the disorientation was complete, with no idea where you were in space, in relation to the ground or sky. I suspect it induces such dislocation that the sufferer feels, at some level of the psyche, as if she or he is dying.

After a week or two Helen was still unable to walk. The punitive attitude of the consultant was offset by heart-warming compassion provided by Simon Latham, a paediatric registrar. I first met him while we were, for some reason, waiting on the ward. Another doctor was jeering at a young child who cried incessantly. Simon frowned at the doctor, picked the child up and carried her around, soothing her distress while continuing to look at charts and make decisions.

Each morning for several weeks Simon left home early to allow time to call at our house on his way to work. He knelt on the floor to encourage Helen to take her first steps. Helping her gain confidence was a slow process but he had endless patience. Gradually over a period of weeks she was well enough to return to school but was still suffering symptoms that made her so frightened that they sent for me on several occasions. As the staff waited for me to arrive, a male teacher would clasp her tightly in his arms and carry her up and down the playground. It is sad to think that the essential comfort of being held when one is terrified might be forbidden now, for fear that it would be misconstrued as abuse.

When Helen had recovered, we went together to Shepherd's Bush market and bought a guinea pig for seven and sixpence. We called her Abbie. Her fur grew in rosettes, typical of her Abyssinian breed. Three days after she arrived she produced five of the most perfectly formed babies. Within an hour they were running around with their eyes open. Ralph named them after Carthaginian generals all beginning with H. It was typical of him to know the historical details of what was to me rather an obscure period of history. The unwieldy labels for such tiny creatures added to their charm.

Moppet, our cat, had come with us from the Isle of Wight but we were concerned about the main road that ran close to our house. Beyond it the railway embankment must have contained plenty of mice. Fearing the cat would venture across, and in the hope of curbing her hunting instincts, we decided to control her fertility. We opted for a contraceptive hormone injection, as none of us wanted to have her sterilised. The method had recently become available for animals but unfortunately the dose was still experimental. She conceived again before either her system or we were ready for another family. Healthy kittens keep their eyes shut for about ten days after they are born. When this litter was born they had their eyes open – with disastrous results. Because their eyelids had not formed properly the fur rubbed on their eyeballs, causing intense inflammation of the cornea.

We were due to travel abroad on holiday so we left Moppet and the kittens with an expensive but brilliant vet. He managed to save just one of them by performing several operations to create new lids with skin grafts. She grew into a charming cat. The pads of her paws were black and Ralph called her Siksika, one of the names the Native American Blackfeet call themselves. She was timid and never managed to catch anything bigger than a spider, but her pride when she brought us such a treasure was as great as that of the most proficient rat catcher.

My memories of work at that time seem blurred, while domestic details stand out more sharply. The blame that I had received for Helen's vertigo concentrated my energies on trying to provide her with the stability and interests that I imagined a good mother would manage with automatic ease. However, from the beginning I found work in family planning clinics very absorbing. I was meeting a group of patients who were in the main fit and healthy but were in urgent need of medical help to control their fertility. I soon discovered that in this personal area of their lives the ideas and feelings of the patient and her partner were more important than the views of any professional. This is not to deny that the doctor had an important traditional role to play, especially with the comparatively new methods. We were trained to take detailed histories, always check the blood pressure and perform a pelvic examination before prescribing the pill. (Later there were many debates about the necessity for this procedure as it could deter women from taking the precautions so necessary to delay or space their children.) If there were some absolute contraindication to a method the doctor had a duty to refuse it, but where there was a relative risk this had to be weighed against the risks of pregnancy and discussed with the patient.

I quickly became fascinated by the challenge of remaining an authoritative doctor when it was necessary, while developing listening skills to try and understand the person in front of me. I had no idea that this body/mind approach was to become the central interest of my professional life.

For the moment I was immersed in my family. I still yearned for another baby but as well as accepting that I would never be a great hospital specialist I was beginning to realise that I might have to be content with only one child. A large room at the top of the three-storey house, one of those outside the walls of the prison that had been provided for us, made a good playroom. I filled it with a slide, Wendy house and various push and pull toys for any of Helen's friends I could entice inside. I encouraged our friends, who were fond enough of Ralph to tolerate his silences, to visit as often as possible. I clung to these visits, and to our holidays, as times when he became more approachable and more interested in us.

Soon after arriving on the Isle of Wight we had gone to Sennen Cove in Cornwall with Dilla and Alan Roberton. For me it was one of the most enjoyable holidays we ever had as a family. Their daughter Jeanie was about nine and showed great tolerance as she played with the three-year-old Helen. Ralph came out of his shell and did more excursions with them than he would have done with us alone. We went to Kynance Cove. As the tide receded he was the first to explore a headland. He came running back.

'Alan, Alan,' he called, 'come quickly.'

For a moment I thought he had found a dead body. I stood still and looked at Dilla as Alan sprinted after him out of sight.

'Isn't it wonderful? The most perfect bay I have ever seen, quite untouched by the foot of any human, animal or bird.'

Instinctively he had wanted to share his excitement with his male friend, but I was so glad to hear the happiness in his voice that I felt no jealousy.

Interspersed with our visits to Cornwall we went to France, often to Biarritz. In the sixties it had a faded Edwardian elegance and was not in the least fashionable. We first discovered the place when Helen was about four, after driving through France with no fixed idea of our destination. Later, when Jeanie was a teenager, we took the Robertons with us. On the way down we stopped at a lake in 'Les Landes', the wide expanse of pine forests in southwest France. Jeanie and I had sailing lessons conducted in Old French. Some of the commands still vibrate in my head (I don't know how to spell the words) along with *beignets abricot*, the call of the doughnut sellers on the Biarritz beach.

Once Helen had learnt to swim, on holiday in Madeira where there was a wonderful sea water pool, we could return to the inland waterways, spending a week travelling down the Thames in a camping punt. At the school in Holland Park she had made great friends with Lucy Crowther, the youngest daughter of an editor at the *British Medical Journal*. Lucy came with us on the river. That trip took place soon after Helen's vestibular neuronitis and the peace was healing for both of us. The two girls sat in the bow of the boat catching leaves and twigs and 'sending them home' to the bank while Ralph punted and I just lay on the cushions in the middle.

Almost despite myself, between these holidays I was becoming more interested in family planning work. It must be difficult for anyone in the twenty-first century, with sexual matters constantly in the media, to imagine the degree of prejudice that had to be over-come both among the general public and the medical profession. But at about this time a number of pioneering doctors, mainly women, were starting domiciliary services in big cities, including Dr Libby Wilson in Sheffield and then Glasgow. Anyone interested in this vital work should read her memoir, *Sex on the Rates*.

I was not one of those medical pioneers who took up the fight, although I admired them enormously. In any venture there are those spirits who forge the new trail, revelling in the fight against prejudice and entrenched ideas. Others follow who consolidate their vision. Both in timing and temperament I was one of the latter.

During this time, a group of family planning doctors were meeting with Dr Tom Main to discuss the psychological influences on contraceptive choice, and the sexual difficulties that often pre-sented during the consultations. Looking back I cannot understand why I was not among them. Tom, who had been analysed by Michael Balint and became a close colleague, had been present when I was interviewed for the GP group eight or nine years previously when we were living in London. At that time they had considered the 'small but essential change in the doctor', necessary for the development of a more psychological approach, took at least two or three years. They had been worried that the single year I was to be in London would only unsettle me. 'Is half a loaf for a starving woman more useful than none at all?' they had asked each other, in my hearing. In the end I had been accepted on the understanding that I might be available to join another seminar at some later date. Yet here I was back in London, making no move in that direction. Perhaps I was too consumed by the need to be a perfect mother and wife, and to maintain what social contacts we had, to be able to face the emotional demands of such training.

In 1968 Ralph heard he had been promoted from Assistant Gov-ernor to Governor class three, and was to be posted back to

Pollington. As far as I know he was the only person in the service to be sent to that isolated spot for a second term. He had to start before our accommodation was ready and wrote to explain that the old hut had been pulled down and a purpose-built detached house allocated to us. Being modern, the rooms were small. The large furniture we had acquired for the three-storey house at Wormwood Scrubs, mainly from my grandparents, would have to be severely pruned. Helen and I were forced to stay on in London for several months and we spent Christmas that year with Helen's friend Lucy and her hospitable family, who have remained good friends.

I viewed the prospect of returning to Pollington with some trepidation, knowing it would be difficult to find work that would dovetail with my home life. Neither did I look forward to being 'the governor's wife'. Dilla filled the role with great aplomb, gracious and friendly at prison functions, acting as a figurehead and often organising the officers' wives club in the places they served. Ralph was extremely fond of her but in general, having met army wives who talked of 'my regiment', he was against what he saw as women who interfered. More importantly, times were changing and such things could be seen as patronising.

I knew I would be no good in such a role. I was still shy at parties, remaining glued to the wall at the mercy of anyone who approached me. The ability to move from one group to another has come to me very late in life, since my analysis, and I still revel in the freedom, enjoying and even looking forward to social functions in a way I never did before.

During that second stay in rural Yorkshire the village school played an important part in our lives. I was slightly ashamed when Helen became something of a teacher's pet but I am deeply grateful for the attention and support she got from the headmaster and his wife. They helped her to regain confidence after her vertigo. She was able to ride her bike to and from school and quickly made friends. It was a small community with some children from the village and the rest from the staff at the camp.

In addition to a few infant welfare and school clinics that I took

114

on with no enthusiasm, I got myself appointed to a couple of family planning clinics a week. If I was not home in time to greet Helen from school one of the other wives took her in. This commitment to work as a doctor provided an acceptable excuse for me to refuse to run the wives' club or even be their chairman. Luckily the wife of the chief officer was happy to take my place.

As the months passed some of the wives came to me with their worries. One knocked on my door in deep distress. I led her into the sitting room. Luckily I was alone in the house as Ralph was at work and Helen at school.

'My father has just been diagnosed with cancer,' she said as tears ran down her cheeks.

I said how sorry I was, and wondered what on earth I could do to help and whether I should make the proverbial cup of tea. In fact I just sat and let her talk in her own time.

After a bit she went on, 'No one in my family has had cancer. What will happen?'

'What is it you are especially afraid of?' I asked, sensing that she needed to talk more than listen.

'I can't bear him to suffer. You see, ever since I was little we have been very close.'

She went on to tell me about times when her mother had been ill and she and her father had supported each other. 'Will he come home to die? I don't know if I could nurse him, I'm not good at that sort of thing. Or will they keep him in hospital? I don't know what will happen,' she repeated.

She was comforted by an opportunity to discuss the possible scenarios and the knowledge that he would be given whatever painkillers he needed. I was surprised to find that I did have enough experience to provide at least some answers – but also to realise that the listening skills I was beginning to develop could be of use. It was far more important for her to share her fears than for me to attempt to offer some immediate panacea in a situation where there were no easy answers.

Perhaps a more useful thing I did on the camp was to start a playgroup. Jo Matthews, a friend and a leading light in the Pre-school Playgroup Association (PPA), came to stay for a few days and gave a talk, suggesting that several mothers should take turns to run the group. The PPA considered the involvement of parents most important and I was grateful for all the help I could get, having no specific qualifications for the job.

Ralph was again working three weekends out of four so that I was left to entertain Helen by myself. I remember how my heart sank each Saturday morning when my nine-year-old asked brightly, 'What are we doing today?' She presumed I would have a plan. We walked a lot in the flat countryside, made small trips into the neighbouring village of Snaith and sometimes into Goole. Even the names now sound bleak and distant, yet I don't remember feeling unhappy. I had still not managed to conceive again but the sadness was fading to a distant ache. During much of my early marriage I hankered after my parents' lifestyle, secretly wondering why I had not married a man like my father with practical hands and a sunny temperament. Now I was changing, embarking belatedly on the process of learning to be myself. I could even feel some gratitude to the mother I had always found so difficult. Her insistence that I enter a profession, especially one where I could earn a reasonable salary in return for part-time work, provided me with flexible options. The knowledge that I could return to a more active medical life when I was ready helped me to tolerate and even to enjoy the confines of domestic life that might irk a professional woman of today.

Although the doctor who had blamed me for Helen's vertigo prompted much of my commitment to my home, I was also ful-filling a need in myself. Over the years I have found that the line between coping and not coping with the inherent tension between profession and home is very fine. At Hewell Grange, during the first three years of Helen's life, I was happy with two surgeries a week but over-stretched when I tried three. Later the breaking point was between seven and eight sessions. My hope is that society is developing in such a way that every woman and man can experience the same freedom of choice that was available to me. Then each individual could discover the pattern best suited to her or his personality and life situation.

Many men in the modern world try to take their share of domestic chores but I still meet women who are carrying a heavy load. My heart goes out to all those who are expected and expect themselves to compete with men without the support of an extended family or the cheap and reliable help that was available in the past.

11

Freedom to Choose

The decision about Helen's future education, which had loomed in the distance, was thrown into sharp focus when Ralph heard he was to be moved to the prison training college in Wakefield. She was not yet eleven and I had to face the prospect of sending her away to school a year earlier than expected.

Ralph started to board at his prep school, Beaudesert Park in Gloucestershire, at the age of seven. He had been happier there than at home, where he was a solitary and rather lonely little boy. He eagerly awaited the start of each term. I was surprised to hear that copies of a book containing 500 facts were among the boys' most treasured possessions. They were carried around and used by the boys to test each other's knowledge. Ralph excelled at competitive regurgitation and believed he acquired more information during his years at that school than at any other time in his life. He was convinced that Helen would enjoy life in a boarding school. I was not so sure. I was not unhappy at St Felix but felt I learned little and had longed for the end of every term. But I was afraid that Helen, as an only child, would suffer from a mother who was too clinging if she remained at home. She would also have had to start at a new school and make new friends every few years. In the event she was pleased to leave home to board at Badminton girls' school in Bristol.

At the time I was not aware that the most intense period of my life as a mother had come to an end. As this memoir reaches the adolescence of my daughter I have made a deliberate decision to neglect the major part she has played in my life. She has her own view of her father and of our marriage, and has generously made no complaint about this account of our family from my point of view. Her own journey into medicine, marriage and motherhood belongs to her and is not mine to tell. My love for Helen is the living centre of my being. But the themes that are developing in this story do not need to include the details of her life or those of her family, although I will not be able to stop them creeping in from time to time.

I find it hard to identify my feelings as the beginning of her first term away from home drew near. I did not believe I had been a very successful mother. I was too anxious and, though I don't like to admit it, easily bored by the unremitting demands of a child. At the same time a fear that my family was falling apart led me to buy a dog. We visited some kennels where a litter of Welsh Border collies waited for new homes. At the front of the cage two male pups scrabbled for our attention while a timid bitch cowered against the back wall. Instinctively I chose her, identifying with her shyness. She was a bad choice, for although charming she grew up to be very nervous, made worse by the fact that she lost an eye due to disease soon after we collected her.

Ralph chose her name. It was not as good as those he chose for the baby guinea pigs and our cats, because Biz is known as Bess in the US, which led to some confusion. But he seldom offered an opinion about domestic details so I never demurred when he did make a rare suggestion. In the same way I was landed with a hideous carpet because he had, in an uncharacteristic moment, agreed to view my choice of floor covering before I bought it. On the way into the shop he saw one with a monstrous green and yellow pattern – and liked it. I acquiesced, too pleased that he had taken an interest to argue.

For the first time we did not live in provided accommodation but bought our own house in Wakefield. It was on a corner with a low wall separating our garden from the pavement. To keep Bess confined we had a fence erected on top. Cadets from the police training college round the corner used to run their truncheons along the struts, exciting Bess to a state of frenzy. She grew up with a fear of all men walking alone and would chase them, barking and snapping, a constant worry when I let her off the lead.

As a child, I squirmed when my mother said, as she did frequently, 'We are animal people.' I could not bear that 'we' for I knew she meant all five of us. She used the term frequently about beliefs and behaviours that I did not necessarily share, though I never complained. In contrast I glowed when one of my grandchildren referred to his family as 'we', giving the impression that he had a safe base from which he would be able to separate with confidence. In his mouth the word was reassuring, while my mother's insistence on unity was stifling. Perhaps this was another reason why I felt I had to give Helen as much freedom as possible, however much I might want to keep the family together.

Another quibble with my mother's assertion that we were animal people is that I have never been as moved by or involved with animals as my sister. Until Biz had her own children she preferred animals to humans. She trained as a zoologist and has run a small herd of cows on her farm in Virginia for most of her married life. She welcomes unusual pets, especially snakes and other reptiles and amphibians. There was often a black snake in her bedroom. Aware of my phobia about things that slither, not helped by the worm Arthur put down my back when I was young, she never insisted that I handle it. Her dining room also contained a small iguana for many years, kept in a cage on a side table. Earlier, when I developed acute back pain during one of her visits, I had shared the green bathroom with her opossum.

I cannot compete with her knowledge and gentleness but fully agree with the belief, which has been passed down the family over at least five generations, that pets add much to a household. Children have a chance to see that even a relatively self-sufficient cat needs regular attention. Animals also offer channels for emotions that we English cannot always express. When my grandsons arrive for a visit, the task of finding and petting the cat eases that awkward moment after the first greetings have been exchanged. Throwing a ball for a dog in the garden, feeding carrots to the rabbit, visiting a neighbour's horse are shared occupations that can bind disparate members of a family who may share few other interests. I am not in favour of kicking one's cat but it is less harmful to shout at him than at one's spouse. In her increasing dementia my much-beloved cousin Jenny has a Labrador who provides a degree of unquestioning devotion that few human beings could offer so consistently to someone who is seriously confused.

Whether my delayed commitment to animals was an effort to maintain the semblance of a family, or to provide a more interesting home for Helen during the holidays, it is clear that my life had entered a new phase. I was continuing the journey to free myself from the need to react against, or conform to, my parents' beliefs. The process had started when I defied my mother by marrying a diabetic in church wearing a white dress. The magnitude of that defiance made it both easier and more difficult to take my own decisions, whether they were about pets or work.

With Helen away at school I had more time and energy for my profession. To the bemusement of my parents I did not consider looking for work in general practice, for I had developed an increasing fascination with the challenge of helping people find a contraceptive method they could use effectively. I was discovering that although doctors and nurses must have adequate scientific knowledge, the skill of helping each individual person is closer to an art or craft.

Unfortunately we still do not have a perfect method of contraception, one that is free of side effects and acceptable to everyone. Choices have to be made. Before the 1960s the only methods widely available in the UK were periodic abstinence (the rhythm method); withdrawal of the penis before ejaculation, known as 'being careful', 'pulling out', 'stopping at Darlington', and other synonyms; spermicides; and the barrier methods of condoms and vaginal devices. By the time I did my training we had oral contraceptives and intrauterine devices (IUDs). Hormone containing IUDs and injectable progestogens did not become available till later.

One of the first things I learned was not to make presumptions about a patient's beliefs. At that time, in the early 1970s, Catholics were supposed to use no 'artificial' method of birth control but to depend on the rhythm method, also called Natural Family Planning. During my work I met some Catholics who would not consider anything other than this method, which depends on abstinence from sex except during the infertile times of the menstrual cycle. The safest time is after ovulation, calculated with the use of a diary, temperature charts and/or monitoring subtle changes in the body.

For those who wanted to use the method it was important to find someone with the patience and time to teach the details and to provide enthusiastic support for its continuing use. Because of the high failure rate many doctors – I was one of them – found this task difficult. Some family planning nurses became experts and the church itself provided counsellors in many places. As doctors we were faced with the task of referring the patient in a non-judgemental way while at the same time weighing and explaining the medical risks for that particular patient if the method failed.

If the doctor herself had a strong religious faith, not necessarily Catholic, the task could be easier. My friend and family planning pioneer Elizabeth Gregson worked in the domiciliary service in Liverpool. She was asked to visit a harassed mother of eleven children. After spending some time in the overcrowded house, she realised that the priest was behind the woman's intransigence. In desperation Elizabeth, a committed Anglican, approached her bishop who spoke to the Catholic bishop who had a word with the priest. The upshot was that the woman could discuss contraception more freely and eventually decided to opt for sterilisation.

Despite their strong faith, Catholic women had many different views. I was envious of those whose religious belief provided the support in their lives for which I have always been searching. However, the experience of resisting my mother's evangelical atheism might have increased my sensitivity to individual variations. Some women were happy to take the pill but could not use any sort of barrier method. Others felt it was wicked to take drugs but they would use condoms and occasionally a vaginal diaphragm. The IUD was particularly acceptable although, because the early devices probably worked by preventing the fertilised egg fixing onto the lining of the womb, the belief that it was a form of abortion could make it unacceptable. Devices containing copper or hormones are more usually used nowadays and probably act by changing the fluids in the reproductive system, preventing fertilisation. Another advantage of all IUDs was that a doctor fitted the device; the patient had to take no active steps of her own. Other women, no matter what their religion, liked it because of the slight but real failure rate. One patient, who felt she should not have any more children for financial reasons, told me she still felt unfulfilled. 'If I did get pregnant with the coil it would not be my fault,' she said, her face radiant with the thought that contraceptive failure, not her own rash behaviour, could give her the additional baby she longed for.

I had been trained to insert coils in London but at that time they were fitted in designated clinics. I never ran one of these and although I became reasonably proficient I knew my limitations. With my dislike of emergencies I always feared that the patient would go into cervical shock, a sudden drop in blood pressure leading to pallor and faintness caused by the insertion. In fact it happened rarely. If it did, the patient usually recovered quickly when laid flat, reassured and given painkillers. Only once or twice did I have to take the device out. I tried to avoid such collapse by referring any patient who might have a difficult insertion, such as women who had not had a baby, to someone more experienced.

Even today Catholic teaching, that only the rhythm method is allowed, is strong in many parts of the world. The recent relaxation of advice from the Vatican, allowing condoms to be used to protect against infection, is more than welcome and long overdue. On holiday in Tanzania, in 1994, I attended a church service and saw the strength of the Catholic faith. The building was packed with the congregation in their most colourful Sunday best, doing justice to the blue electric candles on the altar and the length of the sermon. In the secondary school a nun provided the only sex education. She taught nothing but complete abstinence until marriage. The powerful local priest vetoed all other information. In my chatty way I asked one of our guides if he were married. He told me firmly that the question was impolite, not one to be asked in his country. When I got to know him better he confessed that he had three children, all with different women, but had never been married.

One teacher at the school had already died of AIDS. Someone whispered that the headmaster would provide condoms if he suspected a senior boy was at risk. On leaving, I left a package containing a simple book on contraceptive methods and some money with instructions that it be spent on nothing but condoms. I never heard if my wishes were carried out.

In a recent issue of the *Journal of Family Planning and Reproductive Health Care* there was a discussion about whether nurses should be trained in the use of intravenous atropine for cervical shock. I was impressed to read that some nurses had been fitting IUDs for twenty years. I remember trying to teach a nurse to do a bimanual examination of the uterus to discover its size and direction, an essential procedure before fitting an IUD. I was struck by her lack of familiarity with the feel of the internal organs. As doctors we had been feeling for enlarged livers, kidneys, spleens since our first day on the wards. The resistance of the abdominal wall, the degree of pressure needed, somehow the distance of the organ from the fingers, were all new sensations for the nurse. But I am sure that with adequate training, supervision and experience a nurse will be as safe as a doctor, safer than someone who is fitting them less frequently. The only time, to my knowledge, that the uterus was perforated in my presence was by an overconfident obstetric registrar, someone who should have known how much force to use. The patient had recently had a baby and the uterus can be very soft at that time. She felt no pain, the device being found in the abdominal cavity on X-ray later.

Since the first two years of my marriage, while I was completing my training, relative subfertility and my wish for another baby had removed the need for us to use contraception. My belief that I was therefore not influenced by personal prejudices about the methods was misplaced. Because of my dislike of fitting coils I probably did not promote them as strongly as I should have done. In the same way, because I had not minded using a diaphragm, and enjoyed the simple task of fitting them and teaching their use (a job now carried out by nurses), I was happy when a patient chose to try one. I hope I resisted the temptation to encourage that method over others. One of my colleagues had become pregnant using one and admitted she hated the premeditation and messiness. It must have been hard for her to sing the praises of a method that had failed for her personally. All we could do was to be aware of and try to make allowances for our personal biases.

Helping the individual to assess the risks and benefits of different methods was also difficult. I was beginning to appreciate the difference between the 'theoretical effectiveness' of a method and its 'use-effectiveness'. Bob Snowden, in his foreword to the book *Contraceptive Care*, which I edited with Heather Montford, defines the latter as the 'rate of unwanted pregnancy in terms of the experience of the couples using the product during the emotional and physical somersaults of their love-life'. If someone said they did not want to use a method it was important to find out the details of why she or her partner felt so strongly. One could quote the known failure rates, the possible side effects and the statistical risks compared with those of pregnancy. They made little sense to a patient who said, 'My mother was using a cap when she got pregnant with me.' The girl whose best friend was admitted to hospital with a deep vein thrombosis soon after starting on the pill was not likely to be amenable to reassurance about its safety. On the other hand, if the fear was about gaining weight, then the strength of that fear had to be assessed by her reaction to the information that not everyone did so, and that there was a range of possible pills she could try provided there was no family history that might put her at greater risk.

The feelings of the usually absent partner are also important. There are times, for instance following delivery or while getting settled on a pill, when the use of a condom appears to be the best method. If the woman says 'he doesn't like them' one needs to know if he finds it more enjoyable without, or whether he loses his erection every time he tries to put one on. It could be reasonable to ask him to put up with the first for a limited time but possibly devastating for their relationship to press a method that leads to repeated failure of all attempts at love-making.

During these consultations patients often revealed sexual difficulties. The old adage holds true: contraception is not about avoiding babies, you can do that by not having sex. Thus every request for family planning is an unspoken plea to be allowed a sexual life. From there it is not such a big step to confess that the act is not much fun or doesn't work properly. During my medical training such subjects had never been mentioned. I felt so useless in the face of such human distress that I joined a group in Sheffield.

The leader of the group was Dr Lawton Tonge, a gentle and intelligent psychiatrist, who knew of Tom Main's work with family planning doctors in London. But he accepted doctors, nurses and social workers into his group, while Tom was never in favour of training different professionals together; he believed that the expectations and pressures on each group were very different. In addition he felt that their rivalry interfered with the efficient working of the group. I have always agreed with this view though I realise that the idea of teamwork is now politically correct. Arguments about this subject still rage in training organisations like the Institute of Psychosexual Medicine.

At the first meeting I experienced the typical antagonism of an established group towards a newcomer. Someone grudgingly pointed me to a chair but did not offer me a cigarette when she passed the packet round to the others. I am sure they did not mean to be unkind but the action has remained a powerful demonstration of group solidarity. As I relive the moment I am also surprised that a group of health service workers were openly smoking and encouraging others to do so. The accepted behaviour feels as dated as the Edwardian nicety of calling cards, an equivalent social gesture, yet it was barely forty years ago.

The most lasting outcome of that group was my friendship with Doreen Anderson, who was also a family planning doctor. She introduced me to the lovely woods round Newmillerdam where we walked our dogs together. We had a lot to chat about as we strode out beneath the new green of spring or crunched over fallen leaves in autumn. Doreen is a Scot. When I last visited her in Cumbria, where she has retired, I felt again the attraction of her lifestyle: her love of walking, home-made muesli and abundant vegetables grown by her husband. I envied her stories of mountains conquered and nights spent in her caravan. Ralph had never responded to my interest in camping and insisted that he had walked enough in the army to last him a lifetime. However, my romantic notions of simple holidays close to the earth did not stop me enjoying the expensive hotels he chose and paid for.

He earned a reasonable salary but had, in addition, a small income from a family trust. We were never short of money, yet from time to time I was disgruntled. He paid me a housekeeping allowance that was meant to cover the help I employed in the house, all the bills and food. It never occurred to him that this was anything but generous and apart from an occasional splurge on a new car he spent little on himself. He encouraged me to spend my own earnings in any way I liked. In my view I used much of that personal income to subsidise our expenses; but being too lazy to keep accounts I had no grounds to argue my case. We did not talk about it and I never voiced my vague feeling of discontent. I imagine a modern woman would chide me for being spineless but, if I had cared enough, surely I would have kept the records to prove my point?

In retrospect I wonder if I needed something on which to pin a vague dissatisfaction. We were very different people. I once said to Helen that the bumps on his head fitted the dents on mine. She flashed back, 'The bumps on his head *made* the dents on yours.' My role as the one who did the bending made me look like a martyr, but I was well aware that my dents had always been there. Ever since the days when I looked under the bonnet of cars with my father, or sat with Arthur while he made things, I have needed to tend the men in my life. Because Ralph was the late son of a family who had waited a long time for their male heir, and had been brought up by a doting mother with the help of a clutch of servants, he took the attentions of a devoted wife for granted.

As a tutor at the college, Ralph's daily life must have been very different from that when he was governing a prison, but the subject was not discussed between us. For me, the most important aspect of the way we interacted was that he never, ever, tried to influence the type or amount of work that I undertook, leaving me free to choose the balance of my life to suit my own needs and interests. Throughout this time our holidays became increasingly important. We bought a cabin cruiser and travelled the inland waterways. From the beginning I loved the altered view, as if one had crept inside someone else's skin and was seeing the world through their eyes. Cities were more appealing when seen from the inside, the underside. Looking up at crumbling walls and rusty winches, relics of a time when the canals were commercially viable, the weight of history provided a perspective that ridiculed my anxieties about the small world of work and family. Out in the countryside, the eye-level hedges flashed dog roses, unexpected splodges of simple blooms draped over brambles that would bear inaccessible blackberries in the autumn. Yellow rape seared the eye. Round any corner one might put up a kingfisher or happen on a heron standing motionless. On windless days the arches of old stone bridges completed ovals with their reflections. My obsessive counting of mallard chicks, as many as eleven on one occasion, led Ralph to complain that I did not need to extend my family planning interests into the avian world.

He chose to be entirely responsible for driving the boat and caring for the engine. I cleaned and polished but took pleasure in the fact that he was in charge. The paradox of our life together was that he appeared to be in control, but in our day-to-day life I took the decisions, bought and cooked the food, paid all the bills, changed light bulbs and tightened loose screws. During those waterway holidays, alone or with Helen, he was able to forget his prisoners for a while and pay more attention to us. With the balance of power between us subtly altered, our marriage felt stronger.

12

Family Planning Provision and Training

A network of family planning clinics had been started by the National Birth Control Trust, which changed its name to the Family Planning Association in 1939. The sessions were held in premises designated for maternity and child welfare, and owned by local authorities. The FPA fought a fierce battle to get the importance of family planning recognised, but although the NHS had been introduced in 1948 it did not take over the running of the service until twenty-six years later. Doctors were surprisingly uninterested in this vital aspect of health.

From the beginning, owing to the tripartite nature of the NHS, there was a varying degree of rivalry between community services and general practice. I had been lucky to experience friendly relationships on the Isle of Wight, fostered by the medical officer of health. But in other places there was a feeling that clinic doctors were busybodies who created unnecessary extra work for the GP. Certainly, for many years, working for the FPA and in the community service I was not allowed to prescribe anything other than contraceptives. Any patient who was ill had to be referred back to their 'own' doctor. This rivalry was not helped when GPs finally agreed to provide family planning in 1975 and were paid on an item for service basis – although they refused to become a source of free condoms.

One GP complained that too many women doctors were being lost to medicine by doing nothing but working in FP clinics, that they had opted out of their duty to heal the sick. In our hearts some of us might have agreed with him, for the choice was, to a degree, a soft option. The volume of knowledge required was manageable; we were spared the responsibility of caring for sick people. Yet I was meeting doctors who had spent their lives in the field and who filled me with awe-struck admiration for their dedication and their understanding of human suffering.

In respect to younger patients the FPA was slow to provide a much-needed service. Until four years before they handed the service over to the NHS the clinics were supposed to ask for proof of marriage or intended marriage. The provision for younger people had been left to the discretion of local FPA committees, some not very liberal. Because of their lack of total commitment, special centres to cater for the needs of the young were opened. These included the 408 centre in Sheffield and a network of Brook clinics. I was sad not to have had the opportunity to do more than occasional sessions with these organisations for I enjoyed the young patients who came to general sessions and believed strongly in the work.

Intercourse with a girl under 16 years old is illegal. Guidelines about protecting her from the results of that action have gone through various forms, influenced by the campaigns by high-profile parents, who have tried to insist that they are always informed when an underage person seeks help. The medical decision depends on assessing whether the young person is mature enough to understand what she is doing. Usually this is not difficult. One has to talk about the possibility of involving the parent, but if a girl says she needs contraception she probably does – although one youngster stays in my mind.

A mother brought her thirteen-year-old daughter and demanded I put her on the pill. She had been discovered having sex with a boy on a school outing. After some talk, the mother allowed me to see the girl alone. I got the impression that she had been looking for attention and although compliant had not fully realised what was happening. She told me how her parents favoured her sister and she felt neglected at home. She did not want to take the pill, as she had no intention of having sex again for a long time. When invited back into the room, her mother reluctantly agreed to follow her wishes but it was clear that I would be blamed if her daughter did become pregnant. We discussed ways in which the girl might feel more appreciated and she was thrilled when her mother offered to redecorate her bedroom. At the time we had coffee-making equipment in the clinic where one of the nurses was particularly interested in adolescent children. We encouraged the girl to drop in for coffee and a chat whenever she wanted. A funny sort of contraception, not easy to audit or build into a cash-strapped service. But the result was that she did not need to take the pill for several years and she did not get pregnant.

During my time in Wakefield I gained the FPA certificate to become a training doctor. The organisation continued to offer training to doctors under the auspices of the Joint Committee on Contraception, which was formed in 1973 by the College of Obstetricians and Gynaecologists together with the College of General Practitioners. This joint committee provided reaccreditation for me in 1979 and again in 1984. Theoretical courses were followed by practical experience in designated clinics. When training, a doctor first sat in with a training doctor to observe, then ran the clinic under supervision. A male trainee could cause some difficulty if a patient had chosen to come to the clinic specifically to see a woman. Sympathetic explanation by the reception staff, who worked in a voluntary capacity until the NHS took over, helped most patients accept the presence of a trainee whatever their sex. I enjoyed training and discovered a latent love of teaching, perhaps inherited from my grandmother who started the family school in Swanage.

Within the branches of the FPA, the doctors and nurses had established clinical groups that met two or three times a year for lectures and mutual support. With the hand-over of clinics to the health authorities some doctors felt the need of a national association of doctors working in the field. At that time I was attending the Northern Inter-branch Group in Yorkshire chaired by Dr Kay Reid, who believed that we had to join forces with other groups to maintain standards of practice and training. I supported her idea.

Before the merger took place Ralph was appointed Governor of Maidstone prison and we moved to Kent. I found family planning work in the area with no difficulty and joined the family planning doctors' group in central London. To my disgust they showed little interest in joining with others groups, implying that as they were already the centre of the family planning world they had no need for any expansion. This discussion took place at my first meeting and I was too cowardly to speak up for my provincial colleagues. Afterwards I was so ashamed that I wrote to Kay offering to do anything I could to help form the national group, claiming prowess at licking stamps. The result was that I was asked to serve on the steering committee and later elected to the first council. We decided to produce a newsletter and to my surprise I found my name on the first edition, as joint editor with Michael Smith. I would never have volunteered for such a job, considering my inability to spell an insuperable barrier. But I was not consulted and in the event that offer to lick stamps was another small incident that tumbled me into unexpected opportunities.

The clinical material available for the first few issues of the newsletter was very scanty. Our members were too busy with work and their own families to be interested in promoting their careers by publishing papers. I found myself trying to turn scrappy hand-written observations into articles that looked professional. The important contraceptive research trials, involving large numbers in multiple clinics, were organised by well-known academic figures such as Martin Vessey and were published in established journals. However, in a comparable way to the developments in the College of General Practitioners, we felt there was scope for study and discussion of practice by those doing the clinical work. Above all, I wanted a journal that raised the profile of family planning within the medical profession.

To my surprise I discovered that I enjoyed trying to sort out ideas, and took pleasure in working with one, or at the most two, other people, exchanging views and sparking impressions off each other. I became passionate about the work but Mike could always bring me down to earth in unexpected ways – as when he had to abandon what I considered an important pre-Christmas telephone conversation to catch the live goose running free in his office.

We soon formed an editorial committee and my friend Margaret Corbett acted as unpaid statistician. Her main interest had been in dermatology, but she was developing her knowledge of medical statistics and worked hard, in a voluntary capacity, on our articles although they were not very sophisticated. On one occasion we were flattered to be sent some work by a well-known researcher. Margaret was uneasy about the paper although she was unable to locate the problem. 'It just feels wrong,' was all she could say. The committee was so keen to grab what they thought would raise the prestige of the journal that they insisted we publish it. Later, the whole body of that author's work was exposed as fraudulent.

One of the most important days in my entire medical education was provided by the BMA when they ran a course on Writing and Speaking in Medicine. One hour was devoted to the organisation of a scientific paper. The lecturer started by telling us that there were four questions to be answered by any paper. (1) Why did you start? (2) What did you do? (3) What did you find? (4) What does it mean?

He explained that the abstract should summarise the reply to the last three questions. The first question must be answered in the introduction by a brief review of previous work and the gaps that the present paper hoped to fill. The answers to the second and third questions were fairly clear and should come under methods and materials or some similar title, followed by results. The conclusion was then left for interpreting the results, pointing out the limitations and suggesting possible follow-up studies. Since then the headings have become more direct, starting with 'study question' then 'summary answer' and 'what this paper adds'.

For me, a non-academic, a formalised method of approaching a medical paper, either to write it or read it, was revelatory and gave me a foundation with which to try and make the newsletter, which became for a time the *British Journal of Family Planning*, look respectable. The process was a long, uphill slog.

During this time Ralph and I spent a holiday in Malaysia. We stayed in Penang where I had arranged to meet the local family planning advisor. She asked me to join a meeting being held in Kuala Lumpur the next weekend. By then we would be in Singapore, but I discovered a flight, newly scheduled for business travellers, which would take me there and back in a day. I passed up a chance to drink at the famous Raffles hotel (taken up with Heather Montford years later) in order to make the trip.

Sixteen highly experienced female community workers, non-medical leaders of family planning services in the thirteen states and three federal territories of Malaysia, had gathered for a lecture on, of all things, sexual problems in obstetrics and gynaecology. At the last moment the consultant could not get away so he sent a junior doctor in his place. I was sorry for this embarrassed young man and did what I could to relieve his confusion. At the end we all had lunch together in a café where we ate Nasi Goreng. The conversation was exclusively about female circumcision (now known as female genital mutilation, or FGM). The lecturer bolted his food and left, saying he would collect me later and take me to the hospital.

The assembled organisers represented all three races and several religions and sects. Some had themselves been subjected to various degrees of the mutilating operation – and did not condemn it entirely. For one it had consisted of no more than slight shortening of the outer lips of the vagina, a compromise that satisfied tradition without damaging her chances for a happy sexual life and child-bearing. Others saw it as the abusive and often severely damaging procedure we know it can be. One of my new friends had grown up excited by the expectation of the symbolic act, marked in my own culture by a girl's first lipstick or bra.

After the privilege of being included in these intimate discussions, the lecturer led me through the O and G department, where women in labour sat on chairs as they waited patiently for a delivery bed to become vacant. Once a woman had given birth, and the placenta had been expelled, she was moved back onto a chair with her baby, to wait for a brief spell before being checked and sent home.

I was taken onto the roof where a tutorial was in full swing. Despite the heat, the consultant, who had trained in England, grilled his junior staff without mercy. I had retained little of my under-graduate knowledge of O and G and was completely out of my depth. Thank goodness he didn't ask me any questions. I was impressed by his determination to make the most of his limited resources and his imposition of the most rigorous academic standards.

Under my arm I had a copy of our FP journal, carried in the hope that they might take out a subscription. I approached the senior registrar with the suggestion. His first and only question was, 'Is it listed in *Index Medicus*?' At that time, despite much effort on my part, it was not. He turned away in disgust.

Eventually, in the hands of my friend and talented successor, Elizabeth Forsythe, the journal was included, both in *Index Medicus* and other approved lists of medical journals. After several years of intensive work a Faculty of Family Planning was established at the College of Obstetrics and Gynaecology and the journal took its present name – *Journal of Family Planning and Reproductive Healthcare*. The speciality had arrived.

In addition to training doctors and nurses in contraceptive methods, the FPA ran a variety of courses on subjects such as abortion and vasectomy counselling. The abortion act passed in 1967 provides specific situations in which a woman can obtain a legal termination of pregnancy. The most important provision includes '… the con-tinuance of the pregnancy would involve risk, greater than if the pregnancy were terminated, of injury to the physical or mental health of the pregnant woman or any existing children of her family.' Two doctors had to be satisfied that the criteria were met before signing a form.

Many people believe that abortion should be freely available on demand, especially in the early weeks. In an over-stretched service, and an overpopulated world, this may be unavoidable. Most women have decided what they want and do not change their minds after discussion. But I still believe the opportunity to consider how they might feel afterwards can mitigate later self-recrimination and depression. This sort of benefit is difficult to measure. I would say, 'Yes you can have a termination, I will of course sign the form, but now let's talk about it.' Explaining that the woman did not have to justify her desire to end the pregnancy sometimes meant she was more able to discuss how she might feel about it afterwards. The idea that there was no good solution, only a least bad one, was helpful to some people. Certainly, if one could provide time during a routine clinic to let patients discuss their feelings, before or after the event, they found some relief. One of the letters I have kept in an envelope marked 'Some of my most precious possessions' is from a patient thanking me for spotting her overactive thyroid and also for having allowed her to discuss the termination she had chosen a few months earlier. That piece of paper is a token that I was sometimes the sort of doctor I aspired to be – one who could to some degree care for the body and the mind.

Many of the same arguments held for sterilisation counselling. The FPA had run vasectomy counselling clinics since 1968. I found the challenges fascinating. Often the request was made by a couple who, under the stress of a new baby, felt unable to cope; life had been thrown into total chaos. By choosing the safest method of contraception they could at least be in control of one aspect of their lives. But the operation is not reliably reversible and if they were still young, with perhaps only one child, their request prompted me to try to help them find another acceptable method, possibly an injection or implant, to carry them over the next few months. Once the immediate pressures had eased I was surprised how many couples decided they would like to keep the option of another baby open for a bit longer.

Another striking finding was the wish by many men to 'do their part'. They felt that their wife had done her share by giving birth to the babies and it was now their turn. The fact that her fertility would end naturally, while his could continue into old age, had not usually been discussed between them. If they divorced or the wife died, the man might want to marry a younger woman with no children of her own.

Men were appearing in clinics in greater numbers, both as doctors and patients. Sometimes a man, often angry, would arrive in the waiting room, causing confusion – but providing the possibility of an understanding that had been absent before. One patient told us repeatedly that she wanted to take the pill but as soon as we gave her a supply her husband threw them on the fire. After several visits I heard a commotion outside my door and he burst in.

'What do you think you are doing, giving my wife all these pills?'

'Well, she would like to stop having any more babies for a while,' I murmured, reaching out to save a family photo from the hands of a three-year-old. Four of their six children were rampaging round the room, which I shared with a GP who had left many of his belongings within child's reach.

'What do you mean?' he shouted. 'I planned these children.' Then under his breath he added, 'Are you saying I can't control myself?'

I was lucky to have heard him. 'Do sit down and let's talk about this,' I said.

He sat reluctantly, taking a child on his knee. 'I am man enough you know.'

I began to understand that he was using coitus interruptus and I was casting aspersions on his manhood by suggesting he was not very good at it. In that part of the country it was an important status symbol for a man to be able to satisfy his woman and then pull out.

'Of course you are being as careful as any man could be,' I said. I went on to explain that, however careful he was, a drop of semen could escape ages before he reached his climax, and that this was nothing any man could control. He relaxed, and after I had admired his fractious children for some time his wife was allowed to go home with some more pills.

I do not claim any particular insight into these findings, for they are well recognised by those working in clinics and probably by every agony aunt in the country. For me the effort to understand each individual and each couple, to see where they fitted or did not fit into emerging patterns, was satisfying. As I began to understand some of the complex feelings, both conscious and unconscious, that affect our sex lives, I became a strong advocate for what detractors called a duplicated service.

Choice for patients has become a political slogan in this century. Despite my emphasis in the last chapter on the importance of choice in relation to contraception and to the work/life balance, I feel it is often overrated when we are ill. Most of us want a doctor we can trust, who has personal contacts with consultants working in a good enough hospital within a reasonable distance. We are not usually in a state to weigh all the pros and cons of treatments, consultants and services. But when it comes to our sex lives the situation is different. Sex is messy, both physically and often emotionally. We get carried away and do not always make sensible decisions. Not everyone feels able to talk to their regular doctor, who might have cared for them as a child, the ultimate authority figure called in when the parents could not cope. When I am ill I want my doctor to consider me a sensible person, so that he will take my symptoms seriously and believe what I have to say. But sex puts us in touch with a silly side of ourselves when we often make mistakes. For these reasons sexually transmitted disease clinics have always been open to everyone, with no requirement for referral from another doctor. A special parliamentary statute protects confidentiality in these clinics. In various editorials I have argued strongly that family planning clinics should be treated in the same way, but this has never happened.

Over the years there have been many changes. General practices are larger with many more women partners. Sex is more openly discussed in society. Pharmacists and nurses play a much bigger role in the provision of services and advice, and many supplies are available on the net. But despite this liberalisation unplanned pregnancies still occur in large numbers. In 2009, 189,000 abortions were performed in England and Wales. I hope that, whatever the structure of the future NHS, designated family planning clinics will not wither away. The importance of a sign over the door that says, in effect, 'We are interested in sex' cannot be exaggerated.

Once GPs began providing FP advice for their patients the nature of trainees in the clinics changed. Hospital doctors too were realising that they needed expertise in this field. I was interested in the developments that were taking place in training for general practice and the different ideas about how to analyse the consultation. The fashion at the time was to break the interaction into tasks, an approach that seemed very limited for it did not help the doctor to notice a patient's unspoken communications. For instance, one of the tasks was to explain the pros and cons of any treatment. As one conscientious family planning trainee went through all the possible side effects of the pill I saw the patient's eyes glaze over. After several minutes I intervened.

'You are clearly still anxious. I wonder what is worrying you?'

Relieved, she turned to me and said, 'I am worried that it may be difficult for me to have a baby when I am ready.'

The effect of different methods on future fertility must have been the only subject that had not been mentioned during the exposition.

I was lucky to be asked to take part in a trial weekend designed to develop guidelines for training the trainers in family planning. Together with Gill Cardy and Elizabeth Gregson we planned the course, which was strengthened when Gill's husband Ian, a GP, joined us. We enlisted the help of an educationalist who was adamant that a residential weekend should include group work and a progressive rise in the demands made on the participants. He explained that they needed to be stretched but that the level of anxiety must not become overwhelming.

At this time the concept of recording live consultations with patients, after asking their permission, was fashionable. We thought it important, as tutors, to share our own videos. I was horrified to see that I appeared to wave the clinic notes in front of my face as a shield! I hope the camera had exaggerated this effect but at least when I showed it on the course I could not pretend to be setting a perfect example.

The style of one northern GP was particularly interesting. He appeared to break all the rules, hardly looking up as the patient entered the room. He started the consultation with a string of questions. I felt myself getting hot with embarrassment as I watched his interest confined entirely to his notes. However, after a few minutes he put down his pen, sat back in his chair and looked up. 'Now, tell me about the problem.' His expression was transformed as if, having first dealt with the detritus that lay between them, every cell in his body was at the patient's disposal.

Through the seminars run by the Institute of Psychosexual Medicine, I had experience of working as a member and also leader of various groups. Every scrap of judgement I had acquired was needed as the course progressed. Unfortunately my co-tutor Elizabeth Gregson was taken ill. My own group was working well and I was happy to leave it knowing that my journal colleague Elizabeth Forsythe and Heather Montford, both doctors with great experience in the field, would make sure it continued to run smoothly.

The same could not be said for the group that had been without a leader for a while. By this stage we were engaged in three-way role-play with participants taking the parts of doctor, trainer and patient. I walked in to discover one member lying on a sofa feeling poorly and the floor taken by a GP trainer telling the rest how the consultation should be conducted. The whole point of the session was to simulate the experience of such a consultation, not to give a lecture about how it should be done. The only way I could restore the spirit of the exercise was to introduce a new prepared case. I asked the doctor who had been showing off to play the part of an anxious and embarrassed man sent to the clinic by his wife to collect condoms.

Our format was adopted for several years by local authorities and by John Guillebaud, who ran such courses for the Margaret Pyke centre, an independent organisation. Working as a tutor with Heather on these courses was great fun and we became very good

friends. The first time we cooperated we prepared a series of imagined scenarios, giving all the patients the names of birds. We can
still remember Miss Dove who was a shy soul unable to voice her
problems, and Mr Peacock whose flamboyance hid his deep
uncertainty about his sexuality.

One unexpected effect of this role-play was shown by some
doctors, especially those trained in Asia, who were very authoritarian
when playing the doctor's role. This behaviour easily antagonised the
group. When such doctors were asked to put themselves in the place
of a pregnant sixteen-year-old we discovered they were not lacking
in sympathy. Quite the reverse; they showed a deep and touching
empathy with the patient's predicament, becoming hesitant,
embarrassed and vulnerable. The original impression, caused by
cultural expectations on their part, and probably by many of their
patients, was that the doctor should always be the one to give advice
and make decisions. It has taken all of us a long time to learn that in
the contraceptive field such an approach is seldom in the best
interest of the patient.

The experience reinforced the lesson I had learned when I was a
hospital resident with doctors from different cultures: that individuals are more important than cultural stereotypes. Now, in old age,
I take great pleasure in meeting people of all ages, social status and
cultural background: but if I base my judgements of them on first
impressions and superficial differences I can still make bad mistakes.

13

Body/Mind Doctoring

The body/mind split has been laid at the door of Descartes. I confess I have not read him but, like a jackdaw, I pick up second-hand shiny objects and ideas. Apt quotations have a particular attraction. I collect them in my 'Jackdaw book', where I find a scribbled note about Descartes. Apparently, in his determination to refound human knowledge, he said that the mind and the body were distinct substances. In this way he could reconcile the death of the physical body with his belief in the immortality of the soul.

Although Descartes died in 1650, his thinking still has a profound effect. Only now, with the development of detailed brain imaging, is it possible to begin to grasp the connections between these two aspects of a human being. I am excited by Iain McGilchrist's book *The Master and his Emissary*. He provides a detailed review of the results of recent studies in brain imaging, and is particularly interested in the work of the two sides of the brain. Their different tasks, and in particular the intimate ways in which they communicate with each other, provide both a factual and a metaphorical basis for seeing each person as a unit.

In the day to day work of doctors, the struggle to gain such insight is only just beginning. I believe that the potential for the body and the mind to interact is present at every level: the single cell, the tissues, the organs and the self. But it is difficult to assimilate that belief into my relationships, personal or professional.

One of the problems is that scientific medicine has advanced so rapidly. Pasteur discovered microbes and my ancestor Lord Lister developed some techniques to combat them. Alexander Fleming noticed an absence of mould and discovered penicillin. Crick and Watson unravelled the secrets of DNA. In quite a different room Freud laid his patients on a couch and explored the unconscious.

Medical science has scampered into specialities that keep dividing like an overactive amoeba. As the volume of knowledge expands, the old saw fulfils itself, and experts know more and more about less and less. Such division is the outcome of analytical activity, located in the left hemisphere of the brain. McGilchrist believes that, during the development of the western world, this aspect of humanity has become too powerful.

Science is good at analysis, but not so hot when it comes to synthesis, mainly the work of the right side of the brain. There is a danger that the task of integrating things into a whole is falling into the hands of the crystal gazers, the iridologists (who make diagnosis by looking at the iris of the eye and nothing else), diet fetishists and others. I find McGilchrist's scholarly book an important antidote.

I don't want us to dismiss the scientific method. If we were to do so our luxurious western lives would become similar to those of pregnant Tanzanian women in the hinterland of Arusha. When I visited in 1994, I heard that they had to walk twelve miles to the nearest hospital to give birth. They tell their existing children, 'I am going to the sea to fetch a baby. The way is long and hard and I may not return.'

But the traditional scientific approach in medicine can sometimes lead to consultations and services that are dehumanised. Marshall Marinker, who was Professor of General Practice at Leicester, has suggested that 'not all consultations are problem solving, some are more like a piece of theatre, a celebration or an expiation; not to be valued as crosswords but more as poems.'

My introduction to the importance of the body/mind connection started when I joined Michael Balint's group for general practitioners in 1958. By the time we moved to Kent I was already seeing patients with sexual difficulties in my own time before and after family planning sessions. The patients had revealed their distress to me during the normal consultation and included those who had already identified a problem. Others presented indirectly, often with difficulty finding an acceptable contraceptive method. A woman might discover that touching her own genitals to insert a diaphragm was deeply distasteful, yet taking the pill gave her headaches. The idea of an IUD, a foreign body inside, could produce a fantasy of damage out of all proportion to the true risks of the device. A condom interrupted their lovemaking and the rhythm method was too complicated and premeditated. Following some of my colleagues I began to suspect that it was sex itself that was unsatisfactory. The skill of picking up unspoken clues, observing the mode of dress, eye contact or its absence, feelings of anger, despair or withdrawal, was hard to learn. But if one could remain quiet and give patients the opportunity to talk, they might find a way to get in touch with underlying sexual unhappiness.

A particularly interesting part of the work was meeting those people who developed genuine symptoms, often pain in various parts of their body, or irritations and discharges for which no obvious physical cause could be found. During my traditional medical training such patients were often labelled as suffering from a 'functional' disorder. This word, defined in the dictionary as 'characterised by impairment of functions not organs', was usually spoken in a disparaging tone. Functional has come to mean 'in the mind', or even 'caused by the mind'. It is a small step to those pejorative words 'neurotic', 'malingering', 'imagined'. The conclusion could be reached that functional pain was not real pain: even that the patient was not feeling pain at all.

It is impossible to assess another person's pain. On every occasion it is felt on the body and in the mind. My personal experience of pain has been small. Labour pains were relieved by analgesics and toothache has never lasted very long. I have never suffered from renal colic, said to be one of the most acute agonies, or the persistent, gnawing torment of cancer cells growing within the bones.

Occasional attacks of back trouble have provided my only experience of life-restricting pain.

I was shocked when my daughter said I often developed back pain when she asked me to look after her children. What me? Suffering from neurotic symptoms? Never. On reflection, I saw this to be a simple example of the mind and body intertwined. Before such childcare visits I would spend more time on my feet, cooking food to take with me and tidying my house, straining the ligaments in my back and producing reflex muscle spasm. At the same time, the prospect of being responsible for the children made me anxious, tightening my muscles further. In this example, a few minutes' thought helped me to see the connection. Other ways in which the body and mind are connected lie at a deeper level of the psyche.

During our time in Maidstone, in the first half of the 1970s, I was becoming ever more interested in the patients I was meeting, and I was only too glad that I had no responsibilities towards Ralph's work. Prisoners did not come to work in our garden as they had at Parkhurst. No one pushed my car in the way the borstal boys had done during our first visit to Pollington. Even at Wormwood Scrubs I had been inveigled into helping with the chapel flowers and had been escorted inside the walls from time to time. On our return to Pollington I had run the playgroup; but in Kent accommodation was spread about the town. Staff wives could find company and recreation in the community, removing the need for them to run their own group.

It was here that Ralph met many more prisoners who were serving a life sentence for murder. This detention is for an indeterminate length of time, at least eight years, but can be extended as necessary, determined by the parole board. A governor has to supply a report to this board and Ralph took immense trouble over the task, spending several hours with each prisoner in an effort to make an accurate assessment of his danger to the public if released. The board uses other reports and a close study of the case in order to reach their decision, which is usually right. Of course there are occasional mistakes when a man released on parole kills again. Ralph maintained that the system could never be totally foolproof. If every murderer was locked up for the duration of his natural life, large numbers of people would be shut away unnecessarily and the prison population would explode.

Not long after we arrived, I joined a group at the Cassel hospital, led by Tom Main under the auspices of the Institute of Psychosexual Medicine (IPM). At the time when the majority of family planning services were handed over to the NHS doctors working in marriage guidance clinics run by the FPA felt they needed a special training organisation. They asked Tom Main to be their chairman as he was already running groups to discuss the sexual problems that presented in the clinics. He was a psychoanalyst with a fund of understanding about human beings and a rigorous approach to our study; but he inspired strong feelings of attachment and antagonism. An unsympathetic doctor referred to his acolytes as his 'lovely ladies'. We were in the main women, because the work started with family planning doctors who were almost exclusively female. In addition, something about the nature of the work might have appealed to us more than to male doctors. Many men found Tom's personality overbearing. Prue Tunnadine, the training secretary of the IPM for many years and who succeeded Tom as president, described a 'stags at bay' scenario that could develop between him and some men.

I travelled to London by train with a colleague, Pat Roberts, a gentle, charming person. I was delighted when Ralph asked her to become a prison visitor. Although we were enjoying our life together in a large house and pleasant garden it was good to have a friend with interests in both our worlds. We talked on the terrace, looking out at a trellis of roses running down one side of a lawn with a pond on the other.

After Pat had gained some experience in the prison she gave a talk to the IPM about her role. She explained that she had not been appointed as a doctor or as a person with training in psychosexual medicine. She was only an interested member of the public who wanted to help in any way she could. She had no powers within the prison and no set agenda, other than to be a friend to the prisoner, within the rules of the service. When she had finished her talk someone asked if she had ever felt frightened in the company of men who had committed murder. She said no, but added, 'I have to admit to a small *frisson* when I heard that the charming man who recently offered me one lump or two in my coffee had poisoned two wives.'

In common with most doctors who start training with the IPM, both Pat and I found the seminars frustrating. The acquisition of facts had played such a large part in our previous education. All through my training I had believed that there was a body of knowledge that I must master, either by being told or by studying the recommended books. I could not understand why Tom Main was not teaching me how to help my patients. Doctors are supposed to have the answers and I was not equipping myself with them. The idea that I was learning how NOT to know, to stay in ignorance with the patient, only dawned slowly.

In the world of psychoanalysis and dynamic psychotherapy Tom is probably known best for furthering the idea of the therapeutic community. After serving in the RAMC as a psychiatric advisor he was posted to Northfield hospital to develop group studies in the care of disturbed servicemen. Soon he was appointed medical director of the Cassel hospital where he developed a more dynamic psychosocial role for nurses and where he established a family unit.

Michael Balint had been his analyst and they worked together to develop the group training method for general practitioners which I had experienced briefly in 1958. Some of Tom's seminal thoughts are captured in *The Ailment*, a collection of his papers edited by his daughter. The last three chapters that deal with the defences of doctors and the training method of the Institute of Psychosexual Medicine are of vital importance. His most salient ideas have reverberated in my head down the years.

The clues to an individual's discomfort with his or her sexual feelings or performance lie inside that person. All the doctor can do is to work with the patient to try and discover what these internal feelings might be. Over time I learned that preconceived ideas learned from books or teachers can only muddy the waters. Indeed, Tom was so concerned that his original ideas might be turned into accepted truths that would be passed down and block further thought that his work with us, alas, covers no more than three chapters of the book. But these are of vital importance for psychosexual medicine.

During this time, the mid- to late seventies, the new discipline of Sexual Therapy was developing. Treatment was based on the work of Masters and Johnson who had published their book *Human Sexual Inadequacy* in 1970. They had studied the physical changes that took place during sexual arousal and orgasm, using human subjects in a laboratory. For many years a behavioural approach was advocated with enthusiasm. Men and women were told how to have sex and given exercises to desensitise their hang-ups. Deeply personal and interpersonal feelings were labelled 'Sexual Dysfunction' defined by the frequency and adequacy of sexual performance. A new terminology developed to classify symptoms. Thus impotence became erectile dysfunction, retarded or premature ejaculation. Frigidity was subdivided into dysfunction of the arousal phase or orgasmic failure. Lack of desire was often seen as a hormonal deficiency.

The use of these terms removed the stigma of words like impotence and frigidity, which can imply something about the person rather than a medical condition. Despite this advantage, I disliked the new terminology. The old words were useful and poignant. Frigidity suggests something of the painful sense of being out of touch with one's feelings. The word also helps us to understand the atmosphere that may develop during a consultation. Tom never referred to the transference or counter-transference, preferring 'doctor–patient relationship' and 'atmosphere' as being more descriptive of the dynamic whole.

'Come *on*,' he would say. 'How did the patient look? What was she wearing? How did he enter the room? What was it LIKE to be with this person?'

I might find myself becoming very active, chipping away as if at a block of ice with questions and ideas. Yet, somehow, the patient could let out none of the feelings that mattered to her, except the despair of being how she was. 'I am standing at the sink, he puts his arms round me and I freeze.' The pain of the moment can be powerful and present in the room.

One of the first things I learned in the seminar was the futility of asking questions. 'If you ask questions you get answers,' Tom would say. 'What use are they? You have no idea if the patient is trying to please you, give you the expected reply or fishing for the answer they want. Your question is dependent on your ideas and may be miles from the patient's concerns.'

In the scenario described above, questions would have been useless. If the patient had known why she felt this way she could have remedied the situation herself. At that moment, what she longed for was to have her feelings understood. If the doctor makes a guess, based on other patients or what has been written in books, he or she is likely to be wide of the mark. The best response is to recognise the misery. 'That must be awful for you.' At least then the relationship with the patient has a chance of developing some warmth.

Another early lesson was the destructive effect of reassurance if it is given too early. Unless one can get near the core of the anxiety, reassurance is felt as denial. I remember once, when I was overcome by despair at my inability to help, I told a patient that she was not the only person to have these feelings, other people suffered in the same way. She leant forward and banged the table. 'I am not other people, I'm ME.'

Learning to recognise that our own feelings and actions might be a response to the patient, a signpost to his or her difficulty, was the central idea that Tom brought to our work, which he believed was 'applied psychoanalysis'. At the time I thought it was a ridiculous exaggeration of our skills, but with the passing of time I have come to believe he was talking about an approach so fundamentally different from many forms of counselling and behavioural therapy that he might have been justified.

During training for psychoanalysis and psychodynamic counselling, based on this idea of the relationship, the worker is required to undergo a varying amount of personal therapy with the aim of disentangling emotions produced by the patient/client from those arising from the psyche of the professional. Although some of us decided to have our own therapy this has never been a requirement in the IPM. Tom made a deliberate decision to ban discussion of the doctor's personal feelings in the group. He had no wish to produce some lower species of therapist. His objective was to sensitise and improve our skills during our day-to-day work. (He was always ambivalent about special sessions where I believe important work can be done.) We were to remain, before everything else, doctors. Our personal feelings were not denied, just ignored. Any attempt at self-understanding was to be done outside the training seminar. With hindsight I see that this emphasis acted as a powerful stimulus to keep the consultation focused on the patient. For example, the doctor who admitted he had been angry with a woman in surgery might explain it to himself by saying he was in a bad temper because of an argument with his wife that morning. Tom would point out that he had not lost his temper with the preceding patients, so why this one? After some thought the doctor might say she reminded him of his wife. Instead of wanting to know in what way, Tom would wonder what it was in this patient that led her to ruffle people who were trying to help her.

Much of my professional life had been dominated by my lack of knowledge and by my anxiety that I would make mistakes. The opportunity to concentrate on the patient instead of myself was a new experience and a great relief. For the first time, I was encouraged to think not 'was that right or wrong?' but 'what does that mean in terms of the patient?' In addition, we were listening to stories of the sexual lives of our patients. It was particularly important that our personal lives were not exposed to the group in any way that we might regret later. Our professional selves were being studied, not our whole persons, allowing a more open and honest critique of our work.

The second tenet of the IPM, the study of what became known as the psychosomatic genital examination, emerged during Tom's early work with family planning doctors. They noticed that before, during or after that vulnerable moment when people take their clothes off, they might get in touch with feelings they had not been aware of or had not connected with their symptoms. For most of us, when we lie on the couch, we are concerned to detach ourselves from the embarrassment of the exposure, to act unconcerned and sensible. The idea of further exposure, of feelings as well as flesh, is threatening. I was once asked if I obtained the patient's permission to do such an examination – as if it was some invasive procedure, like an X-ray. It is nothing of the kind, merely an attempt to provide a listening and observing space where feelings can be allowed to emerge if they are pressing to do so. The most one could do to facilitate such exposure would be to comment on tension, sadness or fury evident in the face or body of the patient, or just present in the room.

As I became more confident I began to lecture on various courses. I will never forget being seized by the arm as I stood on an escalator leading to the underground in Stockholm. A young gynaecologist looked earnestly into my face as he asked, 'Just how exactly do you do this psychosomatic examination?' With the crowds surging round us, I was silenced by the impossibility of condensing several years of study and experience into a one-minute soundbite.

The next stage in the development of consultation skills was to learn how to step outside my feelings and interpret them to the patient in a meaningful way. Tom suggested that one cannot feel and think at the same time. The activity must be one of going close to feel with empathy, then pulling away to think, the movement one of rapid oscillation. I continued to struggle to develop this art for the rest of my professional life.

Because the feelings in the consultation were to some extent a product of our own internal worlds, our remarks had to be tentative and patient centred. Not 'You are making me feel sad' but 'I wonder if you are feeling sad'. Or even 'There seems to be a lot of sadness (anger, fear) around.' One colleague found herself almost asleep as the patient droned on. Instead of processing the feeling she said, 'I'm feeling very sleepy.' The patient replied, 'Yes, I have that effect on everyone.' The doctor was immediately interested and fully awake. I cannot decide if her remark was foolhardy or courageous. I would not have been so direct, but in this particular instance the remark freed the patient to let out something real.

Tom Main called the study and use of the doctor–patient relationship the *golden road to understanding*. He departed from Balint by believing that doctors who were not analysts could learn to lead training seminars. I became a leader and attended the leaders' seminars. Although we learnt much about groups, the most striking aspect of these meetings was the way Tom always took the discussion back to the patient. As with the basic training, we were taught no theory, for Tom believed passionately that one learnt by doing, his favourite quotation being from Izaak Walton, *That art was not to be taught by words, but practice.*

I am concerned by a further memory. Tom frequently asked, 'Is this patient suitable for a brief psychosexual approach?' I don't remember asking this in the groups I led and I wonder if I had enough experience of more disturbed people to make that judgement myself. I did refer some patients on for further psychological help so at least I was not trying to cure the world. Tom thought we could help those with a problem in a focused area of their personality. This is not the same as focusing on the sexual problem – that was always secondary to the doctor–patient relationship.

The skills of psychosexual medicine cross the boundaries between the body and the mind. Along with others, I often felt ignorant and ill equipped to help.

'This work is really difficult,' I complained to Tom one day.

'What do you expect? Anything worth doing is difficult. Stick with it.'

That obligation to stay with the here and now of the consultation, to remain in ignorance with the patient, required more courage than I realised at the time.

I have never felt myself to be courageous. Childhood and adolescence were full of frightening things. To my shame, when a gaggle of hissing geese approached, it was my younger sister who intervened to protect me. Since becoming an adult I had been able to avoid doing anything alarming. I only realised how easy it had been to run away from anxious situations when Ralph and I moved our cabin cruiser south from Yorkshire where it had been built. Bringing it by road would have been impossibly expensive, so we found a route via the canals and the tidal Trent. As soon as we passed through the lock into the rushing tide our engine failed. We were pulled back into the calm of the canal and had to wait a whole day while the engine was fixed and the tide reached the required height again.

There was no escape from the wild waters that waited for us. Glad of the pre-exam experience of controlling my nerves, I immersed myself in a novel, walked the dog along the towpath until exhausted, even tried to pray. Ralph read his book of knots, only looking at the engine manual when he thought I would not notice. I was glad he ignored me; we both knew that no words could relieve our anxiety.

When the time came to exit the lock for the second time all went smoothly. I clutched a handrail for support against the movement of our home, now a fragile matchbox in substantial waves. In the late afternoon we passed into the Fossdyke navigation via another lock. Once through to the other side, the scene was transformed. Boats were moored by the bank, motionless in the placid water where moorhens puttered about. Sitting in the still evening sunshine, protected from the fury of a nine-knot tide, made us realise that we knew nothing of the reality of nautical life.

The memory lingers as one of those moments of peace, so often provided for me by a river or canal. Some people long for the sea from which our antecedents, those minuscule creatures, dragged themselves onto the land. Perhaps the expanse of ocean signifies a greater reality into which our beginning and end can merge. For me, the journey is more important than the arrival. From those days on the river Thames with my parents, via our canoe, various punts and then our canal boat, the inland waterways have coursed through my being. Upland brooks still call to me, even though I can no longer walk up the hills to reach them. Rivulets join to form small rivers that coalesce and become waterways, on which we humans can journey, becoming a part of the whole. During those years when I was struggling to learn how to consider the body and mind as one entity, these watery experiences shared with Ralph not only continued to hold our marriage together but fed what, in the absence of a better word, I have to call my soul.

14

Body Fantasies

As I write about psychosexual medicine my voice takes on the tone of the lecturer I became, originally as an occasional speaker on family planning courses, then to various other groups of health care professionals. Telling people about the work, or about my life, appears to negate the idea that listening is important. Perhaps the tension between these two opposites can provide ways to approach the truth. Neville Symington, in his book *The Analytical Experience*, says 'Truth... is a reality that exists between two people seeking it... truth can be seen or glimpsed, not possessed.'

The truth of someone's mental picture of his or her own body is certainly difficult to grasp. The word 'fantasy' often describes a pleasurable journey into an imagined world. It has also come to be used for the more florid misconceptions held about the body. These distorted images may underlie the problem of non-consummation.

The inability to have full, penetrative sex is a fascinating example of the interaction of the body and the mind at different levels. There can be no doubt that social attitudes are very important. Good sex education, a more open approach to the body and relationships and the more enlightened upbringing of children must have reduced the incidence, although accurate figures are impossible to obtain. The difficulty is often revealed during a family planning consultation. A woman might feel she needs a cervical smear but is unable to relax enough to allow it to be taken. The matter is intensely private and may only be forced into the open by the desire for children.

One of the first studies into the problem was published as a book

159

edited by Leonard Friedman under the title *Virgin Wives*, a report of the work of one of Michael Balint's seminars. The group identified different character traits. To quote from Prue Tunnadine's groundbreaking book *Contraception and Sexual Life*, these included the maternally enjoined 'sleeping beauty', the defensive-aggressive destructive 'Brunhild', and the 'queen bee' wishing for virgin motherhood. As Prue points out, these types are often blurred.

I did not use these concepts or talk about them with colleagues. I am left wondering why I shied away from exploring ideas that could have been useful. Perhaps my personal discomfort with the world of myth was partly to blame. I have only recently begun to appreciate the usefulness of story and the part that metaphor can play in the search for truth. On the other hand, in terms of the doctor–patient relationship, the avoidance could have been due to something coming from the patient, encouraging me to think in more concrete terms.

The satisfaction of helping a woman and couple to consummate their relationship is so great that it is tempting to overestimate the success of treatment, whatever method is used. Simple behavioural methods, 'retraining' with graded exercises, may be helpful, although I find the approach uncomfortably authoritarian. I listened once to the description of a woman who had been encouraged to put her finger in a saucer of strawberry jam because the feel was like that of the moist vagina. Not, I thought, very similar at all, and for me an unpleasant image of stickiness and grainy seeds.

The didactic methods employed by many 'sex therapists' fill me with horror. At one meeting I heard such a therapist holding forth about her methods which included a five-page questionnaire. 'You must know the background fully,' she said. I was reminded of the time-wasting nature of questions. In a careful study of 159 cases treated by members of the IPM (Bramley et al., 1983), all of whom had been trained not to ask questions, 60% consummated within six months. Over 80% of these patients had consulted other agencies before coming to us for help and the mean duration of symptoms was 4.2 years.

I don't remember the first patient I saw, or the total number. The successes stay in my mind while the failures drift away like dandelion seeds in a summer breeze. The simile feels inappropriate when the difficulty is such a burden for the sufferer. But the image floated up when I tried to recall my failures – a defensive snapshot, as if the pain of not being able to cure has been converted into something that can be brushed away – although dandelion seeds do have a tendency to cling to one's clothes.

The main thing we discovered by listening to patients before, during or after an attempted examination was the prevalence and variety of body fantasies. These beliefs had usually never been voiced before and were often unconscious. The range and multiplicity of these misunderstandings surprises me to this day. Nothing in the following paragraphs will be new to those who work to uncover hidden fears. I hope they may be of interest to the general reader. However, if you are squeamish I suggest you skip the next section of this chapter for it contains, as the TV warnings say, 'scenes of a disturbing nature'.

The fear that there is a 'block' at the entrance to the vagina is so common that I used the word in the title of my book *Blocks and Freedoms in Sexual Life*, published in 1997. I was writing for the medical and allied professions but I find myself re-reading it now as I address a wider audience. After being away from the work for more than ten years I have to remind myself of the understanding that I was groping for at that time.

Vaginismus, a reflex spasm of the muscles, is often the cause of the apparent block. Occasionally there can be a physical abnormality. The hymen can be unusually thick and tight, as I found in one patient. I warned her that I thought she might need a small operation but she wanted to try and stretch it with her own finger. Within two weeks she had managed to have enjoyable sex – but then, she did not have irrational fears to hold her back. Other very rare conditions include double vagina and the presence of a hymen that extends across the whole entrance, causing abdominal pain in adolescence when the menstrual blood cannot escape.

The hymen and the whole question of virginity have been subjects of interest for thousands of years. One of the medical museums in Vienna has ninety-two hymens displayed in glass jars. Some of these are torn or scarred, some have bands across the opening, some have inelegant skin tags and some are thick with a tiny hole. I went round the exhibition as a medical student, after falling off a horse that had kicked me on the head. I was a bit dazed before the tour started. By the end I was in a whirl, but at least I realised how very difficult it can be, impossible in many cases, especially today when girls use tampons from an early age, to say if someone is a virgin. Yet this diagnosis still remains a matter of legal and emotional importance, especially in some Asian and Muslim cultures. I was amazed to find how many on-line questions were devoted to the subject. Most of the answers depended on the opinion of an examining doctor, which I suggest may be open to doubt. For Catholics the importance lies in the fact that the Pope can annul a marriage that has not been consummated.

Old myths persist. Phrases like 'she hasn't been broken in', and the need for blood on the sheets to prove virginity, add fuel to the fire of unrecognised fears. One patient told me she knew the solid flesh had to be torn through the whole length to make a passage. With her muscles clenched she could not believe a well-lined space already existed. She showed immense courage in her efforts to feel for herself, her terror making her blood pressure fall so she felt faint, visit after visit. Stretching the entrance under anaesthetic, a practice that is still carried out, seldom helps these fears.

When working with such patients I was often the first to use the word hymen and sometimes found it difficult to do so, as if the very word was a sort of rape. The hymen may be considered as one of the guardians of the entrance, not only to the vagina but also to the very self. As I parted the lips of one woman, prior to inserting a finger, she said, 'There is an outer and inner part of me, the curtains have to be drawn.'

The relief, and sometimes the disappointment, when the tip of the doctor's finger is eased inside, can be intense. Even when a patient

162

can insert one or more of her own fingers, she cannot always give up the fantasy of a block. It is as if the hymen retreats up the vagina until it is still lying intact, covering the cervix. Here the image may get muddled with ideas about the need to 'break through into the womb'.

Several of my patients had a fear that the penis would go into the wrong place, usually into the bladder. Many living creatures have a cloaca, an internal space into which the urinary system, digestive tract and sometimes the reproductive organs open. The muddle may be due to the emphasis on animals in the biology syllabus, especially in the past when human biology was hardly mentioned. But I suspect serious misunderstandings arise much earlier in life, when the baby girl is exploring her own body. If so, then it is unlikely that even good sex education will be able to remove those fears that are not available to conscious awareness.

Once through the barrier, or 'gate' as one patient described it to me, a whole range of different phobias may lie waiting, acting like hidden parasites draining the strength of their hosts. Beyond the muscles, the upper part of the vagina can be imagined as a limitless void, a hole with no end. One woman was afraid that if her finger slipped through she would touch her liver. Having never seen a human liver she had no idea how far away it lay, snuggling smooth and glistening under the ribs. Her vision was of a raw, bloody slice in the butcher's window.

If the hole has no walls, things could get lost inside. If tampons went in, how would they get out? This ties in with male fantasies of castration. The most precious and sensitive part of a man's body could be lost inside, broken off or stuck. Even damaged by hidden teeth. One of my patients said he thought the inside was like 'rice pudding'. His facial expression showed how much he disliked that food.

Because men keep their sexual organs on the outside, fantasies about their own bodies are less common than those of women. However, I did meet one young man, a well-built country lad who was brought to the clinic by his girlfriend. Whenever he tried to penetrate he got a sore at the base of his frenulum (the fold that joins the foreskin to the tip of the penis on the underside). He had been given cream, which helped, but the problem recurred whenever he tried to have sex. I examined him and found a small ulcer. Despite my reassurance that everything else looked fine, he made no effort to get up from the couch but continued to lie looking up at the ceiling.

'You still look worried?'

'It doesn't go back.'

'How do you mean, go back?' I had checked that the foreskin retracted fully and easily.

'You know, properly back.' He was touching the base of his penis.

'I wonder why you think it has to go back there?'

'Well, it does in horses.'

Light dawned on us both at the same time. 'You mean, it *all* goes inside?' he asked.

I nodded. No wonder he kept traumatising himself.

Such simple misunderstandings will be less common now the teaching of human anatomy and sex education has improved, but the remaining problems are likely to be more difficult. The depths and type of fantasy, often more than one, are personal to each individual. Any attempt to guess at the picture in the patient's mind will hinder her efforts to get in touch with the unconscious images that are acting as a block.

I have led a relatively sheltered professional life, for I have never seen a woman who has suffered genital mutilation, or been asked to comment on the results of very early sexual abuse. Such trauma to the body, before it has been softened by the oestrogen surge of puberty, can lead to terrible scarring which is particularly difficult to assess in a traumatised child. Such work is for the experts, as indeed is help for recent victims. In psychosexual work we do hear of childhood sexual abuse, and in an audit of my clinic published in 1991, 11% of patients gave such a history. I found that the degree of psychological damage was very varied. Many were helped as quickly as those patients without such a history. However in one study, of the five patients I referred for longer and more extensive psychotherapy, three had suffered abuse. The most important lesson I learned was the care needed in asking about such a history. More than one patient became angry at the assumption that she must have been abused. In some instances this could be a conscious or unconscious denial of the past, but for this reason it was important to let such memories emerge when they were ready to do so. Asking questions only invites denial and may encourage false memories. The doctor often has to accept that the literal truth of what is being revealed may be impossible to prove. What matters are the feelings that have been evoked.

Body fantasies can also emerge later in sexual life, for instance after childbirth. When I had my own baby I was lucky that the delivery was straightforward and that I was in an environment that felt totally safe. My few stitches were inserted with the greatest care and did not cause me any problems. It took time for me to learn that, in those who had not been so lucky, their experiences could trigger a variety of new fantasies, and in particular to appreciate the symbolic importance the body image could hold for one or both partners.

More than one patient has described her vagina as being left huge and gaping, like a 'Wellington boot'. The muscles may be a bit loose but can be improved with exercises and physiotherapy. If the image represents the feeling of being so huge in her role as a mother that she cannot also be the firm, excited and exciting lover of previous times, physical methods alone are unlikely to be helpful.

For some women a tender scar may be drawn forward by muscles tense with fear, so that it is rubbed during intercourse. But again, if the woman believes the stitches have been put in too tightly and that she is now too small, not big enough to be both a mother and a lover, reassurance alone will be useless. One patient had been unable to make love since the birth of her baby three years earlier. With me she managed to insert three of her fingers easily but still looked worried. Only later in the consultation did she say thoughtfully, 'If I had been stitched up as I imagined, after six babies there would be no hole left.' As she spoke she was making a movement with her hand as if she was cobbling up a hole in a stocking. In reality, the stitches only restore the integrity of the wall and entrance and do not reduce it in size.

One of the traumatic memories of childbirth that can become fixed on the body is that of being out of control. Some people need to feel in control of every aspect of their lives. One particular couple came together to ask for an operation to remove the scar on her perineum. As they described it I imagined some grotesque deformity. When I plucked up enough courage to examine her I found a perfectly healed scar, a thin white line, almost invisible. Any operation could only have made it worse. As they talked I began to realise how distressing the birth experience had been. They were a professional, well-organised couple, used to being in full command of themselves and the world around them. Their own doctor had been called away while she was in labour so she was delivered by a stranger. In addition, the person stitching her up was told by a superior that she had not done it properly. The stitches had to be taken out and redone, leaving the couple feeling vulnerable and at the mercy of incompetent people over whom they had no control. The sense of having been damaged by incompetence had become fixed on the scar.

The majority of young people, even twenty years ago, had picked up enough information about the way their body worked for them to use it for love making with few problems. For those who were in trouble, looking at the doctor–patient relationship could be helpful. With many of my patients who could not allow full intercourse I found myself becoming more instructive than usual, asking them to draw pictures of their bodies, encouraging self-examination, even buying and lending a set of expensive trainers, dildos in graduated sizes. All these strategies could be helpful: but not to everyone. I seldom noticed that I was being so bossy, or if I did, I felt uneasy and defensive about it. My sense of being pulled between a parental role and a more adult interaction can be seen as a reflection of the conflict inside the patient where the child was afraid to grow up, indeed a sleeping beauty.

Sometimes the patient's need to be in control, her inability relax and let go of her self and her muscles, could be observed in the doctor–patient relationship. I had been seeing one patient regularly for some time. One day I found myself driving her home. Only when I realised there had been no good reason for me to do so, did I notice that this was the same patient about whom I wrote in my diary, 'Don't be late'. This rather pathetic looking waif of a girl was in fact extremely powerful, controlling all those around her, including me.

The fear underlying the need to control is, I believe, much more than the fear of pain. In my book I explored the idea that sharing that part of the body with another person could pose a threat to the integrity of the whole self. One patient, who had been married for five years with no full sex, said that she had been alone so long that she could not imagine being 'with' him. Another woman, who suffered from severe eczema and had endured many years of painful dressings by others, felt that the inside was the only part of her body that belonged to her.

The idea that every woman needs to 'own' her own vagina, take control of it from her mother, is well established. One of my most vivid memories of Prue Tunnadine is her description of a successful outcome for a couple who have not been able to make love. Hopefully they will want to inform the doctor of their success but then get rid of her. 'Thank you and good bye,' accompanied perhaps by a symbolic gift of chocolates or flowers. The doctor needs to be firmly shut out of the bedroom so that the couple can regain their privacy.

I am not sure if I ever made full use of the doctor–patient interaction in these cases. How much better if I could have stopped and thought, even asked the patient, 'I wonder why you need me to explain to you – why it is so difficult for you to find out these things for yourself?' Perhaps only from the distance of retirement can I see more clearly that my own particularly strong need to help, to cure, to make better, chimed with the need of these patients to be cured and cared for. I never confessed my bossiness in a group when Tom Main was present, for he would have disapproved, chastised me for regressing, without thought, to a more traditional sort of doctoring. At least, that is what I imagined. Perhaps he would have helped me to interpret what was going on. The most important lesson I learned from him reverberates in my head to this day. 'Fantasies must be fully explored and truly valued before they can be buried with full military honours.'

Despite the ubiquitous way that sex is displayed in our culture it remains, for many individuals, a delicate, personal matter, so the choice to talk about it to a doctor in privacy is not surprising. For me, the openness of my parents in their bathroom did not remove an inborn shyness about my own bodily functions. In the first few years of my professional life I would not have believed anyone who suggested my career would culminate in working and lecturing in the sexual field. I had chosen family planning because the hours fitted my domestic arrangements. The pressing misery of patients then drove me to listen to the stories of their sexual despair. However, the discipline of listening, and discussions within the IPM, have given me a superficial ease about such matters. When my grandchildren were small I was discussing the possible sex of the fish in my small pond, thinking that I was being usefully zoological. Helen burst out, 'Oh Mum, can't you think of anything but sex?' It was difficult for my family to tolerate the work I did. My mother in particular, despite her own emancipation, did not like to use the word 'sex' to her elderly friends. I too would hesitate and talk about medical gynaecology, unsatisfactory when an increasing number of patients were men.

When I started the work I was not helped by an American sex therapist called 'Dr Ruth'. She appeared on a series of TV programmes demonstrating the sort of prescriptive behavioural therapy that I most abhor. I suffered a certain amount of teasing by friends and patients. I am sure she did help some couples, perhaps those with a streak of exhibitionism similar to her own.

I find it hard to choose words to express my thanks to all those in the IPM, and to Tom Main in particular, who helped me to acquire some skills that fitted my personality. I was beginning to listen with my eyes as well as my ears, my feelings as well as my thoughts. Slowly, I was changing into a doctor who could find the way to some truths by learning the things that patients were able to teach me.

15

Back to General Practice

Although I enjoyed the psychosexual and family planning work, and my frequent journeys to London, in some way I did not feel a proper doctor. I was not the only family planning doctor who was concerned that by choosing preventative work rather than a healing role we were following a soft option. Although I was not aware of it at the time, I had a nagging sense that I was letting my father down by not working in general practice. His interest in contraception had been driven by his knowledge that the chances of producing healthy, undamaged babies were higher if they did not arrive too early or too close together. Although his passion was obstetrics, the major part of his time was spent caring for the sick, while my patients were, in the main, fit and well.

He had developed chest pain and began to fail before we left Wakefield. Biz came from America to visit him. I hate to imagine her misery when she had to return over that large expanse of water, knowing she would never see him again. My brother Arthur and I went home as often as we could. On one of my visits, Father complained that even the weight of his pyjama jacket on his sternum was painful. As soon as I got back to my own home I made a wire cage, sewing strips of foam round the struts in the hope that it could rest on the sides of his chest, holding the material away from the skin.

As I bent the wire and covered it with padding – and tears – I remembered the splint he had made to support the ankle of the boy with osteomyelitis. He always took infinite care with small, practical details. In the days before disposable syringes and needles, he sterilised them in a glass dish of methylated spirits. Each needle had to serve for many injections. The point could become blunt, or even hooked. I can see him now, holding one up to the light, then rubbing it on a fine whetstone until the point was sharp enough to slip painlessly under the skin again.

My frame was not a success. It tended to slip and cause more pain. But my father persevered with it for a while and I like to think that he appreciated my efforts. He always wanted me to be as practical as any boy.

A consultant physician from Bath visited on a number of occasions. When my father eventually asked if he had carcinoma of the lung he was told, 'I can't think of a better diagnosis,' an apt reply from one doctor to another. Five days later my father was found dead in his chair, his glasses on his nose and the paper on his lap. I have wondered whether, during his time in India, he had, perhaps unconsciously, found an eastern way to let go. If only we could all arrange to depart so neatly.

My mother had nursed him with great care. On hearing the news of his death, Arthur arrived first. Later in the day, I pulled into the drive, full of foreboding about my mother's state of mind. We both knew she would have nothing to do with the funeral. She dealt well with sickness – but death sent her into a frenzy. I had heard stories of how my Aunt Pip had asked her to fetch something from the room where my paternal grandfather lay in state. As my mother hesitated, Pip, who was not a doctor or a nurse, said, 'Sorry, I'll go. For a moment I forgot that you could not cope with dead bodies.' When D, my mother's own beloved father died, the whole family were on tenterhooks in case she exploded in a fit of anger about the ceremony or something the vicar said. She managed to control herself but her white face and tight lips revealed to everyone her revulsion and horror. I think her anguish about death was tied up with her fear that she might find herself wanting to believe in some sort of afterlife. For her, that would have been a betrayal of her absolute belief in the non-existence of God or of any spirit separate from the physical body. Her passion meant that she had to face her losses with no help from any faith or ritual.

As soon as I arrived at Green Gables she disappeared into the kitchen to make me some tea, giving Arthur and me a quiet moment together. He had not brought his wife with him and it had not occurred to me to ask Ralph to take time away from work. We both sensed that this was a moment when it would be easier to deal with our mother on our own.

'Do you want to see his body?' Arthur asked. 'They are leaving the coffin open until I let them know your wishes.'

I said no, almost without considering my options. Since then I have had moments of regret. Did he look peaceful? I wish I knew. At the time all my energies were focused on my mother and how we were going to get her through the next few days. A funeral must be arranged and we were both aware that she would not attend any sort of ceremony. I am sure some of his old patients would have liked to pay their respects and must have thought it strange that no details were announced in the local newspaper.

When my father was obviously approaching the end my mother had sent for his cousin Sylvia Guthrie, of whom they were very fond. In the end she stayed at home with my mother while the two of us went alone to the crematorium. I did not envy her the role she had so kindly offered to fill. We chose the simplest service in the book with a few prayers and no music. Under stress, my bladder becomes irritable. Driving into Bath, Arthur was patient with my need to stop at every ladies' loo we passed. He is not a great one with words but on that occasion, as on others, he was a substantial rock by my side.

A delayed reaction to my father's death might have driven me back to general practice, but it was not until Ralph was posted to head office in London that I made the move. The accommodation provided was in Coulsdon, Surrey and I was again faced with looking for work in a strange place where I knew no one. The house was smaller than the previous one so our furniture did not fit. By this time Ralph was within ten years of retirement and in anticipation we bought our house in Bath and furnished it with surplus belongings. The move was complicated, with two furniture vans, two cars, two cats and the dog. After packing for days I went to Bath with the dog to receive some furniture there, while Ralph took the cats to Coulsdon. I remember sleeping on the floor in the empty house clutching the dog as cramp seized the inner muscles of my thighs in the worst attack I have ever had. The long-suffering dog stood quietly as I clung to her black coat and screamed. For the first time I understood how people who get cramp in the water could drown.

It took me a few weeks to sort out both houses before I looked for work and found a job as assistant in a four-man practice in Caterham, five miles away. Having been out of mainstream medicine for so long I was extremely nervous, but the partners were supportive and tolerant of my many questions. In an effort to boost my self-confidence I studied for membership of the College of General Practitioners and passed the exam in 1979 at the age of fifty. Since then I have not exposed myself to any other exam, although I have considered a musical one to see what grade I have reached on the flute – but have not yet found the courage.

Even with the letters after my name I did not feel properly qualified and still felt something of a fraud. For instance, I had never been in a position where I had been forced to section a mental patient; that is, to sign the papers for him or her to be committed, by force if necessary, to a mental hospital.

For many years my dreams contained scenes where I had chosen to go back to Bristol as an undergraduate and should be spending more time on the wards. In the dark of those nights I am about to start back at university but have not found anywhere to live. Now when I wake in my own room, the pipes ticking as the central heating comes on, the tracery of branches on the Castanea tree beyond the window becoming sharper as the sky lightens, I try to imagine what it must be like to be a displaced person, a refugee without the solid foundation of one's own place and family. The reality of my good fortune flows through me.

When I felt more confident running surgeries, and had learned my way around the district by doing home visits, I started a special family planning session in the practice. It was a salutary experience. Despite the fact that I was a woman, enthusiastic and experienced, a considerable number of patients continued to attend the local authority clinic in the building opposite. My belief that general practitioners cannot fulfil all the needs of their patients was confirmed, especially if those in search of help are not comfortable with their sexuality.

The doctors in the practice knew of my interest in psychosexual medicine and responded in characteristic ways. The senior man was keen to delegate and sent me straightforward couples wanting to be sterilised whom he could have dealt with himself. The next in the practice was a sensitive doctor who soon realised that I was becoming overwhelmed. I was grateful when he stopped using my services. The third was a jolly 'man's man' who considered anything starting with 'psych' was nonsense. He slapped his patients on the back and said their impotence was temporary, due to drink or overwork, and that they would get better. Many of them did. Only the newest arrival, young and trained in family planning, was sensitive to the sort of problems and people who presented in that setting. He sent me patients I could sometimes help.

But the experience I had gained, my comparative professional ease with sexual matters, helped me in unexpected ways. I was caring for an old man who was dying at home, nursed by his devoted wife. I called each day as he slipped into long periods of semi-conscious ramblings. One morning his wife was distraught. I followed her into the front room where we sat for a few minutes. Through her tears she said, 'I must tell you doctor, last night for the first time, he wouldn't let me... you know... help him with my hand.' For her that sexual withdrawal was the moment she truly lost him. When he died three days later she was all brisk efficiency, washing sheets and paying bills.

It may seem strange to some readers that several doctors working in psychosexual medicine have moved into terminal care. The

175

sensitivity honed by listening to sexual unhappiness can illuminate end of life decisions. I was greatly moved by Judy Gilley's work on intimacy and terminal care. To paraphrase two of her cases, she described one man who pleaded for his dying wife to be allowed to stay at home. 'I want to hold her in my arms for one last night,' he said. Their home was snug having a 'faded glamour, with much gilt and pink lampshades'. The other patient was a man who lived in a tidy and sterile house. He started to suffer panic attacks after being diagnosed with cancer. The wife said that he wanted her to do 'dreadful things'. Imagining these to be intimately sexual the doctor was surprised when she learned he wanted his wife to comb his hair.

It is difficult for me to understand how a woman can feel so distant from her man, although I can relate it to my feelings about my elderly mother. After washing her hair I would comb the tangles with exaggerated care, and it is only as I write that I am reminded of how impatient she was with my own hair when I was small. Another job was to squeeze a cyst behind her ear. It filled up gradually over two or three months with a blackhead at the centre that she hated. My father had done this for her over the years. When I took his place I had to marshal every particle of control to stop myself from gagging. Yet I had done much more distasteful things for patients without any feeling of disgust.

Another memory of my time at Caterham is of a nurse attached to the practice who was trained in terminal care. As well as orga-nising the loan of equipment, commodes and hoists, she attended to small details with dogged patience, suggesting tinned baby food for a woman who could not cope with lumps, a small adjustment to a bedside table, a different arrangement of pillows. In addition she discussed treatment regimes with the doctors, and by listening to our anxieties helped us to bear our feelings of inadequacy, comforting our sadness at being so ineffectual in the face of death.

After about two years I discovered my mother had suffered a transient ischaemic attack (TIA) while visiting Biz in America. She had told no one, but put her name and my address on a label round her neck in case she became unconscious during the journey home.

The effects had been slight weakness in one hand and minimal slurred speech. Over the next few weeks I noticed occasional facial weakness on one side especially when she was tired. As I was finding night work very wearing I used her potential illness as an excuse to leave Caterham and take a part-time job in Purley where I was not required to do any nights and only a few home visits.

Here I met many Jewish families, reminding me of my time in Hendon all those years before, where if one visited on a Saturday one had to creep in at the back. In very orthodox households one must use no energy on the holy day. The ring of the front door bell would desecrate this taboo. A strong sense of family tended to produce anxious parents and we were often called to children who were not very sick. However, the patient I remember most clearly in Purley was not Jewish. She came every day to the surgery, often twice or three times, always with a new symptom and always in a state of anxiety, insisting she must be seen. I found her a great trial. Patients who cry 'wolf' can develop a real emergency that goes undetected, so I felt the need to examine her every time.

While I was struggling with her and hoping that Ralph might soon be moved again so that I could escape, I read an article in the *New England Journal of Medicine*. The best thing about it was the title, 'Taking care of the hateful patient'. The admission that doctors, who were supposed to be ever loving, could hate an occasional patient was a great relief. The authors suggested that obsessional attendees like my patient could be helped by being given a definite time for their next appointment, increasing the gap between visits very gradually. I followed the advice with scrupulous care, starting with appointments the same afternoon, then the next day, two days for several weeks and then three days. All went well until I lengthened the gap to four days. She was back that afternoon, her confidence shattered, never to be regained during my time in the practice.

My boss was a charming man from Sri Lanka who would go out on a limb for his patients. One day he asked if I was busy on the following Saturday, as he wanted some help. He had arranged the adoption of a baby within his practice. Doubts about the legality of such a thing made me hesitate but he had checked that the new regulations forbidding such personal intervention had not yet come into force. With great trepidation I went with him to the maternity ward where we found the young mother weeping over the baby and taking photos. After a while her own mother led her away and we were put into a side ward with the baby in a crib.

There we stood, a short, dark Sri Lankan and a tall blonde English woman, somewhat incongruous in those days. He rubbed his hands in pleasure. 'Now we are the parents.' For the few moments before the new parents arrived we were legally responsible. The baby lay quiet as we gazed down. After a few moments the door opened and a couple came in. They advanced slowly to the crib, not daring to touch their new child.

'Would you like me to lift her?' I asked.

They nodded. I put the bundle into her outstretched arms, moved almost to tears by their tentative joy.

After nearly four years working in London, Ralph was posted to Leyhill open prison in Gloucestershire. The previous governor had not lived in the designated house, which was now occupied by another member of staff. Ralph suggested we could live in Bath and he would commute. The Home Office agreed.

I was delighted to move into our retirement house four years earlier than expected. A succession of student tenants had neglected the garden. Ground elder ruled the flower beds and despite my efforts over the next thirty years, the leaves still push up through the soil with depressing frequency, reminding me of the roots below that are as impossible to eradicate as the child lurking within every adult.

The medical establishment in Bath was not easy to breach. The wives of many of the consultants were medically qualified and had snapped up the available part-time work. I was forced to travel to Bristol and into Somerset for sessions in family planning, although it was not long before I was appointed to a new psychosexual clinic in Bath. After a while, in addition to this work, I helped out in the general practice in Radstock, eight miles away. The town had been the centre of an area of open-cast mining and the small remains of the stalwart mining community were very different from the Surrey population I had recently left. Within the first two weeks I was reminded of the patients in Pontefract, the Yorkshire town where I had first become a doctor.

A late-middle-aged man came into my surgery saying he had a bit of tummy ache. His pulse was rapid, his blood pressure low and his abdomen rock hard. He was walking about with a perforated appendix. Another man rang towards the end of evening surgery asking for a call in the morning, as his wife was unwell. I offered to go that evening. 'We don't want to trouble you, doctor.' I left for the house as soon as surgery was finished and found a greatly distressed woman with advanced heart failure.

It was during this time that I became an IPM seminar leader. The first group I led was in Bristol where there were enough applicants to start two groups. Elizabeth Gregson, my stalwart friend who had climbed the high rise stairs in Liverpool to deliver condoms, led the second one. The power of group dynamics was shown very clearly when one of her members decided to come to a session I was leading. She was an outsider in my group, who had already bonded with some force. They gave her a rough ride. I was too inexperienced to be fully aware of what was happening and did not intervene appropriately. Luckily she is a strong person who could look after herself.

One way in which Tom Main tried to focus the training on our doctoring was to insist that during the seminar and the leaders' workshops we called each other Doctor so and so, not Ruth or Mary or Heather. He did this deliberately and openly, not to be nice or nasty but to address the professional ego. At the end of the training session we could revert to the terms used between friends. In today's world where such familiarity is ubiquitous, used by one's bank manager, solicitor and milkman the rule is archaic and would do nothing but arouse suspicion or mirth.

But I still feel strongly about the subject. One of my clinic secretaries sent an appointment to a referred patient addressing her as Susan although the referral letter had called her Miss Blank. I was furious, and not a bit surprised when she did not arrive to see me. I learned from the letter that she was an unmarried teacher in her forties who had never been able to have sex. Of all people to patronise in that way!

After a couple of years Elizabeth retired and I took over her part-time lectureship. When she held the post it was called 'lectureship in family planning'. I insisting on adding 'and psychosexual medicine' to try and raise the profile of the work. The job included a psychosexual clinic in gynaecology outpatients. By this time more men were being referred to me, which was very awkward as the electronic system of registration did not include 'Mr'. A man often had to suffer the double embarrassment of being the only male in the waiting room and of being called over the Tannoy as 'Ms'. I soon insisted that I would fetch each patient myself, whatever their sex.

I went on to lead several groups in various parts of the country, including one of obstetric and gynaecological physiotherapists. Despite the fact that their role requires them to give a lot of advice they were responsive to the idea that they could learn to listen in the consultation. Many of their patients were postnatal, with bladder and pelvic floor problems. The idea of 'de-briefing' is useful after childbirth. One definition of the word is 'to relive an experience with someone else to make sense of it'. Feelings about the labour and delivery may take a few weeks to develop and the physiotherapist is ideally placed to listen to the woman's story. I was sad to hear recently that no training in this aspect of their work has been included in their curriculum.

My life had become over-full and the time had come to give up my general practice work once again. I never regretted my short foray back into what I still thought of as the 'real' medical world, for it gave me more legitimacy to lead groups where an increasing number of the trainees were combining their family planning and psychosexual work with general practice or hospital medicine. These doctors were learning to integrate their psychosexual work into their healing role. However, I can't help wondering if the deep understanding of emotional problems, unearthed by the detailed work of those who remained focused in family planning and psychosexual medicine, would be possible in today's management-driven NHS.

16

Taking the Reins

After my father's funeral Arthur and Sylvia went home. I stayed on for several days. During that strange interlude I became the adult to my mother for the first and only time in my life. I was the one to suggest we should take my father's blankets to be cleaned, I chose what we would eat, and opened and listed the condolence letters for her to answer later. This position of power was surprisingly satisfying. My mother had always been the boss of the household, and of our lives, with no chink in her efficiency that would allow her children to provide genuine help. Now, in her grief, my mother truly relied on me and her need made me stronger. But my own grief demanded some outlet. Using my dog Bess as an excuse for a walk, I took an hour off every afternoon. Striding down gypsy lane and across the fields where we had walked so often as children I wept, not just for the loss of my father but for my departed childhood. The pond with the bullrushes at the end of the second field remained as I remembered it. The pill-box left from the war still smelt of stale urine. The path went over a tributary of the river Avon and down the side of the Nestlé factory as it always had done. I encouraged my tears, for they relieved the ache inside, but it was easy to stop them at will, in time to allow my eyes to recover before facing my mother again.

One day our friends Dilla and Alan Roberton, with whom we had spent holidays in Cornwall, arrived to take me out to a pub lunch. During that meal I learned something of the needs of the carer. Until then every fibre of my body had been concentrated on helping my mother survive, hour by hour. The warmth of their concern and the opportunity to talk about my own grief gave me the strength to go on.

After about ten days my mother seized back the reins of her life and I went home to Ralph. It was not long before she threw herself into converting the surgeries at Green Gables into a flat where she had a selection of different tenants. Then she built a smaller house in the grounds. A pleasant couple bought our family home, but they eventually sold it to a developer, who divided it into four flats and built seven houses in our lovely garden.

For me, the moment of parting from the house I loved so much came when all the furniture had been removed. I was standing at the nursery window looking out at the empty swimming pool with its cracked walls. I remembered the soggy leaves that always lurked at the bottom, full of worms, making me afraid to put my feet down. (My parents didn't acquire a vacuum pump till many years after I had left home.) As I stood there, a single sob shook my body. One of Daisy's nieces, who still helped in the house, was by my side. She laid a hand on my shoulder but said nothing. There was nothing to say.

My mother had always enjoyed planning houses and insisted on having the new house designed round her favourite furniture. This included her Globe Wernicke bookcases, bed, oak desk, and her 'by-me', a small mahogany piece with shelves, a drawer and cupboard opening on both sides and made to stand between two beds. The resultant house was a plain building, light but utilitarian. Her architect, who had wanted an elegant house with windows in the shape of cabin portholes, lost every battle.

During my mother's time in that house, my father's cousin Sylvia Guthrie, who had been such a stalwart support when my father died, became very frail. I had always been in awe of her. Her husband had died early in her life but despite being a single woman she had been allowed to adopt two children. The rules were not so rigid in those days and the fact that she was a respected paediatrician in Manchester might have helped. My parents had chosen her as one of my

Godmothers. After taking Arthur to be christened my mother had felt physically sick, so when it was my turn she had delegated the task to Sylvia. Biz was never christened and I often wondered if she felt a bit deprived.

It was not until Sylvia was fading in body and mind, when I visited her in her home, that I appreciated the person she was. I found her sitting up in bed reading one of Enid Blyton's 'Famous Five' adventures. She had been something of a legend in the paediatric world and the humility with which she accepted that she could no longer keep up with the latest medical advances, yet had found a book she could still read and enjoy, was impressive. She told me she had been close to Michael Balint in her youth but to my great disappointment was not willing or able to elaborate on one of the most important gurus in my life.

On moving back to Bath in 1980 I had found the local accent very evocative. My gardener and many of the girls who served in the shops spoke in Daisy's voice, carrying me back to my earliest memories. Travelling to London, on what used to be the Great Western Railway, the first stop was Chippenham. For years I looked out of the window on every journey, searching the entrance where my father would stand, hat on his head and gloves in his hand, waiting for me to arrive home from school or university. He was always sent to fetch us, for my mother hated meetings and partings as much as I do.

During the last years of her life Daisy continued to live with another of her nieces in Chippenham. I only saw her occasionally, though she was an integral part of the person I am, present in the deeper recesses of my mind and my memory. Eventually she became very frail and was moved into a care home. The day before she died I took my mother to visit her. We were shocked to find her semi-conscious, but dressed and sitting outside. Protocol demanded that old people should be mobilised at all cost; but we were sad she had not been allowed to lie peacefully in her bed for her last few hours. My mother was upset that Daisy was dying first. In her will she had left all her tweed coats to this person who had given the most loyal service to the whole family over so many years. What would she do with the coats now?

Ever since Daisy first arrived at Green Gables, and I had peeped at her round the banisters, there had been a love–hate relationship between the two women. My mother was often irritated by her, especially when she insisted on continuing the story she was telling to the bitter end, never deterred by the interruptions that would have silenced others. But she was fond of her and was totally reliant on her practical help during the war. Daisy admired her employer's intelligence and dedication to her work. Neither woman would have admitted how dependent they were on the other.

Needless to say, my mother would not consider going to her funeral. I had to represent the family, at the same crematorium where we had taken my father. In sharp contrast to his minimalist ceremony, Daisy's service was well attended. I managed to get a seat by the wide window where my mind could escape over the rolling Somerset hills. All such sorrow-filled places should have an expansive vista. Despite my atheism – not as rabid as my mother's for I am not anti-church, just not able to believe in an 'out-there' God – my favourite devotional line, based on the 121st psalm and set to music by Mendelssohn, is 'Lift thine eyes to the mountains whence cometh help'. The hills, together with the intervening valleys and their rivers, hold for me that sense of mystery that others find in religious belief.

That day of Daisy's funeral I again witnessed the tradition of placing the flowers from the top of the coffin on the ground in the courtyard, in the shape of a body. Her pile lay as one of a row with those of others who had been cremated during the day. The custom was for the mourners to linger, reading the messages of condolence while talking, at times with some animation. When Arthur and I had scuttled away from my father's dispatch there had been no such niceties, for we had no flowers and no mourners other than ourselves.

As I stood awkwardly among Daisy's friends and relations a

middle-aged man approached me. 'I think you are Ruth, aren't you? I remember your house and parents so well.' He was one of Daisy's many cousins and told me the following story with glee. Remembering seemed to give him as much pleasure and amusement as listening gave me.

'During the war, when I was about seven, I was walking up your surgery path. You remember, it was a long path used by your father's patients to get to the surgery entrance. We always went that way when we visited Daisy.'

I nodded, enjoying his memory of the path that I had used so often on the obligatory afternoon walk as a child.

'I had a friend with me, young Jack, he's dead now, rode his motorbike into a wall. As we were going up the slope, kicking the leaves, he saw something at the side of the path. It was like a round tube. We knew it must be an unexploded bomb.' He paused for effect. In the solemn surroundings I had to suppress a giggle.

'We looked at it from all angles, then prodded it with a stick. It didn't move. Should we go on and tell Mrs Hickson? Or just run home? In the end we decided the right thing to do was to take it to the police station. I had a piece of string in my pocket so we tied it to the end of a stick to keep it as far away as possible in case it exploded.'

The vision of these two small boys, solemnly walking through Chippenham High Street, arms outstretched with what was probably some sort of empty cartridge case tied at the end of a stick, was a good story to take back to my mother.

By the time Daisy died my mother had moved into the rooms she had added to the back of our house in Bath. It had been built in the late 1950s of imitation Bath stone and is a plain rectangle with two projections on the back. The cupboard under the stairs has been extended to make a study in which I still write at my computer with a view of the garden, enclosed on two sides by an ancient wall. I was told that it had been part of an orchard belonging to an old monastery. In the corner where the two walls join, a shed contains a small stone grate. Half the floor of the shed is raised a few inches above the rest. Could it have been a bakery, or was a fire used to heat one of the walls, which shows the remains of coping-stones and whitewash, suggesting greenhouses? The ground is full of broken glass and clinker. When we first viewed the house its simple style combined with the site's long history made it irresistible.

The other addition at the back was a large playroom. With some trepidation we had invited my mother to join us. She turned the playroom into her living room and built on a bedroom with a kitchen and bathroom beyond, creating a 'granny annexe'. She applied the same principle of building it round her furniture. In her eighties she continued to be in charge of her own affairs. But she was living in my house and I had a growing sense of responsibility for her wellbeing. She had given up her car and although she could, for several years, get to the town on the bus, I drove her to visit friends and family who lived further away. From the passenger seat in my car she could see the rev counter, hovering between 30 and 40, which she mistook for the speedometer. I never enlightened her for she would have been horrified by my speed. Adjusting to the faster speed of all traffic was as difficult for her as getting used to the rising cost of everything as the years passed.

My mother matured with age, like a good wine, becoming less tart. To my surprise we were able to live together in peace. Sometimes I could even share some of my inner feelings without fear of being shattered by her temper in the way I had been as a child. On one calm day in June, when lupins and delphiniums were flowering against the backdrop of grey stone, I told her that the garden felt like a space where I could face whatever life threw at me. So far that has proved to be true – though I have not been required to suffer the devastation of untimely death or serious illness among my younger loved ones. The loss of a child or grandchild must be the ultimate horror.

During that time, when my mother was living with us, I edited my first psychosexual book. For several years the proceedings of the

IPM leaders' workshop were recorded and transcribed. I was no longer editing the family planning journal and I missed the task of trying to sort ideas. I began to pick out themes and to choose extracts as examples. In those days I worked with a pair of scissors, cutting out relevant pieces, stapling them onto plain paper and then photocopying them at the local paper shop. After a few months I sent a sample to Tom Main, fearful of the scathing comments I expected. His reply included the following: '... *I had no enthusiasm for the idea when you first mooted it... but your headings make the discussions punchy and even exciting reading... if the fumbling is plain and the occasional errors or superficialities also plain these accounts have one virtue – They have an authenticity, unpolished and even crude, that makes them a model of reportage.*'

His letter lives in that envelope marked 'Some of my most precious things'. This package contains a number of other messages of appreciation, including a postcard of a stylised cat and kitten with the words:

Dear Mum
One kitten safely weaned! Thank you for a wonderful wedding.
Lot and lots of love
Helen

Although I do not often take out these small tokens I still value them. The need for appreciation never dies.

I discussed the edited transcripts with Jimmy Matthews, Ralph's longstanding friend, who worked as a small-time publisher producing a directory of legal businesses. He became intrigued and we decide to continue the project that eventually became the book *Psychosexual Training and the Doctor/Patient Relationship*.

The text was divided into three main sections: the individual doctor and psychosexual training, the group and psychosexual work, the leader and the group in psychosexual training. To my great delight Marshall Marinker agreed to write the forward to the book. He described the three levels in the following terms. 'In the distance we may catch a glimpse of a man and a woman locked in some

189

personal unhappiness... Nearer and less muffled we hear the voices of doctors talking in their training seminars... Closer to hand is the Workshop where the leaders meet to discuss their leadership of these seminars...'

I have been surprised at how much I learned about group behaviour and the technique of helping the group to work. Many years later I was on a course at Schumacher College in Devon, sited in the grounds of Dartington Hall, where they run courses relating to the environment and sustainable living. All sorts of different people attend, including those from abroad and businessmen who want to conduct their affairs in a more ethical way.

The particular course I joined lasted for three weeks. The experience was not a happy one for me. The emphasis on a holistic approach to life's problems was set in opposition to 'relativism' where things were divided into small pieces in order to study them. The members of the group seemed to equate that word with scientific method, in which I believe with passion. I became the token 'bad' scientist, castigated for not knowing all the details of the sheep dip that poisoned farmers back in the 1970s. However, towards the end of the time we were broken into smaller groups to work on some project. Our discussion was becoming heated and going nowhere when one member left the room. The others immediately started attacking her. We had no leader but without thinking I suggested we should wait until she returned and try to find a way of airing these views in her presence. When we did, she was able to put her points more clearly and we produced a result of sorts.

I experienced a very badly led group on a weekend course at the Tavistock Clinic, where I had expected them to be experts. My small group had only one man. When the discussion turned to sexual abuse he was attacked and, not surprisingly, became defensively aggressive. Tom was not in favour of making group interpretations and always took the discussion back to the doctor and the patient, the work task. Perhaps the trouble with the Tavistock group was that we did not have a well-focused task – I don't even remember what it was.

Bion's writing about small groups suggests they function in one of two modes, the *work group* and the *basic assumption group* where members act out unconscious strategies to avoid painful work. Tom never referred to any theories, but the workshop digests demonstrate many of the difficulties met in helping trainee doctors to belong to the former group.

Over the years I have led groups in many parts of the country. My travelling was comparable to that of many participants who, especially in the early days, paid their own expenses. I certainly paid for all my travel during training, only being reimbursed and eventually paid a fee when I started to lead. Like most of my contemporaries I was a woman working part-time with a husband who provided basic financial support for the household. We were happy to give our time and money for the unique training that grabbed our attention and filled a gap, not always recognised as more than a vague dissatisfaction, in our understanding of patients and their needs.

Now, most women doctors can get other part-time work and their households have been designed with the expectation of two salaries. Sexual problems are recognised as underlying much unhappiness and some illness. All doctors are expected to have some training in the recognition of such difficulties and to be aware of places to which their patients can be sent for help. Some doctors apply to the IPM for training because their employing authority has sent them or because they like the idea of another qualification – with such motivation they are unlikely to gain much insight.

The publication of the workshop transcripts was an important step in my working life. Although I was never an innovator, I had taken on the job of trying of capture the highly original ideas and method of training that was developing within psychosexual medicine. In both my family and my professional life I was on my way to becoming a member of the senior generation.

When my mother fell and broke her femur I was in London to present a paper at an IPM meeting. She was in her flat and managed to crawl to one of the panic buttons we had put in each room. Ralph went through to find she had a bag ready packed for such an eventuality. The ambulance took her to a private clinic. I caught the next train home, to find she had been prescribed bed rest in the hope that the simple break would heal itself. During that time she appreciated being called Dr Hickson by the staff. She enjoyed the care, the tasty meals and the single ward with a view over fields, the flowers and letters from well-wishers. But a week later her fracture showed no sign of healing. Her consultant decided he must operate. I went with her to the door of the operating theatre where she looked into my eyes and clutched my hand. I reassured her that I would be waiting for her when she came out. I was, once again, the adult to the frightened child – as I had been for those few days following the death of my father.

Back on the ward she floated on the edge of consciousness. After twenty-four hours we were told she had sustained a massive heart attack under the anaesthetic and was not going to recover. Arthur sat with me by her bed while a nurse did everything she could to make her comfortable, keeping her mouth moist and every part of the body supported in a comfortable position. Half an hour before she died the nurse asked me what my mother's first name was. When addressed as 'Joan' her eyes flickered. I was deeply moved. This passionate, powerful woman who had been my mother had regressed to the stage of an infant. I am comforted by my belief that hearing her name in those last moments ensured that she did not feel deserted or alone. I held her hand and Arthur held mine, a line of support I tried to extend across the Atlantic when I phoned Biz later. She, however, was in the middle of hosting a dinner party and with typical stoicism continued being polite until her guests had left and she could share the news with her husband and seek what comfort he could offer.

I mustered some words to thank the nurse for her sensitive care of my mother during those last few minutes of her life. She told me she had nursed her own mother to the end and that the personal experience had taught her the importance of adjusting one's responses to the moment by moment changes in each patient as they slipped towards death.

Again, Arthur and I were faced by a funeral. Knowing our mother would hate to have even the simplest prayers said over her, we asked the undertaker how it could be done. He said quite simply that the coffin would be in the crematorium. We could go in and sit down. When we wanted it to disappear we should stand up. So we did just that. She always hated bought flowers, they were a waste of money, garden bunches were much nicer. So, after forcing the buds to open by putting them in a warm oven, I placed three Iris stylosa blooms on the plain wood. They only last a day so it was appropriate that they should burn with her.

As we drove back to Bath after the 'non-funeral' I told Arthur about the time, only a few months before, when our mother had climbed into one of my compost boxes, made of wooden planks, in order to paint them with preservative. She loved to help in the garden and I did not resent what I would have considered intolerable interference earlier in my life. I tried to suggest simple tasks that she could manage easily and had meant her to treat the wood from the outside. But she was determined to do the job properly. When I came home she told me, with a laugh, 'I found myself wishing to die at that moment, in that place. Then you would not have the trouble of moving my body but could build me into the layers of compost.'

Arthur and I managed to laugh too, at our practical but impossible mother, whom we had loved despite her tempestuous temperament.

17

Surviving

After the publication of the workshop transcripts, Jimmy and I published a multi-authored book *Introduction to Psychosexual Medicine* under the same imprint, Montana Press. The name occurred to him one day as we sat with Ralph in the garden near a prolific clematis that had draped itself round a pear tree, one of the last of the monastery trees, not destined to live for many more years. Among my favourite photos is that of Helen and her new husband Simon, taken in front of that tree with its mantle of white flowers, soon after their return from honeymooning in Africa.

Ralph retired from the prison service when he was sixty, in accordance with the regulations. The year was 1984, appropriately synchronous with Orwell's book. He would have found the prison service with its modern ethos of privatisation a difficult place to work. In retirement I had expected him to become a keen member of the Bath chess club for he had played by post for many years. However after attending a few times he stopped, preferring the distance of correspondence and the impersonality of a computer. In the hope of prying him out of his chair into the open air I acquired a replacement dog. Bess had died a couple of years before. Cassie was a collie/Labrador cross with her own problems. She had eczema and the steroid tablets needed to keep it under control gave her a ferocious appetite. She stole any food within her reach. If allowed to run free in the fields above our house she disappeared into the bowels of the skips at the back of the university, where they chucked waste food. I was not firm enough to train either of my dogs.

On the second occasion Ralph took Cassie for a walk he sprained his knee and the excursions never resumed – but he could walk into the town to buy tobacco for a variety of pipes. He stopped smoking at frequent intervals but was always so miserable that I had difficulty waiting in silence during the few days before he restarted. Although I hate the smell of tobacco now, at that time I trained myself not to notice. After he died I buried my head in his tweed jacket, straining to reach a whiff of memory, with as much effort as Cassie strained for her stolen food.

Thus I have come to the moment I can no longer avoid – the plunge into the well of memory that leads to widowhood. 1990 was my *annus horribilis,* despite the fact that it started so well with the safe birth of Alec, my first grandson. Six weeks later Jimmy Matthews died suddenly of a ruptured aortic aneurysm. In November Ralph had a heart attack. He had spent a restless night, feeling sick and uncomfortable but not complaining of severe pain. As soon as it was time for our doctor's surgery to open I phoned and asked for a visit. 'If he says it is just indigestion I will smash his face in,' said my husband who, since his discharge from the army, had never raised his hand to anyone, and who could not kill a wasp.

Our GP had just come in from another urgent visit and was about to start morning surgery. I had an image of his waiting room filling up with restless patients. 'Do you want to see a few before you come?' I suggested, identifying with his predicament. 'I could give Ralph an aspirin in case it is a heart attack.'

Luckily he heard the panic behind my words and was on the doorstep within a few minutes with his ECG machine in his hand. The tracing confirmed our fears. Dr King stayed with me until the ambulance arrived to take Ralph to the Intensive Care Unit at the Royal United Hospital.

The treatment he received was meticulous. He was quite poorly for several days. I remember sitting with Helen in the small relatives' waiting room, unable to let go of her hand as she tried to comfort the mother of a boy who had crashed his motorbike and suffered a severe head injury. Corralled in the bubble of my own pain and anxiety, I could not utter a word.

During his time in hospital Ralph turned to Helen for comfort and reassurance. He relied on her medical knowledge and trusted her in a way he never trusted me. She was wonderful, bringing small offerings each day but more importantly just the reassurance of her presence.

After about three days the various tubes were removed from his body. I was sitting by his bed when the nurse in charge (she was probably no longer called a Sister) asked if anyone had washed his feet. When he said no she fetched a basin of water and descended to the floor.

'Surely you must have a minion who could do this?' Ralph asked. 'You are much too senior for such a lowly task.'

'Good enough for Jesus, good enough for me,' came the reply, as she soaped between his toes.

When he was eventually moved onto a general ward the contrast was harsh. Here, we could have entered a third world country. The floor was not very clean with the beds close together, the room crowded with visitors who arrived early and stayed all day bringing food, flowers and titbits of gossip to entertain their relatives. The ward was for diabetics and the ever-changing staff had no idea how his exercise level should be graded after a heart attack. I tried to work it out with Ralph, not sure if I should allow him to walk to the toilet or fetch a wheelchair, uncertain when he should be encouraged to try a few stairs.

One kind act stays in my mind. A bed next to the window became vacant and a nurse suggested he might like to move into that privileged place. The change made an enormous difference to his comfort. Now he could turn away from the people and the noise and let his eyes travel up to the skyline where clouds moved, fast or slowly depending on the wind, in ever-changing patterns.

I never wrote the letters of thanks that I planned to the intensive care staff or to that nurse who had noticed that he was suffering, perhaps more than some of the others, a hermit confined in close proximity to a sample of seething humanity.

His stay was made worse by the fact that it was a mixed-sex ward. A few years before he had been admitted to a male ward for an operation on his Dupuytren's contracture, a thickening of the tissue in the palm that pulls the fingers into a claw. I had been afraid he would find a general ward difficult but when I visited a few hours later he was in charge of the tea trolley. 'Over here, Gov,' the men were calling. 'Two sugars for me, Gov.' He was back in an all-male society that he understood, and had instinctively taken the role of the officer caring for his men.

A couple of days before he came home after his heart attack, I was standing at the sink thinking that the one person I would like to see was my sister. The idea startled me for we had never been very close. In my despair I was searching for some contact, any contact, with the world of my childhood where I had been safe and where it never occurred to me that any tragedy could touch my family.

I turned from the dishes – and there was Biz walking in at the front gate. Her husband Jim had insisted she came to support me and she had leapt onto a plane in Virginia and come. Surprise and gratitude overwhelmed me.

Where Americans are able to show their sympathy, our British reserve makes it difficult. I am ashamed of the time when I did not visit a relative whose husband was dying of dementia at an early age. I had told myself that there was nothing I could do. Now I know that just being there is something – only cowards are paralysed by their own inadequacy.

Biz stayed for a few days making welcome-home posters for Ralph. After his return home she peeled vegetables and disappeared to her room at appropriate intervals. When she left I was torn between the wish to spend time with him and my duty to return to work. Helen insisted I stay off for at least six weeks and ever since I've been grateful to her for helping to solve that dilemma. Those six weeks were very important for us a family. We had the baby Alec to stay while his parents had a night away. Ralph was afraid to pick him up, as he had been all those years ago with Helen. He had not met a baby since that time, thirty years before. But he would kneel down and make faces and baby noises to entertain his grandson whenever I left them together. One picture remains vividly in my mind. After taking Alec into our bed in the morning, I had gone downstairs to make a cup of tea. When I returned the two chaps were lying in our big bed, their heads side by side on the pillow.

Supported by Helen, we grew very close. Ralph read poetry, sometimes aloud. He took short walks in the garden, a place he had seldom ventured when he was well. Until that time he had declared that he would be happy with green concrete. After six weeks he died suddenly, sitting in his chair. Again, I planned to write to the hospital to explain that, although they might feel his death so soon after discharge from hospital had meant their efforts had been in vain, the importance of the time they gave us could never be explained in words. Perhaps this was the reason the letter was never sent.

Much has been written about bereavement, yet my experience suggests that the advice is often misplaced. 'Stages of grief' have been described, with rules for the time each stage should take. My sense is that there are no rules, every person survives, or does not survive, in their own way. Talking to friends who have lost their partners we agree that the complete process can take up to six years, perhaps even longer for some. Until the end of that time I felt that part of me was still buried with his ashes in the crematorium. I would sit up in bed after I woke, my favourite place and time for remembering, weeping and putting some thoughts onto paper. On the sixth anniversary of his death I wrote a poem and when it was finished I knew I had dragged myself out of his grave and was now a whole person again.

Looking back from my vantage point twenty-one years later I wonder if the poem was the result – or the cause – of the healing. At the time I had been in analysis for four years. I had cried during much of my time in that room, without being clear what I was crying about. In the rare sessions when I did not cry I was left parched, as if the day held no possibility of new life, like the dry, infertile days of the menstrual cycle. As far as I can understand it now, much of the work had been concerned with differentiation from my mother, a necessary step in the process of separation from my husband. Writing this memoir and reliving some of the past has extended that process... I am free to love him with even more of myself.

During this period there were of course times when I forgot and could enjoy immediate activities. These intermissions became more frequent and the time between patches of hopelessness grew longer. I was only sixty-two when he died and still had enough energy left over from grieving to devote to the struggle back to a new life. Very old people with reduced energy levels find the effort doubly hard and I am not surprised that many die within a short time of their loved one.

I had dealt with day-to-day family finances all our married life so the practical tasks of paying bills and running the house were no burden. More difficult was deciding what bread I wanted to buy. As with all food, Ralph had been fussy: square, processed white or nothing. I wandered round the supermarkets with no idea what I wanted to buy. In the end I closed my eyes, walked a few paces and reached for the first loaf I touched, only putting it back if it was square and white.

With little understanding of my motives I found myself making a collage of four women and their babies from sixty years of photos kept jumbled in a suitcase. In the top left-hand corner all generations are shown together. My grandmother sits on a garden seat holding Helen, a few weeks old. I stand behind in a floral summer dress, inherited ivory beads round my neck, which I seldom dare to wear in public. The killing of elephants for their tusks is quite unacceptable but this material was culled many years ago and I can't put it back. Luckily it never occurs to people to consider that it is anything but synthetic. The line of my gaze blends with that of my grandmother, both of us besotted with the baby. My mother also sits on the seat, looking straight ahead with a stern expression.

Below this generational group are pictures of each woman with her offspring. My mother at about two years already looks rebellious. Where she is holding me I can just make out an arm round my waist, she would not actually wish to drop me, but the more obvious hand is reaching down to her beloved dog Jimmy by her side. In other pictures two toddlers sit on different doorsteps. One is myself with curly hair, looking happy. Once, on being shown a picture taken by one of my mother's friends, I had burst out, 'But I was a pretty child.'

'Of course you were,' my mother snapped, 'but we would *never* have said so to you or anyone else.'

Helen, on her doorstep, has very short hair and could be mistaken for a boy. Her expression is searching and not easy to read. Next to that image she is smiling as she holds her own baby aloft, the most joyous mother of us all. The men are all present but mostly in the background. The only way I can understand my obsession at the time is to notice the emphasis on babies, as if in the presence of death I needed to remind myself of the cycle of life and the possibility of new beginnings.

My career did much to help me through those years. Most evenings when I returned from a family planning or psychosexual clinic I found a message asking me to lecture, not only to doctors on family planning courses but to a variety of nurses and other health professionals. The first talk I had ever given was to a group of officers' wives at Pollington when we were first married. I had been ridiculously nervous. The pill was not yet freely available so I dealt with barrier methods and periodic abstinence. I used to blush furiously and had none of the ease that developed as I became more familiar with the subject.

Once I moved onto subjects related to the emotional aspects of sex I began to enjoy the discipline of preparation. First, I would write the lecture out in full and read it through several times to memorise as much as possible. Then I summarised the themes onto cards, highlighting particular phrases to remind me what came next. I was determined not to read any presentation. The task of holding the attention of an audience is easier with eye contact. Although sex is a fascinating topic there were often two or three listeners who thought all this 'psych' nonsense was a waste of time. They would do their utmost to rubbish whatever I was saying and I had to use the more sympathetic members of the audience to argue my case for me.

During the time I was adjusting to a solitary life I was busy looking for a publisher to take on two more books that Jimmy and I had been planning. We had asked Rosemary Lincoln, a psychosexual colleague of mine, to edit another multi-author book. She selected a wider range of contributors than I had used and I felt the book was an important addition to the scant literature on psychosexual medicine. Both Rosemary and I had the advantage of hearing papers given at IPM clinical meetings and drawing on the expertise of the best speakers. (I have already quoted from Judy Gilley's chapter on intimacy and terminal care.)

The second book in the planning stage was called *Sexual Abuse and the Primary Care Doctor* by Gill Wakley. She points out that within the population of any one practice there are likely to be a handful of children currently being abused, but large numbers whose lives have been blighted by past experiences. She covers many aspects of relevance to the work of a general practitioner.

Jimmy had died before he published either of these books. After hawking them to a number of other publishers I found an editor at Chapman and Hall who showed some interest. She was a retired nurse. I would have preferred to see it promoted especially for doctors but had to make do with a list designed to appeal to a wider medical audience. At least I now had a professional publisher interested in the subject. Alas, they did not sell particularly well. Like others in the series they barely covered their costs, which saddened me for I considered them important – but I was biased.

Gill went on to lead seminars and to follow me as chairman of the IPM, a job in which I was greatly helped by Heather Montford who was secretary at the time and did most of the hard work, especially the letters and visits to the Charity Commission that were needed in order to get the training organisation accepted by them. Jimmy's wife Jo Matthews had served on many committees while a member of PPA and other voluntary bodies, chairing several of them. She lent me a useful book on the art of running a meeting. One piece of advice stays in my mind; members must be allowed to have their say but if there is something you particularly want them to pass, put it late on the agenda for they will be much more likely to let it through when they are tired and hungry.

Writing about these old friends I am assailed by one particularly poignant memory. Gill and Jimmy and I were sitting in the garden on a summer's day under the cherry tree. We had been working on ideas for her book for some time, when Ralph appeared carrying a tray of iced drinks and nibbles. He seldom took on a domestic role of any kind, often appearing unsociable and not overly hospitable. My surprise was mixed with delight. In some way, perhaps because Jimmy was an old friend from their Oxford days, his reserve had melted so that he could find a reason to join us. While we sipped our drinks I felt a complete person, happy in every section of myself, my professional and personal lives merged for one brief, sunlit moment.

18

Safe Spaces

The last ten years of my life as a doctor, which coincided with the last decade of the twentieth century, were a time of personal consolidation and professional development. My psychoanalysis was both time-consuming and expensive but it gave me the confidence to adapt to widowhood and live more fully.

In addition to deciding what food I liked to eat after Ralph died, I had to discover how I wanted to spend my holidays. The first spring, Helen and Simon took me with them to the Lake District. In the back of their car, where I was not able to hear their conversation, I was freed of responsibility, a child again sitting behind her parents. My elder grandson Alec, raised in his car seat by my side, took the place of my sister Biz, with whom I invariably argued. My mother used to keep barley sugar sweets and peppermints in the front pocket to pass back when our squabbles became shrill.

In the rented house near Windermere I took Alec out in his pushchair while his parents did the chores. A stream ran through the village. One morning two mergansers were diving in the fast-flowing water. They were new birds for me and when I identified them from the book I felt a flutter, the first spark of interest in anything since Ralph had died.

During the twenty-one years since, I have travelled with several different friends. One year, in early September, I was standing with Jo Matthews by our hired car in Alberta. The huge expanse of yellow stubble stretched in every direction. As I absorbed the scale of the place, a skein of geese appeared over the lip of the huge horizon.

Turning, I saw another coming up in the distance behind us, then another and another as if they had been called from every compass point. After converging towards us they circled, before disappearing into a dip in the ground that hid their rendezvous. The noise of sibilant wings gave way to a swelling chatter, each individual seemed driven to share the story of his day.

What makes this image so magical? Is it the symmetry of their lines, their unerring sense of direction, their mastery of an element into which the earthbound human cannot enter? I did not realise at the time that the merganser and the geese were premonitions of one answer to the question of my future holidays, an interest that had been latent since a family holiday during the war.

We had been staying on the east coast of Northern Ireland in a cottage belonging to Professor Hugh Meredith, my mother's bearded cousin with whom we had been allowed to eat ice creams in Chippenham High Street. He was there with his second wife. Biz and I had to share a bed. As usual, when forced into close contact, we fell out. After one row, my mother shouted at me and I went down to the beach where I watched a flock of small wading birds running back and forth with the waves. I now suspect they were sanderlings but at the time I had no idea of their name, only that their instinctive behaviour was soothing. When I was calm enough to go back to the others, Hugh's wife took me on one side.

'I saw what happened with your sister,' she said. 'You did not start it.'

I loved her for noticing – and for the tactful way she healed my feelings.

Dogs and birds do not mix so I put my renewed interest in birds on hold for several years until after Cassie had died. She had been such a difficult pet that I was aware of her absence for weeks, turning to see what food she was stealing, moving to shut her away when the door bell rang. I was reminded of a patient who had become sexually frigid after the death of her dog. She had lost her mother two years before. At that time, her husband had been sympathetic and she had soon been able to make love again. As she talked about her dog it was clear that her old grief had been aroused. She had not connected the two losses and was filled with fury that she could not express when her husband said, 'How can you be so upset about a *dog*?'

The year my dog died I joined a birding group to the Scilly Isles, where I met my first real birders. They keep lists of sightings in the day, the week and each year, as well as life-long lists. The first ever sighting of a new bird is very important. On that trip a couple of people had two new birds but many felt lucky to get even one. I was in the enviable position of the new girl, whose ignorance was tolerated with amused patience when I admitted that my list ran to twenty-five.

Since that time I have spent several holidays with such groups. I am not an obsessive or knowledgeable bird watcher. The appeal of scanning the boundless sky, the depth of a reed bed or the expanse of a dry, flat plain is hard to express in words. It is not the human company, for some of my happiest moments have been spent alone. Nor is it merely the thrill of recognition, with the help of the book if necessary. No, the call is to that part of me that was so moved as a schoolgirl when I found my private place in the grounds of Hinton House, where I could look out over the fields, or contemplate a leaf. Sitting in a hide or crouched by the side of a lake or estuary, the hues and contours of the countryside sink into my being. Watching the almost imperceptible change in the reflected clouds or the ebb of the water, a flutter of wings or a flash of colour tames the impersonal space with evidence of individual life.

I cannot imagine looking out at my garden and finding it bereft of birds, those fluttering creatures who decide, of their own free will, to visit me. When I was first alone that space was also made safe for me by the naval tenants to whom I let my mother's flat. The accommodation suited sub-lieutenants, who were all married with wives and small boys living elsewhere. This meant that for most weekends they left the house on Friday morning and did not return till Monday evening, an ideal arrangement as I and my birds had the garden to ourselves.

I have kept in touch with several of these men. Chris moved in within a year of Ralph's death. I was so grateful to him for the tactful way he ignored my frequent red eyes, making no comment but suggesting a drink by the pond, where we talked of anything but death. David came later and was a vegetarian who liked his rum. I would see him stalking across the garden to put the outside leaves of his greens in my compost. One wet weekend, when his boys were visiting, I lent him my Buccaneer, a game where you sail little boats about collecting treasure. It was an old set of Ralph's and even though the cloth 'board' was very worn the treasure was beautiful. The gold bars were lead, painted gold and heavy enough to be real, the barrels of rum were made of wood and the glass diamonds and rubies sparkled. In modern sets all the treasure is plastic. The following Christmas David made his own set using half toggles for the barrels. Such imaginative dexterity warmed me with memories of my father.

After my father had died someone suggested to my mother that strangers could be helpful. She took tenants into the surgeries at Green Gables and again into the new house she built in the grounds. In my turn, I found the friendly but non-invasive company of the naval officers with whom I shared my house, and in particular my garden, helped to detoxify the grief that could have overwhelmed me. Eventually the naval establishment in Bath began to move over to Abbey Wood north of Bristol and the supply dried up. Now I am dependent on the university for tenants and have to adapt to a variety of students. I aim for those in their fourth year or studying for a PhD in the hope, sometimes realised, that they will be mature enough to need little attention from me, either in a caring or disciplinary role.

Floundering in the turmoil following Ralph's death my work provided another safe space where the routine forced me to keep in touch with the world and my place in it. I gave up my job at the University the year after he died, but continued to have a very full diary and to drive my car a great deal. Not only into Bristol three or four times a week to see my analyst but down into Somerset for clinics, into Wiltshire and Gloucestershire and Devon to lecture or lead psychosexual seminars. Once a year Heather Montford and I tutored on training courses for family planning trainers, often under the auspices of John Guillebaud of the Margaret Pyke Centre. The interest and pleasure of working with Heather provided some of my happiest moments since Ralph had died. Out of these experiences we conceived the joint project of editing a multi-author book.

Heather wanted to call the book *Psychological Factors in Contraception*. I insisted on *Contraceptive Care*. In retrospect, I can see that her title would have been better. The idea of 'care' was going out of fashion, associated with a paternalistic view of doctoring that was being challenged by the concept of more autonomy for patients. 'Shared care' was a phrase used, not just for sharing between different professionals but between the doctor and patient who should be allowed to make choices. In addition, the more scientific sounding name would have helped our fight to have the subject fully recognised as a special branch of medicine.

Several years passed before I understood that the decision about the title was an example of my voice being heard more powerfully than I realised. I had never considered myself to be a forceful person, one whose opinions would carry weight. Now, perhaps because I had led seminars and edited books, I caught myself holding forth and being listened to with respect. I had to step back and be more obviously prepared to change my point of view. As someone who had always believed that I saw too many sides to any question and was lacking the ability to make judgements, this required a startling re-assessment.

As my psychoanalysis progressed I began to see that I was neither as bad as I sometimes imagined, nor as good. I realised that the pervasive sense of 'not being good enough' was a sort of inverted snobbery that carried an undertone of needing to be better... better than I had been, better than my sister, better than others. I leant to accept that my position at school, hovering somewhere in the middle of the class, was about right. For the first time I could consciously counter the awful sense of not being worthy of respect, affection or love, with a more realistic idea that I was not that bad... nor in any way outstandingly good.

The question of evaluating my own views and work comes to a head as I try to assess the value of *Blocks and Freedoms in Sexual Life*, the book that I wrote on psychosexual medicine and published in 1997. At the time I was reading a lot of psychoanalytic literature. This is reflected in the list of references, which my analyst said I used defensively but which I think were there for a reason.

Tom Main had died in 1990 and the IPM was in the difficult position of any organisation that loses a charismatic founder. I thought my book was needed because of the danger that the insights we had gained over our long training were being lost. Psychoanalytic theories were becoming unfashionable. During a listening consultation, where the body and mind can be considered together, the patient can sometimes break through barriers in the most surprising and rapid way, cutting short a chain of referral to different specialists, as was shown by the research into non-consummation.

Pressures were building to widen the scope of understanding and training to include behavioural ideas that were so fashionable at the time. Injections for impotence were coming onto the market, with Viagra on the horizon. Quite rightly, doctors in the IPM realised that they needed to be fully up to date with these advances. At the same time another society, which became the British Association of Sexual and Relationship Therapists (BASRT), was running multidisciplinary training meetings with a very behavioural bias. I remember being asked to speak at one meeting where the participants, including doctors, were being encouraged to take a full sexual history and give advice, both activities at which those in the medical profession are very accomplished. My own suggestion that, in a busy surgery, one needed to listen, pick up unspoken messages and follow the patient, was given a very rough reception. That association has now become the College of Sexual and Relationship Therapists (COSRT) and I am sure has a wider understanding of the aetiology and possible approaches to sexual problems.

I divided my book into three parts. The first dealt with aspects of doctoring with especial reference to the psychodynamic use of the consultation and the genital examination. The following section of the book considered various feelings that may underlie the presenting symptom. In the last two chapters I try to make more philosophical connections between the mind and the body.

The reviews of the book when it was published make interesting reading for me, particularly the one from the *Journal of Sexual and Marital Therapy*. The reviewer considered the viewpoint 'individualistic, almost idiosyncratic', and complained that there were no references to the behavioural literature. It will be clear to the reader that I did not value that work enough to quote from it. I was also surprised at his suggestion that this was a personal idiosyncrasy, whereas I was representing quite a large group of doctors whose work I admired. He did, however, say that the case histories were useful. Re-reading some of these now I am no longer sure which stories were taken from my own practice and which borrowed from the experience of others. All doctors working in the IPM at that time had either changed practical details to preserve the anonymity of patients, or got their permission to share their story with colleagues. In addition, I put the following sentence at the beginning of the book: 'If any reader believes that they can recognise themselves in the histories, it is likely that they are identifying with aspects of someone else's story. In any event, they can rest assured that no one else will be able to recognise them.' I sincerely hope that this has proved to be the case.

In the *Journal of Psychoanalytic Psychotherapy* the reviewer points out that I retreat from lists as soon as I have made them, being more interested in the uniqueness of the individual. When Heather asked me to co-edit her book *Psychosexual Medicine, An Introduction*, published in 2001, I tried to ignore my dislike of boxes and tables. I realised that an up-to-date book, written in a modern style, was needed. But I was not the person to do it and should have declined her invitation. In my heart I do not believe one learns skills from lists and bullet points. Possibly a case history can shed some light, but my own insights have been gained from experience with patients and well-directed discussions with colleagues.

I am reminded that Joan Chodorow, talking about dance therapy, found it useful to '... keep feelers out for the fourfold crisis emotions: grief, fear, anger and contempt/shame. More often than not the first three are named – the fourth is the missing one.' In my section on symptoms and feelings I dealt with these emotions under different headings. The first, 'I'm not that sort of girl – or boy' is the one on shame. The feeling, that one's own sexual arousal is dirty, can be present from the earliest stages of life. It can also be precipitated by many later events: by marriage, childbirth, disease, especially genital infections, or indeed many other life experiences. I would be most interested to know how big a part this plays in psychosexual medicine now, during the second decade of the twenty-first century. With sexual matters so pervasive and explicit one might expect shame to be a thing of the past. But my hunch is that the roots often lie in very early experiences. If this is true, then changes in social mores are unlikely to have much effect on the feelings of the individual. Indeed, the social ease with which the subject is discussed could make it more difficult to admit one's own feeling of dirtiness and inadequacy.

Personally, the messages I had received from my father and mother were very mixed. Their almost blatant exposure of their bodies in their bathroom, and their comfort with bodily functions, contrasted with my mother's hesitancy about sex. I was introduced to the facts of childbirth by sitting next to our cat as she gave birth to her kittens. My parents covered the mechanics of intercourse and contraception with cool precision. But sexual arousal and pleasure were never a matter for discussion: I would have been deeply embarrassed if they had been.

I was a virgin when I got married although, even if my mother had believed me, it would not have lessened her abhorrence of my white dress. Ralph was also fairly inexperienced. As my marriage progressed I was lucky to have little difficulty getting in touch with my own sexual feelings. In addition, I learned from Tom Main to feel easier with sexual matters and to value a 'good enough' sexual life within marriage. Our discussion and efforts to understand our patients helped me to keep an interest in that side of my life throughout the ups and downs that Ralph and I negotiated during the years. Without this help my passion might well have cooled as happens to so many people. Even to myself I am only able to acknowledge this personal side effect of the work from a safe distance – after more than twenty years of widowhood.

Much has been written about the effect of childbirth on the sexual life of individuals and couples. In my chapter on the subject I find one of the few tables in the book. What I notice at this point is that the first three feelings identified by Chodorow, grief, fear and anger, are so often inextricably mixed, especially after childbirth. I identified another feeling that seems as important: that of vulnerability. The loss of control during childbirth can be terrifying. Good sex also requires us to 'let go', laying us open to feelings of hurt or ridicule.

Another of my chapters deals with 'Sex, anger and the couple'. I was well aware of the inhibiting effect of unexpressed anger in my own marriage. I remember a specific night when I could not respond to Ralph's advances. I found myself thinking, 'Tomorrow, I will *make* him listen,' and my body was freed.

It is often said that to resolve sexual difficulties both partners must be seen, for the problem may be collusive. In non-consummation a frightened woman is often attracted to a timid man with his own inhibitions. Tom Main believed, with some passion, that when a patient chose to consult a doctor and came alone, we should respect that decision. By the use of a one-to-one interaction, and the opportunity to examine the body, we could reach a deep but restricted area of the psyche. We should not be attempting to help those with more global disturbances of their personality. I hear him asking again, 'Is this a suitable case for a brief psychosomatic approach?'

Sending for the absent partner can be seen as a defence against uncomfortable feelings in the doctor, patient or both. Blame is shifted and can be explained by the psychoanalytic idea of projection. I recognise simple examples of this in my own life. One day I was fuming round the house counting the piles of papers Ralph had left about, collecting the dust. Only when I had the sense to count the larger number of my own piles was I able to smile. His piles were a sign of untidiness, mine were work in progress. In the same way, when my mother was living in the granny annexe I found myself standing alone in my kitchen saying, out loud, 'I must tell my mother not to talk to herself, people will think she is crazy.' Who was crazy? In our everyday life we frequently project our uncomfortable feelings into others where they can be despised or sometimes tolerated more easily than in ourselves.

If we ask to see the partner we often end up with two patients. Together with many of my colleagues, I realised that I knew very little about the interaction of couples and had no skills to help them. I had analysed my own practice in 1991 and discovered that I separated couples more often than I sent for the absent partner. Looking at the case histories I used in my chapter about the couple I find that all the patients presented alone. The safe space of the consultation allowed some of them to get in touch with their anger, connect it to their sexual difficulty and then deal with it more directly at home. However, couples still sometimes chose to come together and my feeling of inadequacy led me to attend an introductory term at the Tavistock Institute of Marital Studies (TIMS). My experience gave me some insight into the complicated nature of relationships and subsequently, when a couple came together, I tried to focus on the relationship between them. Only if I suspected there were body fantasies or other fears that could not be expressed in the presence of a third person, would I split them up.

Soon after publishing my book I wrote an article for the *Journal of Sexual and Marital Therapy* that I called 'Emotional contact and containment in psychosexual medicine'. In this article I explored the idea of holding bodily and emotional anxieties together in the safe space of the consultation. When this article was republished in 2001 in a book *Brief Encounters With Couples*, edited by Francis Grier, I felt I had come of age. I had mastered enough psychotherapeutic ideas to hold my own in the company of some of the exalted staff at TIMS.

In the final section of my book I try to suggest ways of looking for a theory of our work. It is here that my references become more wide reaching and I could be accused, and accuse myself, not so much of using them defensively as of trying to be 'clever-clever' or showing off. Because I am aware of being ignorant in so many areas I get particular pleasure from knowing things. Yet I am not prepared to rubbish the work for that reason. I remember Tom Main saying that most mental health nurses choose their occupation because they need help themselves, but if it were not for them we would have no mental health care. Even if our careers satisfy some need in ourselves, that does not necessarily negate the value of the work.

Fifteen years later, I find one or two quotations that still seem pertinent. Carl Rogers quotes Lawrence Henderson: 'The physician must have first, intimate, habitual intuitive familiarity with things; secondly, systematic knowledge of things; thirdly, an effective way of thinking about things.' Our traditional training had given us the first two of those requirements but Tom, perhaps because the work was so new and exploratory, had actively discouraged us from perusing theory. Now, in his absence, I believed that we needed to strive for ideas with which to think about our work. My book falls far short of providing any answers. It seems that I was groping for a language in which to conceptualise our experience without being pulled sideways into that of psychotherapy or behaviourism.

Re-reading my work now, I am struck afresh by the idea of therapeutic space and the need to keep it free of too much theory. A quote from Peter Brook, writing about producing plays in his book *There Are No Secrets*, hovers in my mind: 'In order for something of quality to take place an empty space has to be created.' I see now that the idea of keeping both the consultation and the training group free of theory is in opposition to my own search for ideas to explain and further the work. I can only hope that this dichotomy produces a tension from which further understanding can develop. Marshall Marinker, in a lecture to the IPM, said that 'exciting things happened at the boundary'. I am becoming aware that the space between knowing and not knowing has ever-expanding boundaries.

Before starting to write this chapter I could not imagine how to comment on the book that was the culmination of my professional life. As I sit at my computer looking out at the garden I think back to those months when I was first alone, with no one here but my naval friends. Re-reading some of the things I have written, I am hopeful that the safe space I am now in will allow new thoughts to emerge that will help me to face my remaining days with fortitude.

Writing a memoir is an exercise in making oneself vulnerable. For me, this is not about revealing desperate personal traumas, for I have been mercifully free of those, but about exploring the relationship between my personal and professional self. Until now, my training encouraged me to keep these two sides of my life in separate compartments. In order to put them together I am learning to trust that space of unknowing within myself, in the way I learned to trust it in the consultation, and from which (to my great surprise) the next chapter of my life erupted.

19

And Then There Was Fiction

Once my book was published I had nothing more to say about my work. The sense of emptiness was made worse by my approaching retirement. The local authorities had made it clear that at the age of seventy they would no longer employ me in their clinics. I was only seeing one or two private patients a week. If I continued to work from home the need to clean the mud from under my fingernails, and the cat's hairs and dead mice from the consulting room, would be a tiresome constraint. I also knew that without a steady stream of patients on whom to spread my concern I would become over-anxious.

Having decided to stop all clinical work I needed to retire from the Institute of Psychosexual Medicine. Although nobody suggested I should do so, I had learnt that training groups work better if all members are prepared to be equally vulnerable. The observer who can criticise, without receiving a reciprocal critique of their own work, alters the balance of power, creating eddies of unnecessary resentment. Without work I would be such an observer. My skills as a leader would diminish if I were not facing the same day-to-day stresses as the members.

Two years before I retired I was already wondering how to survive without the profession that had, to a large extent, defined the person I was. I had loved the work with patients and colleagues, and imagined their loss would be a bereavement. Aware of my ignorance in the arts, I considered taking an Open University degree. Good fortune led me to mention my dilemma to my friend Elizabeth

Forsythe who introduced me to the Open College of the Arts (OCA), an organisation described as 'a creative arts college that specialises in distance learning'. I chose the Starting to Write course. At the beginning of my folder for the course I find a scrawled note. 'Having had the course material for two days I feel as if I am in love! Moments of excitement are followed by hollow despair when it seems so difficult and tiring.'

This introductory course gave me an opportunity to try poetry, prose and script writing. A chapter in the course book introduced each of the six assignments. My work had to be sent off with a covering letter of comment to my tutor Irene Rawnsley. She is a poet who always followed the educational precept of giving praise before offering criticism. Having my work considered seriously by a 'real writer' was a heady experience and my excitement is clear from my replies.

Re-reading those assignments is more problematic. I recognise some of the characters and situations for I have built them into subsequent stories, but I cannot always remember how they have developed or where they have finally come to rest. Some images recur, each time described as if I was seeing them for the first time. The sweet chestnut tree outside my bedroom window that I am gazing at now, the prickly husks swelling each day, the sky behind turning from black to indigo to pale blue, is there in that first folder. I also meet it in my bedside diary, in half-filled notebooks and on scrappy bits of paper. The mind worries at images and ideas as if sucking at a drinking straw, hoping to extract the last drop of liquid from the bottom of the glass. I now see the returning light at the start of each day as holding out the repeated hope that such clarity might dawn in the world of my understanding.

The following year I embarked on the short story course. Trying to make some sense of the material I have found on my computer is a lengthy process. Most stories have at least two titles and several drafts, for I appear to have re-worked them diligently, the good girl as always, in response to each letter of critique. Names and some situations are half-recognisable from my later novels. I sent a couple out to agents who showed no interest. One, who was looking for commercial stories for women's magazines, was dogmatic that a couple must never meet over an animal – not a dog, a donkey or even a stick insect.

The six stories I wrote got longer as the course progressed. Towards the end the tutor suggested that the form might not be suitable for me. I must have taken that comment to heart. By the time I enrolled on the MA course in creative writing at Bath Spa University, two years later, I had the first draft of a novel in my hand.

The year was 1999. I celebrated my seventieth birthday with a party that I arranged for myself. As well as family and friends I invited a number of medical colleagues in an attempt to ease what I had expected to find a traumatic parting from my professional life. By the time it happened I was so enchanted by the idea of the new writing course that I hardly noticed.

Helen would have liked to organise a party for me but because I insisted on arranging it for myself she substituted a mystery tour the next day. I thought we might be going to France for the night but she said I did not need a passport. At the end of the party, my brother Arthur and his wife Ruth left – I thought for their own home in Cheshire. I imagined we would drive north and meet them somewhere between our two houses. When we turned south I was mystified but hid my disappointment. Biz had come from America and was with us in Helen's car so at least I had one sibling by my side. At lunchtime we had reached Devon and turned into the car park of *The Nobody Inn*. To belie its name, three of the other most important people in my life were sitting outside: Arthur, his wife and my beloved cousin Jenny. After the meal I discovered that Helen had arranged for us all to go on to a luxurious hotel on Dartmoor where I was greeted by flowers fit for a bride, more champagne, a sumptuous dinner and much loving banter.

It is for the people gathered at that dinner, and especially for Helen and her family, that I try to be as independent and happy as possible. An idea from the novel by R C Hutchinson, *Testament*, has reverberated in my mind for many years; that one has a duty to be happy – for one cannot make others happy if one is not happy oneself. I was born with a reasonably contented nature, a 'glass half full' sort of person. The effort needed to be content is not so great – indeed, my relative happiness can be a matter of smug self-congratulation. I have to remind myself that the difficulty of judging the struggle another person has to find contentment is as great as trying to assess the degree of someone else's pain.

Before the MA in creative writing started, I stayed for five days at Lumb Bank, one of the residential Arvon centres for creative writing. The eighteenth-century house once belonged to Ted Hughes and is at the top of a steep lane with wide views over the Yorkshire countryside. The tutor who influenced me most was the poet Michael Laskey. When he visited Bath recently I was touched and amazed that he remembered a hate poem I wrote about my mother. I spent some time trying to write poetry but surprised myself on the MA by choosing prose modules. I probably realised that I had not read enough poetry to be much good in that form.

By the time the course started I had became addicted to the discipline of writing. If I do not write for a few days I get itchy inside, as if I am deprived of a necessary antihistamine to soothe an urticarial rash. Despite constant battles with my poor spelling, my lack of dexterity with words provides a challenge as well as moments of intense pleasure. Apart from giving birth to a baby, the course was the most exciting thing that has happened to me in my life. I was at least twenty years older than most of the others in the year, but because we had a common goal the generational differences did not seem to matter. I spent my time rewriting the novel and trying some more short stories.

After the MA course ended I enrolled on a third OCA course, this time in poetry. My tutor, Robert Drake, reminded me of my father. Robert's first collection of poems, *A Line on Stone*, moved me greatly, for it drew on his experiences with stone and included building the dry stone walls that my father strove to perfect.

At the same time I found myself writing a second novel. I sent the two novels out to agents. Their negative responses did not deter me and during the first decade of the new century I wrote five novels in all. I was lucky to have the help of Lindsay Clarke's tutorial group during some of this time. He was the most demanding of all the teachers I have met in my struggle to become a writer. I am greatly in his debt. Leaving the group after four years was hard. I was influenced by Tom Main's idea, that after three or four years doctors in psychosexual training needed to forgo the support of the group and go out into the world to practise what they had learned. He believed they were professionally independent people who had to be responsible for their own work. He encouraged them to re-join a group later for a 'top-up', in order to unpick bad habits, like mistakes in a knitted garment, and to halt the tendency to backslide into more traditional forms of doctoring. The same dangers may lie in waiting for the aspiring writer.

The seeds from which my fictions germinated were most often psychosexual problems. Heather says there is nothing interesting or exciting about sex gone wrong. I disagree. Sex is a central part of the human condition and no one can divorce themselves from its drives and complications. The problem is to find good enough ways to write about it. I am surprised and hurt when told that my characters do not come alive or feel real, for I believe that professionally I have touched 'reality' in the depths of many people. I would like to blame Tom for my inability to flesh them out. His training, concerned as it was with 'deep penetration on a narrow front', probably blinded me to many aspects of a character. But the reason is more likely to be my own underdeveloped writing and imaginative skills. My need to rationalise and control my material might be even more of a handicap. Lindsay told me on more than one occasion, 'Put down your pen and close your eyes. Go back into the scene and see it better, in all its details.'

Since the end of the MA course a small group of us has continued to meet at my house every four to six weeks. The company has dwindled to four and I am deeply grateful to the others, who arrive through all weathers and at whatever personal inconvenience. After a shared meal we workshop our writing in a disciplined way. The critical edge of our eyes and ears has sharpened over the years. Without their company and belief in my work, their encouragement and critique, I could easily have given up the struggle.

My second novel *Parallel Journeys* was eventually published, but not under ideal circumstances. After many refusals I was put in touch with an agent who suggested a publisher in the north of England. I was excited of course, and when he explained that I would have to pay a considerable amount of money I did not demur. His letter, which arrived with the formal agreement, was very explicit about the number of copies I would have to sell to cover my costs, the many people worldwide to whom he would send review copies and the amount I might expect to make per copy. I was totally naive and saw the arrangement as somewhere between vanity publishing, or to use a kinder word self-publishing, and the real thing. I did not even realise that the book would be published 'on demand'.

I have no evidence that any review copies were sent out. I enjoyed working with the sub-editor and the production team. The Bath branch of Toppings bookshop arranged a launch party to which I asked friends and ex-colleagues. This gathering was the highlight of my publishing career. Ninety people turned up to listen as I read some extracts, a tribute to the loyalty of my friends rather than the literary quality of the novel.

Since then few copies have sold and my fiction publishing has ground to a halt – but I have continued to write. Despite the disappointment, and the financial loss, I am glad I got something into print. My stories are about human relationships, with an underlying serious idea. In the published novel the theme was the temptation for businesses to cut corners to make money. I set it in the research and development department of a drug firm. Unfortunately one of my friends thought I was getting at all such companies and she pointed out, quite rightly, that without them we would have no drug research. My intention had been to show that unscrupulous people are to be found in many different settings.

I have enjoyed researching for the books, especially one about an environmentalist who believes the only way to influence people would be to blow up the Thames river barrier. One icy day in January the barrier was expected to rise for its routine check, and I set off at 6 a.m. wearing five layers of woollies and carrying my grandmother's walking stick. By this time I was in my mid-seventies and not too happy on slippery ground. I travelled on the Docklands Light Railway for the first time, and arrived on the north bank of the river. Entering the Thames Barrier Park I found an imaginative place that had been opened in 2000. It has a sunken green area to represent a dry dock. It was still early but I ignored the cold, being on a high, feeling like an explorer, my senses heightened by the need to look, listen, smell and feel for the sake of the book. The writing that followed that visit has etched the experience into my mind, enhancing the power and enjoyment of the memory despite the fact that the barrier never rose. My one human contact, a man walking his dog, told me it had been used for a high tide the day before and the routine check was not needed.

I also consulted a friend I had met on my first birding trip who was a waterman's daughter and had lived close to the barrier all her life. She knew every craft that had ever travelled on the Thames and had helped with some of the surveying for the barrier. When I sent her a draft of my story she felt I had used her experiences in such a way that she might be confused with one of the characters. I hastily made some changes.

My anti-hero swims down to attach limpet mines beneath the water. I wrote to the Imperial War Museum and had a most helpful answer about how limpet mines could be disguised in a variety of objects including boat fenders. These mines were used during the Second World War to blow up enemy ships moored off Bordeaux. That story has been immortalised in the fictional film *Cockleshell Heroes*. I also had a lesson with the Bath Sub Aqua Club, where the instructor was friendly and helpful. The equipment was heavy, especially out of the water. I managed to float for a few minutes between the surface and bottom of the pool and the freedom was intoxicating. If I were younger I could become addicted.

My fifth novel started differently, sparked by the terrorist incident at Glasgow airport. A group of doctors and other medical personnel had driven a car into the terminal doors. I had no ideas in my mind apart from my horror of fundamental religious belief. I can imagine I could become a violent terrorist if I had suffered great deprivation, or my family had been killed or tortured. But I could not, and still do not, understand how such privileged people could have been radicalised in this way. I decided that I did not know enough about Islam to write about it, so I chose a Church of England vicar for my main character. I had no idea what was going to happen and was greatly surprised when he got severely beaten up in the second chapter. I still have hopes that some publisher might be interested in this story in the future, but I need to re-write it to make the characters more realistic; not so 'naïve and nice', as Heather says.

Writing has filled a part of my life that I believe is occupied, to some degree, by religious practices or meditation in those who cultivate their inner life. Within a minute or two of taking up my pen, or re-reading something I have written, I am detached from my surroundings. The immediate buzzing in my mind is stilled. The discipline cannot take over if I am really worried or depressed – or if there are other people in the house – but given a moment of reasonable stability and isolation, the magic works. The concentration needed to find the best word, something that Lindsay Clarke says can take him half the morning, becomes an absorbing task. I do not claim to be so dedicated, but exploring the thesaurus has become a very important part of the work. The height of excitement comes when I find an image or a form of words that carry a metaphor or meaning that I had not consciously put in when I first wrote the text. That demonstration of my unconscious mind in action is the highlight of the experience, providing as it does an access to a deeper layer of my psyche – although I do not understand why it should evoke such overwhelming joy.

As I begin on the downward path towards real old age I treasure the extended boundaries that writing has provided. My day to day experiences are richer, I look more closely and make more effort to remain open to new people and ideas. Reserves of energy, un-available for other occupations, are released in a surge that only occurs in response to this itch that needs to be scratched – by the act of writing.

20

Mining the Past

Indian philosophy divides life into three parts. The first is spent growing up and fitting oneself for life in work and family. The second is devoted to earning one's living, taking an active part in society and raising one's children. During the last third one has to learn to let go of precious things and prepare oneself for death. When I first came across this idea the divisions each lasted twenty-five years. Given the length of modern training, and our increasing life span, thirty years might be more appropriate for the present day – at least for those of us living in the west. However, many of the activities that have brought me greatest satisfaction – editing the later psychosexual books and writing my own, followed by the world of fiction – have taken place since I was sixty.

As I admit that fact, I feel a stab of disloyalty. Ralph died when I was sixty-one. I am loath to admit that being forced to live alone has freed me in any way. My marriage was not easy, but I know it was a good one.

A friend recently asked me if writing this memoir was therapeutic. The question feels strangely irrelevant. The inner thirst to free myself from early constraints was quenched during my analysis. Yet I am still searching to understand my marriage. While writing these chapters it has felt increasingly like writing a love story, although there is quite a lot of complaint about Ralph and I am sure there are places where he does not emerge as a very sympathetic character. I need to understand how my marriage worked, to find some basis for my conviction that it was good, for the devastation I felt when he died and for the changes that have taken place since.

Ralph was not naturally gregarious. Once I was alone I could take chances. I was more hospitable and invited people to stay with less caution. If they were not congenial I was the only person who had to tolerate the discomfort. These varied visitors have enriched my life. My younger American nephew, Will, is a maths professor who took a while to get his PhD, for his passion lay elsewhere. He put me in touch with his amazing world of jugglers. If any of them want a bed, in any town in the world, they ask on the net and someone responds. He sent four to stay with me. They arrived on bicycles from Heathrow, their juggling clubs on trailers behind. They had camped on the way and arrived in the pouring rain, grateful for my hot soup and cheese. Although they were all charming they were very different characters, held together by their dedication to their craft. I was astonished that they had no idea Will was a professor. They knew nothing of his family or background but admired him because he could juggle six clubs. It is the most classless society I have ever encountered, its hierarchy determined by nothing but the skill of its members.

For a fortnight, in three consecutive years, I hosted a different Spanish teacher. The organiser of the trips was born in Leicester of Cypriot extraction, and now lives in Pamplona teaching English. He brings groups of children on exchange visits to a school near my home. The children lodge with the families of their exchange partners, while the staff find other accommodation. I have delighted in the company of these teachers and hope to make a return visit.

I have also hosted various interns working in the Liberal Democrat office. Living in Bath, where the Labour party is very small, the Liberal Democrats offer the only challenge to the Conservatives. Although I am not very politically active I am a member of the Liberal party. My sympathies have never been as left wing as my mother's in her early days, but like her I have, during the ageing process, swung slightly to the right – but I have never voted Conservative. Within any capitalist system the population as a whole is said to become wealthier, but whichever party has been in power in this country during my lifetime, they have not been able to prevent the gap between rich and poor becoming wider. In a world with finite resources, any system based on continued growth will be unsustainable. My hope is that, as this realisation spreads, a more egalitarian system will emerge without excessive or heavy-handed state control. Probably a vain hope, but I am an optimist. Meanwhile, despite its weakness, I remain loyal to a party that attempts to follow a rational, middle way. I am frightened by the extremes of both left and right to which, in an uncertain world, more people turn.

My varied visitors have been stimulating, but thinking back I see that my belief that I am freer now I live alone is flawed. On at least two occasions during our marriage we invited young people to lodge with us for several months. When we were in Maidstone, the daughter of a medical colleague got a job in the area and Ralph encouraged me to invite her to stay until she found somewhere to live. Earlier, during our second stay at Pollington, one of the prison officers was moved away. His son stayed with us until he had taken his O levels (GCSEs for today's reader). The boy had lived a fairly restricted life but when he was offered a chance to camp for a weekend on the Yorkshire moors, Ralph encouraged him to go. We were both amazed at the changes when he returned full of excitement. His world had been transformed by his taste of the wild countryside. Ever since, I have subscribed to an organisation called CHICKS – Country Holidays for Inner City Kids.

Ralph had been aware of my need for company since the early days of our marriage. Christmas in the prison service could be difficult for families. We could never go back to our parents for Ralph was always on duty. At the time when family ties are most keenly felt, he was especially concerned for the men and tended to bring their misery home. He was aware of my loneliness and encouraged me to invite a young French woman, living in Britain but alone over the holidays, to stay for the festivities. Marie Therese came many times, bringing her husband with her after her marriage. Helen's first trip abroad without us was spent with them in Paris.

After Ralph died I spent one Christmas in that city with my friend Elizabeth Forsythe. We stayed in a hotel near the Gare du Nord, sharing a small double bedroom. We were not used to such close contact and we pushed the beds apart.

'How will we know when it is morning time?' she asked.

'That won't be a problem,' I assured her.

In the event, it was. I woke in the dark, excited for her to open the small stocking of presents I had brought. I went into the en-suite bathroom to turn on the light without waking her, only to find I had shut the door with the light switch on the outside. To try and see my watch by the glimmer from a high window I stood on the toilet seat – which broke.

At breakfast I apologised to Madame in my inadequate French. She shook her head as, with a serious expression, a stream of words that I could not follow flowed out.

Elizabeth translated. 'On Christmas morning, in France, we only dance on the toilet seats in the country, never in Paris.'

Madame would accept no money for its repair. The story served to break the ice at the lunch party to which Marie Therese had invited us.

But this freedom to travel was nothing new. Ralph had been happy for me to go to Greece for a week with the Matthews, while he stayed to manage the house, Helen and the animals. He never tried to influence my actions. He believed in individual autonomy and I can still hear him saying, 'You must do what you want.' My problem was that I seldom knew what I wanted, or if I did, I could see no way to fit it in with my first concern – to keep him happy. I am convinced that this feeling was not culturally determined, but an inner need. My mood went up and down with his happiness or misery. At the same time I wanted the impossible, for him to realise what I wanted and bend to my unspoken wishes with enthusiasm.

Looking back I find the psychological concept of projection helps me to understand my sense of being to some extent fettered. From a distance I can see that I pushed some of my internal constraints onto Ralph and resented them in him. But the one area where I felt completely free was in my professional life. The messages imparted by my parents, about the importance of training to work in a profession, had been built into my psyche with enough force to withstand all uncertainty. I always chose when to work and in what field of medicine. Although, in keeping with the values of those times, Ralph expected me to run the house, he supported every decision I made about the balance between my domestic and professional life. Only now is it clear that, when I was certain what I wanted, he did everything in his power to help me obtain it.

In John Daniels' book *Looking After* he says, 'Memory is not a record of the past, but an evolving myth of understanding the psyche, which spins from its engagement with the world.' My thoughts about the restrictions and freedoms in my marriage feel like an evolving explanation of the truth of the love that grew between us.

Very late in our life together – for the first and only time in the whole marriage – I lost my temper. I learned then that when I could voice my own needs Ralph was freed to be different.

Being a diabetic he had occasional attacks of hypoglycaemia, 'hypos' we called them, when his blood sugar dropped too low. It happened if he did not balance his insulin with enough food or if he had taken an unusual amount of exercise. Personality changes are known to occur and a story is told of how a loving man killed his wife when he was in this state. When Ralph became hypo his normal wit took on a sarcastic, almost cruel edge. The change was subtle, not usually noticed by strangers. But Helen and I knew; and both hated it. This was not the man we loved. I was frightened, not because I thought he would be violent but just by his strangeness. I sometimes wondered if he did it on purpose so that he could let out some of the negative feelings towards me that he never showed.

On two occasions he needed intravenous glucose and I had to send for the emergency doctor, for I never gave him an injection myself. The first time was after playing cricket all afternoon and evening with his borstal boys. He was too tired to eat much and became unconscious during the night. On the other occasion he had been travelling up to London from Coulsdon and somehow forgot to eat. Again, he became restless during the night and I could not rouse him.

The day I lost my temper was after we had retired to Bath. I found him slumped in his car, but managed to get him into the house where he collapsed onto the floor in the corner of the dining room. He could still swallow so I fed him peppermint creams, a form of glucose that he enjoyed, followed by tea laced with sugar. Once he was almost back to normal I looked down at him in fury and shouted, 'I cannot bear it any longer. You *frighten* me when you're hypo.'

He made no response and I had no idea whether he had registered my anger. But something changed. He continued to get occasional hypos but after that explosion his behaviour was different when they occurred. Either he realised that he needed sugar sooner or he controlled his speech and behaviour more carefully. Whatever the mechanism of the change, he never frightened me again. We did not talk about it, but both of us had discovered that if I could allow my real feelings to show he could change, even when he was in the altered mental state caused by low blood sugar.

After he died I learned that he had said to a friend, 'I give my wife a hard time, but she understands me.' He cannot have felt very comfortable, knowing he gave me a hard time. I wish I could have been more demanding, but something in me needed to do all the giving. Even writing the word 'demanding' makes me feel insatiable, as if however much he had given I would only have wanted more. I am reminded of my mother's style of breast-feeding, using the scales to stop each feed as soon as possible. Again I can imagine her distaste when my small fingers wanted to play with her breast, to delay the moment of parting – to grasp and cling, only to be rejected.

During my analysis I bought many books by analysts and psychotherapists of various schools. Stuffed with knowledge, these books crowded my shelves. I dipped into them but reached the end of very few. Any attempt to integrate the ideas into my ongoing experience was unproductive. I remember, from early chemistry lessons, the definition of osmosis, *the passage of liquid from a weaker to a stronger solution through a semi-permeable membrane.* My purchases were fuelled, not just by the intention to read them, but by the vain hope that the reverse process, where the wisdom in the books would filter through my skin into my brain, would take place.

Once I reached the end of my analysis I lost interest in theories. Within a year or two I donated almost all the books to the IPM and concentrated on the rewards of writing. As I try to assimilate the experience of writing this memoir a flicker of interest stirs again – but in a different form. My analyst described himself as eclectic. I had the sense that he was sympathetic to the views of Melanie Klein (which might account for the connection I have made about the origin of my insatiable needs). But one of his strengths was that he never used any specialist language – there was no psychobabble. His comment on any dream was always the same, 'What do you connect with?' He never put his own interpretation on the material or tried to link it to a general idea of what a dream might mean. I understood he had been working to help me 'free associate', to say the first thing that came into my mind as a way of exploring the unconscious, a technique I found incredibly difficult. If I try the exercise by myself my mind races past any first thought to comment or wonder about its meaning. I do not find the occupation very illuminating, but during the sessions it was different.

At the time I was particularly glad he was not a Jungian. I had sensed that those theories would be too vague for my practical way of seeing the world. I was not interested in the universal unconscious, in archetypes or the search for deeper understanding of the soul. I thought that what I was looking for was a way to deal with the grief of Ralph's death, while being aware that I also needed to escape from some of the legacies of the childhood that had confined me to particular ways of being. When writing about Jung, Anthony Storr says, '… the patient… might not have any associations at all [to dreams with mythological content]. Jung did not hesitate to supply his own associations, culled from his own extensive knowledge of mythology.'

My own dreams may lack mythological content because I am ignorant of the stories. One example of a response to my silence on the couch followed a vivid dream in which I was at the tiller of a small dingy, rushing down a river with the wind behind me. I could make no connections. Eventually my analyst said, 'You are travelling very fast. I wonder what is passing on the banks as you speed along?' I was filled with the warmth of his whole attention. This concentrated regard is a love unlike any other, for it is contracted, paid for, confined within the time of the session and without the need for some adaptation of the self demanded of normal love. Books such as *Care of the Soul* by Thomas Moore arouse my suspicion that Jungians may refract the beam of concern by reference to universal archetypes and mysteries. Vibrant colours of the imagination might be released by such an approach, but for me the feeling of being 'special' was the experience that allowed me to live more fully. My belief is that the healing properties of all therapies probably depend on the ability to provide a feeling of empathy rather than on the analyst's particular intellectual approach.

As part of my quest to understand my marriage I have recently read Deirdre Johnson's book *Love: Bondage or Liberation?* I was alerted to this publication by a notice of a meeting in Bristol about love in the psychosexual clinic. Alas I saw the notice too late to attend, but I have spoken to the organiser, Cathy Coulson, an IPM doctor I have known and admired for many years. She gave one of the lectures, which was about the absence of the concept of love, however one defines it, in our work. This observation is striking. I cannot remember the word in any of the books I have edited or in my professional writing. Cathy explored the idea that when sexual intimacy is lost the playfulness and creativity of the relationship is also lost. She suggested that in those couples where the bond could be repaired, early attachments for both of them might have been stronger.

I believe my patients were sometimes in the process of moving from the state of being in love to a relationship of a more mature kind where a different love could develop. Cathy quoted from *Captain Correlli's Mandolin*: 'Love itself is what is left over, when being in love has burned away.' Much of Deirdre Johnson's book is devoted to the state of falling in love. For me the wide reach of her analysis was a helpful guide to lines I might pursue as I try to understand my past. Two narrative angles particularly interested me.

I experienced the reality of her intrapersonal approach during my analysis. Any complaint about Ralph, and there were many, was met by an interpretation focused on me. My analyst never leapt to his defence or tried to explain the interaction between us.

Being relieved of the compulsive feeling of 'I am not worthy', with its unacknowledged counterpart of being better than others, I had the courage to try new things. To enjoy writing while being aware that I am most unlikely to get published; to practise my flute despite knowing I will never be good enough to play the first part in an orchestra. Above all, to live more fully in the moment and take delight in small things: the quality of evening light casting shadows across a green lawn, the mixed flocks of adolescent finches on my feeder, the taste of peas picked an hour before from the garden, the surprise of finding the apposite word or hidden metaphor in what I have written.

Deirdre Johnson's chapter on individuation caught my attention. Quoting Jung, she defines the word as 'the process by which a person becomes a psychological "individual", that is, a separate, indivisible unity or "whole".' She expands the idea by saying it is a process within the human being that causes them to become what they uniquely have the potential to be.

I sense that Jung is saying something important but I have difficulty grasping his full meaning. A book by Adolf Guggenbuhl-Craig, a Swiss Jungian analyst, called *Marriage Dead or Alive*, makes a distinction between a state of wellbeing leading to happiness and Salvation which involves the question of life's meaning and seems to be in some way equivalent to individuation. The word is taken from a religious context. For me the word 'soul' comes trailing an odour of personal afterlife that I cannot believe in. He considers marriage can be a way for some people to find Salvation but he believes in the institution much less than I do, saying that there are many people for whom it is not a productive way of living.

My cousin Jenny believed that the natural state for human beings was in couples. I do not go that far, but I think many people could find their way to fulfilment and the rewards of love if they stuck to the work of marriage. I am glad that I was brought up to believe that marriage was for life, and it never occurred to me to consider the possibility that we might part. *Marriage Dead or Alive* was published in 1977 and carries echoes of that time. The author implies that unitary marriage has no pre-eminence for raising children, that they can grow equally well with a single woman or in a commune. Observing the number of young people who marry when they decide to start a family, I think his view is not shared very widely. I am old-fashioned enough to believe that the unit of one man and one woman, who get on well enough together without mental or physical cruelty, provides the best holding ground for a child. Having said that, I am sure a good relationship between two people of the same sex provides a more fruitful background for a child than a bad heterosexual atmosphere; but such an unconventional household creates complications. Both these aspects are brought to life in Jackie Kay's wonderful poem 'Mother and Donor and Deirdre'.

Guggenbuhl-Craig also suggests that married couples should share, and when possible live out, their sexual fantasies. I find this idea shocking. My own erotic fantasies, masochistic in nature, are essentially private and far removed from any actual sex play that would give me pleasure. One might see these fantasies as connected to my feelings of inadequacy, as though I was in some way deserving of punishment. However, the erotic effect of such imaginings cannot be explained so easily. I suspect they have very early foundations that could only be uncovered during a much longer and more intense analysis than I experienced. For me it was enough to be able to accept their presence without shame or confusion.

I can now see that my own marriage was a success because the projections that took place between us provided a good enough fit. I find it difficult to imagine what parts of Ralph he unconsciously pushed into me. When I try, I am reminded of the pet names we used soon after we were married. I became Pooh, a bear of very little brain. He was Tigger, a bouncy adolescent. Neither of these images is accurate, for my brain is not that little and he never bounced – but the use of these words released great tenderness between us. Perhaps I carried his fear of not being intelligent, and he my wish to be vivacious, the life and soul of the party. However this is understood, our collusive marriage provided a setting in which deep parts of ourselves could be fulfilled.

With the passing of time I become ever more grateful for one of his qualities that irritated me the most. His passion for the underdog, his tendency to put his prisoners before his family, often left me feeling neglected and unappreciated. Now it seems to me to be essential that in any couple there should be room for one or other, perhaps ideally one alternating with the other, to be free to devote their energies to the wider world. The nuclear family is, in my view, the best place for a child to develop. But society needs those who can act with altruism, thinking of others outside their small, personal circle. I take pride in the fact that Ralph was one of those people.

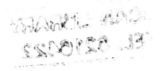

21

The Past in the Present

As a doctor I was fortunate to remain employed in clinical practice meeting patients until I was seventy years old. Ralph chose not to strive to go higher in the prison service, for he did not want to lose touch with individual prisoners. My brother Arthur left his job in engineering because he could see no upward path on which he could continue to work with his hands.

These thoughts suggest that there is a time in life when many people are faced with the choice between following earlier ambitions and settling for different goals. I never aspired to reach the top of anything and was glad that my peripatetic life, moving from prison to prison, provided an excuse to remain a medical generalist. My increasing confidence in the field of psychosexual medicine, where the number of new facts to be assimilated each year was not overwhelming, brought considerable satisfaction. But it was only after my analysis and the widening of my world through music and writing that I developed a hunger to be better at both, becoming ambitious at a time of failing stamina.

Basil Hume, one-time Catholic Archbishop of Westminster, said that the worst thing about getting old was the fatigue. My family is a long-lived one and I am blessed with a long-lasting constitution. At eighty-three I am fit, still reasonably sane and mobile. While my friends collapse around me I go on living an independent and full life. A shudder of unwarranted pride runs· through me when strangers say I do not look my age – as if my looks were somehow my doing rather than the genes my parents bequeathed to me.

But... I cannot deny my age. Nothing works quite as well as it did. My feet and the end of the garden are further away. I lose things more often, finding my glasses in the fridge and the butter in my toolbox... I exaggerate, but only a little. After mislaying the notebook with ideas for this book I spent twenty-four hours searching, only to look again in its designated place – an old drug company folder – and find it tucked inside, grinning at me. Recent memories become fuzzy like a television set on the blink. The picture may disappear beyond recall. Then it can blaze into view as an unconscious connection mends that particular electrical circuit in the brain.

The loss of energy is exasperating. I used to work in the garden for four hours without a break. Now, after an hour, I find myself wandering round looking at the weeds and the dead heads on the roses. I have learned to read this behaviour as a sign that I need to sit in my chair. There, I have exchanged the cryptic for the concise crossword.

People say one makes one's own luck. I cannot agree, for it was not my own effort that prevented me being born in the deserts of Somalia at a time of drought. But my nature helps me to see the best in situations and I try to foster such an outlook. I remember, more than twenty years ago, deciding to compose my face into, not exactly a smile, but an expression that held the promise of a smile. I was surprised by the resulting friendliness of those on the tills of supermarkets, on buses and in queues.

An important bulwark against the depression of old age is to accept that the slope is not steadily downhill. A sudden slip: incapacity takes a step nearer. Then the fall levels out and one adapts to the new limits. For a while Jenny and I talked with animation about these shared experiences, agreeing that the changes were of interest, both of us trying to adapt and laughing when we failed. Alas, she can no longer remember her recent words and has no ability left to analyse her situation. Having said that, I am grateful that she still knows who I am and we can still re-live our shared experiences, though in ever more repetitive sentences.

Having survived Ralph's death and been relieved of much

generalised anxiety as a result of psychoanalysis, I stopped asking myself about the meaning of life. Previously I had been assailed by questions about why we are in the world, and by the anguish of not being able to explain the horrors and pains of existence.

For the last ten years I have lived much more in the present, getting what spiritual nourishment I needed from the attempt to write and from the simple pleasures of family, friendship and daily living. Was my previous interest in the inner life driven by nothing but a search to escape from feeling stupid and clumsy? I have wondered if I am in some way less sensitive. Worrying about such matters had brought no answers but now the reality of death draws nearer and I have to face the trials of old age. I am trying to make sense of the past and to find some fortitude to live the rest of my life.

I hope that the musings in the last chapter and this one may be of interest to readers who are also coping with retirement and on the path into old age. Perhaps they too find their curiosity about the inner life roused once again. Returning to Jung's idea of individuation I find it is suggested that such a state can be approached in many ways – for some through marriage, for others via creative activity or a passion for something outside oneself. I asked one of my friends, who seems to be the most complete person I have ever met, how she did it. Her answer was immediate. 'Until I discovered Beethoven I lacked self-confidence and felt I should be like other people. My love of music drove me to be myself.'

Perhaps for my parents that passion was medicine. Their experience in the same medical school provided an opportunity for shared gossip and memories of their teachers. Although they recognised some poor practice and some bad doctors, their belief in the rectitude of the profession and its value to society underpinned their lives and their relationship. As I search for meaning in my own life I realise that their belief in medicine took the place of allegiance to a religion. Instead of finding friends from within a church congregation, their somewhat limited social life was almost entirely among doctors. Their role models were all medical men they had known or read about.

No teacher at medical school inspired me with any passion until I met Michael Balint. Then I became genuinely excited by the possibilities of my work. Today's training prepares doctors for the enormous difference between hospital medicine and the unorganised chaos of a general practice surgery. I had no such preparation and the only experience I could turn to was that of my pragmatic father. When I read Balint's book *The Doctor, His Patient and the Illness* I discovered a father figure interested in the uncertainties that I had not been able to formulate into questions. He was prepared to look at ideas about why the patient had come and what the doctor's role might be. This distancing of the doctor from the immediate situation allowed for the consideration of emotional factors and the possibility of the body/mind approach, which has given me so much satisfaction.

I knew from many of his patients that my father's traditional, paternalistic method of working had been of the greatest help to many people. Indeed it is a style of doctoring that has great strengths. I can imagine that when I become seriously ill I will want a doctor whose opinion I can trust and who does not offer me too many choices. But I also know that one or two of my father's patients felt neglected when he rushed into advice about hobbies or activities instead of listening to their troubles.

When faced with the undifferentiated complaints and minor illnesses that make up the bulk of a general practitioner's surgery, I was different from my father. I found myself more interested in the unspoken messages that were the concern of Michael Balint and later of Tom Main. For me, those teachers added meaning and depth to my life as a doctor. But I did not worship the practice of medicine in the way of my parents, and continued to search in a rather unfocused way to find reasons for living.

Although I was a bridesmaid three times as a small girl, I attended my first routine church service when I left home for boarding school. There I was faced with the dilemma of faith that confronts all children who are brought up in a godless household and then exposed to traditional Christian worship. One of my grandchildren reminded me of my confusions when I was driving him home from some outing. We stopped at traffic lights.

'Granny, do you believe in God? Mummy doesn't.'

The lights would change at any moment. 'Well... it depends what you mean by God.' Not a very satisfactory answer for a six-year-old.

I had asked much the same of my father in a letter during my first term at school. I wish I had kept his reply for it was typical of him. He explained in very plain language about his Quaker background, the difference between his view as an agnostic and that of my mother, a fervent atheist. He made it plain that when I was older I would be free to make up my own mind, and that whatever I decided to believe, or do with my life, would make no difference to the strength of their continuing love for me.

My response was to be confirmed into the Church of England at the age of about sixteen and to try to find some way to pray and find meaning in the teaching and services. I failed in both, always feeling self-conscious and haunted by my inability to know what I believed. I had absorbed my mother's abhorrence of humbug and insincerity so that I could never enjoy the beauty of church music and buildings without feeling a fraud. The idea that one could see the teaching as a metaphor, which could contain truths without being 'the truth', is something with which I still struggle.

On marrying Ralph I met a philosophical outlook very different from that of my parents. Their beliefs were in the practical values of honesty, hard work and conscious attempts to live a good life. Ralph mistrusted words and never discussed moral codes or how to live an ethical life. He had no time for the Christian teachings I had been exposed to at school. Instead he had developed an interest in eastern thought, and especially the ideas of Zen Buddhism, several years before they became fashionable and were taken up by the New Age movements.

I did not understand his outlook, at times finding it cold. If I began to agonise too much about some passing upset he would say, 'You take your emotional temperature too often.' His belief that one should 'do the next thing' made him appear somewhat uninterested in making plans or in reminiscing about our shared holidays. He told a story where a professor held up a box of matches and asked what it was. When someone called out, 'A box of matches, Sir,' he replied, 'No, no. It's *this...*' and threw it across the room. '*Matchbox* is a noise. Is *this* a noise?' Ralph took pleasure in the story but I found the demonstration that a Word was not the same as the Thing difficult to understand.

It took me many years to appreciate the strength that he gained from his beliefs. When Helen drank the cough medicine, and when she developed vestibular neuronitis, he was strong and supportive as he 'did the next thing'. When he was in hospital for the operation on his hand, and later to have his diabetes stabilised, he was cheerful and uncomplaining. Most impressive of all was his acceptance of his heart attack and the restrictions it placed on his life for the few weeks before he died of the second attack. Now, when I open *The Way of Zen* by Alan Watts – one of his simpler books on the subject, bought in 1958 according to a note inside the cover – I find much that resonates with ideas that I am exploring again. The phrase 'to see the good without evil is like up without down' (p. 115) chimes with Jung's Yin and Yang.

One of the most difficult things for me to accept was Ralph's scoffing at my efforts to be good. Following his death I discovered an enthralling writer, Marion Milner. She was a psychoanalyst but her technical writing is very dense. However, a three-volume autobiography, based on ideas about keeping a diary, had me spellbound. The first two were written in the 1930s and she was much admired by some of the Second World War poets. I read the second volume *An Experiment in Leisure* first, in an edition published by Virago in 1986. She writes, '... the observation that if I did my job with any uplifting enthusiasm for "doing good" what I did was badly done.' For many years I have felt that good should be performed, rather as my father felt about helping people to die, with the left hand not knowing what the right hand was doing. (With greater openness and more people involved in the dying process this option is, perhaps rightly, no longer available to doctors.)

Milner also writes about '... the long struggle to develop an inner life that was not just an escape from reality, but the only means by which I could face it.' Recently, when starting on a holiday with a group of people who did not feel immediately congenial, I found myself thinking, 'I must go inwards if I am to survive this.' The thought helped me to distance myself from the company and freed my senses to look and feel and smell the new experiences. I remember aping a mantra that Milner used, a gesture of inner poverty, 'I am nothing, I have nothing, I want nothing. The readiness is all.' This helped me to cope with the conflicted feelings of unworthiness and superiority that had been so crippling before my analysis.

Another of her phrases that has stuck in my mind is 'the eye has interests of its own'. In the same way that I found facts boring, I have always been blind to the world about me, absorbed in the feelings aroused in myself and others rather than in the things themselves. Milner described her technique of deliberately adjusting the focus of her eyes for near or far vision. Even at this late stage in my life I would like to be able to train myself not only to look in these different ways but also to allow my eye to have interests of its own.

My friend Elizabeth Forsythe is determined to give things up while she still has the choice to do so. She recommended a book by Helen Luke called *Old Age: Journey into Simplicity*. The author re-examines some great literary texts and her conclusion, reached with immense artistry, is that we must learn to let things go.

With my wish to be less stupid, present since my earliest days, I find it difficult to give up the battle for wisdom. But Adolf Guggenbuhl-Craig, in *The Old Fool and the Corruption of Myth*, draws attention to the gap between reality and some of the myths of living. He says that the old are not necessarily any wiser than the young, for their experience is not always relevant to the present day. He maintains that the myth of the wise old man or woman should be complemented by the myth of the old fool. Our role is to accept the limits of our decline and learn to play and enjoy doing nothing. In this way we renounce any claim to power and avoid becoming self-righteous and vain. I am reminded of my pleasure on seeing my eminent godmother Sylvia sitting up in bed enjoying the Famous Five with no medical journal in sight.

But the lesson to stop striving is a hard one. I want to live each day as fully as possible. During one session with my analyst I had a vivid image in which I was holding his brain in my hands. The object, with its convoluted surface and inner mystery, became the world – and I was determined to explore its fullest depths until it was time to die. Then I wanted to be able to open my hands and let it go. This need to keep exploring, to keep trying to understand, is something that I am not prepared to relinquish. Yet I am filled with a curious relief on reading that I have a place in society as an old fool. I can relax when my energy level is low. I do not want to take my own life too seriously and in old age I can occasionally tell a snippet against myself that raises a smile. But as I do so I feel the danger that I am 'showing off', that most heinous of English middle-class sins. I cannot tell if the act of writing this memoir has worked for or against my aim to touch my memories lightly.

Helen Luke and other authors suggest that myth and metaphors help to develop an inner life. I have always found the Greek myths difficult to grasp, their Gods are so complicated. Metaphors from Christianity come embedded in beliefs I cannot embrace. New Age writings and even some respected organisations appear to denigrate the scientific approach. My experience at Schumacher College, where I was vilified for being a reductionist scientist as opposed to the holistic virtues claimed by the other members of the group, was discouraging.

But I am attracted to the idea of mystery, to those things that are explained better in poetry than in methods dependent on measuring. Jenny and I always agreed that, rather than God making man in his image, mankind had created a God in his own image, projecting the best and the worst of themselves into him. The best, as seen in architecture, music and ethical behaviour, the worst in religious genocide and torture, seem too large to have originated within the human brain.

If I am to continue to explore the sense of mystery, within myself and the world, I may have to re-evaluate the word Soul. However I have recently discovered another word that I find more acceptable. In James Hillman's *The Force of Character* I read the words Soul and Character as synonymous. I would recommend the book to anyone who feels his or her old age serves no purpose. While looking with clear eyes at the disintegration of our bodies and the growing confusion of our minds he reclaims this time of life as having value. I particularly liked his definition of memory as imagination – that is, images – qualified by time, which resonates with Wordsworth's definition of poetry as 'Emotion recollected in tranquillity'.

Many of those who write about soul use the concepts of archetypes and the collective unconscious postulated by Jung. My understanding so far has been based on a misunderstanding – that his ideas thrust people into categories instead of seeing each as an individual. With the help of Anthony Storr's primer on Jung in the Fontana Modern Masters series, I can see that the archetypes can be equivalent to the internal objects of later analysts. Their language, with which I feel more comfortable, puts more emphasis on nurture rather than nature, although with the explosion in genetic understanding the balance is shifting again.

Storr suggests that the purpose of myth is to give shape, form and often artistic expression to emotional experience, to make it more coherent, and that every man needs a myth to live by. A friend recently asked me how to change one's personal myth. For me the myth that I was stupid, ignorant, no good etc. was changed by the 'love' during my analysis, using the word in its special sense in that setting. But I am sure there are other ways of changing the story. These include the use of the body, for instance in dance, or even with techniques such as *focusing*. Gendlin, in his book of that name, describes a method of learning to listen with one's whole body and find words to describe what it is telling you. The claim that the method will change the world appears overblown, but my experience of trying to help patients find words for their body fantasies makes me hesitate to rubbish his ideas. The brain imaging described by McGilchrist suggests that the ability to use words is located in the left hemisphere but the concepts are conceived in the right side, with complicated connections between them. I can imagine that striving to find a word that exactly matches a whole body feeling might in some way reduce its intensity.

The concept that we live by myths without fully realising that we do so makes me wonder if my fictional characters are hollow because they do not embody archetypes that resonate with the reader. It has been suggested that such archetypes are different energies that are not part of a system of right and wrong. Perhaps imagining my characters from a different archetypal view would give them more body and help them to be less 'nice and naïve'.

Thus I am brought back to the power of the imagination. For me, the creative work of writing, an activity released by my analysis, has brought immense pleasure in my old age. Any creative act does, I believe, feed the soul, as does experiencing the natural world with one's senses alert. While accepting that one should no longer strive to achieve or be clever, I see no reason why one cannot continue to enjoy exploration in old age. McGilchrist's book *The Master and his Emissary* excites me and the experience of being excited is particularly rewarding when it is comparatively rare. I wonder if old age has to be an either/or choice. One could aim for a 'betweenness' as suggested in his book – something between giving things up and continuing to strive. The process of individuation is said to be circular, not linear. The circles may get smaller as the world contracts but if the right side is allowed space perhaps the circles will be no less valuable. As I regress back to a second childhood, when the reliability of balance, breath and bowels is more problematic, perhaps I can also regain some of the wonder of the growing child, and with Blake 'Kiss every joy as it flies'. This may be the reward of *growing* old, with the acceptance of pain that Helen Luke describes, rather than merely sinking into the ageing process.

I hope to go on exploring ideas, perhaps now with the help of myths, and reading poetry, even trying to write some. At the same time I know that when life gets really tough I will return to those maxims most deeply embedded within myself. 'Stop taking your emotional temperature, do the next thing,' from Ralph. 'Try to get a good night's sleep, you will feel better in the morning,' from my practical and loving father. So with T. S. Eliot:

> We shall not cease from exploration
> And the end of our exploration
> Will be to arrive where we started
> And know the place for the first time.

'Little Gidding'

Bibliography

Apley, John, *The Child and his Symptoms* (Blackwell Science, 1968)

Balint, Michael, *The Doctor, His Patient and the Illness* (Churchill Livingstone, 1957)

Bion, Wilfred, *Experiences in Groups and other papers* (Routledge, 1991)

Bramley, Brown, and Draper, 'Non-consummation of marriage treated by members of the Institute of Psychosexual Medicine', *British Journal of Obstetrics and Gynaecology* (1983)

Brook, Peter, *There Are No Secrets* (Methuen Drama, 1993)

Daniels, John, *Looking After* (Counterpoint, 1996)

Drake, Robert, *A Line on Stone* (BaD Writers Press, 1991)

Eliot, T. S., *Four Quartets* from *Collected Poems* (Faber and Faber, 2002)

Friedman, Leonard, *Virgin Wives* (Tavistock Publications,1962)

Gendlin, Eugene, *Focusing* (Rider, 1978)

Gilley, Judy, (Ed. Rosemary Lincoln), *Intimacy and Terminal Care in Psychosexual Medicine* (Chapman and Hall, 1992)

Grier, Francis, *Brief Encounters With Couples* (Tavistock Marital Studies, 2001)

Guggenbuhl-Craig, Adolf, *Marriage Dead or Alive* (Spring Publications, 1983)

Guggenbuhl-Craig, Adolf, *The Old Fool and the Corruption of Myth* (Spring Publications, 1991)

Hillman, James, *The Soul's Code* (Random House, 1996)

Hillman, James, *The Force of Character and the Lasting Life* (Random House, 1999)

Hutchinson, R. C., *Testament* (Faber and Faber, 1938)

Johnson, Deirdre, *Love: Bondage or Liberation?* (Karnac Books, 2010)

Kay, Jackie, *The Adoption Papers* (Bloodaxe Books, 1998)

Lincoln, Rosemary (Ed.), *Psychosexual Medicine* (Chapman and Hall, 1992)

Luke, Helen, *Old Age: Journey into Simplicity* (Parabola Books, 1987)

Main, Tom, *The Ailment and other psychoanalytic essays* (Free Association Books, 1989)

Masters and Johnson, *Human Sexual Inadequacy* (Little Brown, 1996)

McGilchrist, Ian, *The Master and his Emissary* (Yale University Press, 2009)

Milner, Marion, *An Experiment in Leisure* (Virago, 1986) [first published 1937 under the name of Joanna Field]

Montford, H. and Skrine, R., *Contraceptive Care* (Chapman and Hall, 1993)

Montford, H. and Skrine, R., *Psychosexual Medicine, An Introduction* (Arnold, 2001)

Moore, Thomas, *Care of the Soul* (HarperCollins, 1992)

Nixon and Hickson, *A Guide to Obstetrics in General Practice* (Staples, 1953)

Norell, Jack, *Six Minutes for the Patient* (Tavistock Publications, 1973)

Rilke, Rainer Maria, *Letter to a Young Poet* (Penguin Classics, 2011)

Skrine, R., *Blocks and Freedoms in Sexual Life* (Radcliffe Medical Press, 1997)

Skrine, R. (Ed.), *Psychosexual Training and the Doctor/Patient Relationship* (Montana Press, 1987)

Skrine, R., *Parallel Journeys* (Hallmark Press, 2008)

Storr, Anthony, *Jung* (Fontana, 1973)

Symington, Neville, *The Analytic Experience* (Free Association Books, 1986)

Tunnadine, P., *Contraception and Sexual Life* (Tavistock Publications, 1970)

Watts, Alan, *The Way of Zen* (Thames and Hudson, 1957)

Wakley, Gill, *Sexual Abuse and the Primary Care Doctor* (Chapman and Hall, 1991)

Wilson, Libby, *Sex on the Rates* (Argyll Publishing, 2004)

Index